LIVING LANGUAGE®

COMPLETE
ITALIAN
THE BASICS

Written by
Antonella Ansani

Edited by
Suzanne McQuade

Published in the United States by Living Language, an imprint of
Random House, Inc.

www.livinglanguage.com

Editor: Suzanne McQuade
Production Editor: Carolyn Roth
Production Manager: Tom Marshall
Interior Design: Sophie Chin

First Edition

ISBN: 978-1-4000-2415-5

Library of Congress Cataloging-in-Publication Data available upon request.

This book is available at special discounts for bulk purchases for sales promotions
or premiums. Special editions, including personalized covers, excerpts of existing
books, and corporate imprints, can be created in large quantities for special needs.
For more information, write to Special Markets/Premium Sales, 1745 Broadway,
MD 6-2, New York, New York 10019 or e-mail specialmarkets@randomhouse.com.

PRINTED IN THE UNITED STATES OF AMERICA

10 9 8 7 6 5 4 3 2 1

A mia madre, e alla memoria di mio padre.

ACKNOWLEDGMENTS

Thanks to the Living Language team: Tom Russell, Nicole Benhabib, Christopher Warnasch, Zviezdana Verzich, Suzanne McQuade, Shaina Malkin, Elham Shabahat, Sophie Chin, Denise De Gennaro, Linda Schmidt, Alison Skrabek, Lisbeth Dyer, and Tom Marshall. Special thanks to Giuseppe Manca.

COURSE OUTLINE

Welcome to *Living Language Complete Italian: The Basics*! We know you're ready to jump right in and start learning Italian, but before you do, you may want to spend some time familiarizing yourself with the structure of this course. It will make it easier for you to find your way around, and will really help you get the most out of your studies.

UNITS AND LESSONS

Living Language Complete Italian: The Basics includes ten *Units*, each of which focuses on a certain practical topic, from talking about yourself and making introductions, to asking directions and going shopping. Each Unit is divided into *Lessons* that follow four simple steps:

1. *Words*, featuring the essential vocabulary you need to talk about the topic of the Unit;

2. *Phrases*, bringing words together into more complex structures and introducing a few idiomatic expressions;

3. *Sentences*, expanding on the vocabulary and phrases from previous lessons, using the grammar you've learned to form complete sentences; and

4. *Conversations*, highlighting how everything works together in a realistic conversational dialogue that brings everything in the Unit together.

The lessons are each comprised of the following sections:

WORD LIST/PHRASE LIST/SENTENCE LIST/CONVERSATIONS
Every lesson begins with a list of words, phrases, sentences, or a dialogue. The grammar and exercises will be based on these components, so it's important to spend as much time reading and rereading these as possible before getting into the heart of the lesson.

NOTES
A brief section may appear after the list or conversation to highlight any points of interest in the language or culture.

NUTS & BOLTS
This is the nitty-gritty of each lesson, where you'll learn the grammar of the language, the nuts and bolts that hold the pieces together. Pay close attention to these sections; this is where you'll get the most out of the language and learn what you need to learn to become truly proficient in Italian.

PRACTICE
It's important to practice what you've learned on a regular basis. You'll find practice sections throughout each lesson; take your time to complete these exercises before moving on to the next section. How well you do on each practice will determine whether or not you need to review a particular grammar point before you move on.

TIP!
In order to enhance your experience, you'll find several tips for learning Italian throughout the course. This could be a tip on a specific grammar point, additional vocabulary related to the lesson topic, or a tip on language learning in general. For more practical advice, you can also refer to the Language Learning Tips section that follows this introduction.

CULTURE NOTES AND LANGUAGE LINKS
Becoming familiar with the culture of Italian-speaking countries is nearly as essential to language learning as grammar. These sections allow you to get to know these cultures better through facts about Italian-speaking countries and other bits of cultural information. You'll also find the links to various websites you can visit on the internet to learn more about a particular country or custom, or to find a language-learning tool that may come in handy.

DISCOVERY ACTIVITY
Discovery Activities are another chance for you to put your new language to use. They will often require you to go out into the

world and interact with other Italian speakers, or simply to use the resources around your own home to practice your Italian.

UNIT ESSENTIALS

Finally, each Unit ends with a review of the most essential vocabulary and phrases. Make sure you're familiar with these phrases, as well as their structure, before moving on to the next Unit.

The coursebook also contains a Grammar Summary and Additional Internet Resources to be used for further reference.

LEARNER'S DICTIONARY

If you've purchased this book as a part of the complete audio package, you also received a Learner's Dictionary with more than 15,000 of the most frequently used Italian words, phrases, and idiomatic expressions. Use it as a reference any time you're at a loss for words in the exercises and discovery activities, or as a supplemental study aid. This dictionary is ideal for beginner or intermediate level learners of Italian.

AUDIO

This course works best when used along with the four audio CDs included in the complete course package. These CDs feature all the word lists, phrase lists, sentence lists, and conversations from each unit, as well as key examples from the Nuts & Bolts sections. This audio can be used along with the book, or on the go for hands-free practice.

And it's as easy as that! To get even more out of *Living Language Complete Italian: The Basics*, you may want to read the Language Learning Tips section that follows this introduction. If you're confident that you know all you need to know to get started and prefer to head straight for Unit 1, you can always come back to this section for tips on getting more out of your learning experience.

Good luck!

If you're not sure about the best way to learn a new language, take a moment to read this section. It includes lots of helpful tips and practical advice on studying languages in general, improving vocabulary, mastering grammar, using audio, doing exercises, and expanding your learning experience. All of this will make learning more effective and more fun.

GENERAL TIPS

Let's start with some general points to keep in mind about learning a new language.

1. FIND YOUR PACE

The most important thing to keep in mind is that you should always proceed at your own pace. Don't feel pressured into thinking that you only have one chance to digest information before moving on to new material. Read and listen to parts of lessons or entire lessons as many times as it takes to make you feel comfortable with the material. Regular repetition is the key to learning any new language, so don't be afraid to cover material again, and again, and again!

2. TAKE NOTES

Use a notebook or start a language journal so you can have something to take with you. Each lesson contains material that you'll learn much more quickly and effectively if you write it down, or rephrase it in your own words once you've understood it. That includes vocabulary, grammar points and examples, expressions from dialogues, and anything else that you find noteworthy. Take your notes with you to review wherever you have time to kill—on the bus or train, waiting at the airport, while dinner is cooking, or whenever you can find the time. Remember—practice (and lots of review!) makes perfect when it comes to learning languages.

3. Make a regular commitment

Make time for your new language. The concept of "hours of exposure" is key to learning a language. When you expose yourself to a new language frequently, you'll pick it up more easily. On the other hand, the longer the intervals between your exposure to a language, the more you'll forget. It's best to set time aside regularly for yourself. Imagine that you're enrolled in a class that takes place at certain regular times during the week, and set that time aside. Or use your lunch break. It's better to spend less time several days a week, than a large chunk of time once or twice a week. In other words, spending thirty or forty minutes on Monday, Tuesday, Wednesday, Friday, and Sunday will be better than spending two and a half or three hours just on Saturday.

4. Don't have unrealistic expectations

Don't expect to start speaking a new language as if it were your native language. It's certainly possible for adults to learn new languages with amazing fluency, but that's not a realistic immediate goal for most people. Instead, make a commitment to become "functional" in a new language, and start to set small goals: getting by in most daily activities, talking about yourself and asking about others, following TV and movies, reading a newspaper, expressing your ideas in basic language, and learning creative strategies for getting the most out of the language you know. Functional doesn't mean perfectly native fluent, but it's a great accomplishment!

5. Don't get hung up on pronunciation

"Losing the accent" is one of the most challenging parts of learning a language. If you think about celebrities, scientists, or political figures whose native language isn't English, they probably have a pretty recognizable accent. But that hasn't kept them from becoming celebrities, scientists, or political figures. Really young children are able to learn the sounds of any language in the world, and they can reproduce them perfectly. That's part of the process of learning a native language. As an adult, or even as an older child, this ability becomes reduced, so if you agonize over sounding like a native speaker in your new language, you're just setting yourself up for disappointment. That's not to say that you can't learn pronunciation well. Even adults can get pretty far through mimicking the sounds that they hear. So, listen carefully to the audio several times. Listening is a very important part of this process: you can't reproduce the sound until you learn to distinguish the sound. Then mimic what you hear. Don't be afraid of sounding strange. Just keep at it, and soon enough you'll develop good pronunciation.

6. DON'T BE SHY

Learning a new language inevitably involves speaking out loud, and it involves making mistakes before you get better. Don't be afraid of sounding strange, or awkward, or silly. You won't: you'll impress people with your attempts. The more you speak, and the more you interact, the faster you'll learn to correct the mistakes you do make.

TIPS ON LEARNING VOCABULARY

You obviously need to learn new words in order to speak a new language. Even though that may seem straightforward compared with learning how to actually put those words together in sentences, it's really not as simple as it may seem. Memorizing words is difficult, even just memorizing words in the short term. But long term memorization takes a lot of practice and repetition. You won't learn vocabulary simply by reading through the vocabulary lists once or twice. You need to practice.

There are a few different ways to "lodge" a word in your memory, and some methods may work better for you than others. The best thing to do is to try a few different methods until you feel that one is right for you. Here are a few suggestions and pointers:

1. AUDIO REPETITION

Fix your eye on the written form of a word, and listen to the audio several times. Remind yourself of the English translation as you do this.

2. Spoken repetition

Say a word several times aloud, keeping your eye on the written word as you hear yourself speak it. It's not a race—don't rush to blurt the word over and over again so fast that you're distorting its pronunciation. Just repeat it, slowly and naturally, being careful to pronounce it as well as you can. And run your eye over the shape of the word each time you say it. You'll be stimulating two of your senses at once that way—hearing and sight—so you'll double the impact on your memory.

3. Written repetition

Write a word over and over again across a page, speaking it slowly and carefully each time you write it. Don't be afraid to fill up entire sheets of paper with your new vocabulary words.

4. Flash cards

They may seem elementary, but they're effective. Cut out small pieces of paper (no need to spend a lot of money on index cards) and write the English word on one side and the new word on the other. Just this act alone will put a few words in your mind. Then read through your "deck" of cards. First go from the target (new) language into English—that's easier. Turn the target language side face up, read each card, and guess at its meaning. Once you've guessed, turn the card over to see if you're right. If you are, set the card aside in your "learned" pile. If you're wrong, repeat the word and its meaning and then put it at the bottom of your "learn" pile. Continue through until you've moved all of the cards into your "learned" pile.

Once you've completed the whole deck from your target language into English, turn the deck over and try to go from English into your target language. You'll see that this is harder, but also a better test of whether or not you've really mastered a word.

5. Mnemonics

A mnemonic is a device or a trick to trigger your memory, like "King Phillip Came Over From Great Spain," which you may have learned in high school biology to remember that species are classified into kingdom, phylum, class, order, family, genus, and species. They work well for vocabulary, too. When you hear and read a new word, look to see if it sounds like anything—a place, a name, a nonsense phrase. Then form an image of that place or person or even nonsense scenario in your head. Imagine it as you say and read the new word. Remember that the more sense triggers you have—hearing, reading, writing, speaking, imagining a crazy image—the better you'll remember.

6. Groups
Vocabulary should be learned in small and logically connected groups whenever possible. Most of the vocabulary lists in this course are already organized this way. Don't try to tackle a whole list at once. Choose your method—repeating a word out loud, writing it across a page, etc., and practice with a small group.

7. Practice
Don't just learn a word out of context and leave it hanging there. Go back and practice it in the context provided in this course. If the word appears in a conversation, read it in the full sentence and call to mind an image of that sentence. If possible, substitute other vocabulary words into the same sentence structure ("John goes to the *library*" instead of "John goes to the *store*"). As you advance through the course, try writing your own simple examples of words in context.

8. Come back to it
This is the key to learning vocabulary—not just holding it temporarily in your short-term memory, but making it stick in your long term memory. Go back over old lists, old decks of flashcards you made, or old example sentences. Listen to vocabulary audio from previous lessons. Pull up crazy mnemonic devices you created at some point earlier in your studies. And always be on the lookout for old words appearing again throughout the course.

TIPS ON USING AUDIO

The audio in this course doesn't only let you hear how native speakers pronounce the words you're learning, but it also serves as a second kind of "input" to your learning experience. The printed words serve as visual input, and the audio serves as *auditory* input. There are a few different strategies that you can use to get the most out of the audio. First, use the audio while you're looking at a word or sentence. Listen to it a few times along with the visual input of seeing the material. Then, look away and just listen to the audio on its own. You can also use the audio from previously studied lessons as a way to review. Put the audio on your computer or an MP3 player, and take it along with you in your car, on the train, while you walk, while you jog, or anywhere you have free time. Remember that the more exposure you have to and contact you have with your target language, the better you'll learn.

TIPS ON USING CONVERSATIONS

Conversations are a great way to see language in action, as it's really used by people in realistic situations. To get the most out of a conversation as a language student, think of it as a cycle rather than a linear passage. First read through the dialogue once in the target language to get the gist. Don't agonize over the details just yet. Then, go back and read through a second time, but focus on individual sentences. Look for new words or new constructions. Challenge yourself to figure out what they mean by the context of the dialogue. After all, that's something you'll be doing a lot of in the real world, so it's a good skill to develop! Once you've worked out the details, read the conversation again from start to finish. Now that you're very familiar with the conversation, turn on the audio and listen to it as you read. Don't try to repeat yet; just listen and read along. This will build your listening comprehension. Then, go back and listen again, but this time pause to repeat the phrases or sentences that you're hearing and reading. This will build your spoken proficiency and pronunciation. Now listen again without the aid of the printed dialogue. By now you'll know many of the lines inside out, and any new vocabulary or constructions will be very familiar.

TIPS ON DOING EXERCISES

The exercises are meant to give you a chance to practice the vocabulary and structures that you learn in each lesson, and of course to test yourself on retention. Take the time to write out the entire sentences to get the most out of the practice. Don't limit yourself to just reading and writing. Read the sentences and answers aloud, so you'll also be practicing pronunciation and spoken proficiency. As you gain more confidence, try to adapt the practice sentences by substituting different vocabulary or grammatical constructions, too. Be creative, and push the practices as far as you can to get the most out of them.

TIPS ON LEARNING GRAMMAR

Each grammar point is designed to be as small and "digestible" as possible, while at the same time complete enough to teach you what you need to know. The explanations are intended to be simple and straightforward, but one of the best things you can do is to take notes on each grammar section, putting the explanations into your own words, and then copying the example sentences or tables slowly and carefully. This will do two things. It will give you a nice clear notebook that you can take with you so you can review and practice, and it will also force you to take enough time with each section so that it's really driven home. Of course, a lot of grammar is memorization—verb endings, irregular forms, pronouns, and so on. So a lot of the vocabulary learning tips will come in handy for learning grammar, too.

I. AUDIO REPETITION

Listen to the audio several times while you're looking at the words or sentences. For example, for a verb conjugation, listen to all of the forms several times, reading along to activate your visual memory as well.

2. SPOKEN REPETITION

Listen to the audio and repeat several times for practice. For example, to learn the conjugation of an irregular verb, repeat all of the forms of the verb until you're able to produce them without looking at the screen. It's a little bit like memorizing lines for a play–practice until you can make it sound natural. Practice the example sentences that way as well, focusing of course on the grammar section at hand.

3. WRITTEN REPETITION

Write the new forms again and again, saying them slowly and carefully as well. Do this until you're able to produce all of the forms without any help.

4. FLASH CARDS

Copy the grammar point, whether it's a list of pronouns, a conjugation, or a list of irregular forms, on a flashcard. Stick the cards in your pocket so you can practice them when you have time to kill. Glance over the cards, saying the forms to yourself several times, and when you're ready to test yourself, flip the card over and see if you can produce all of the information.

5. GRAMMAR IN THE WILD

Do you want to see an amazing number of example sentences that use some particular grammatical form? Well, just type that form into a search engine. Pick a few of the examples you find at random, and copy them down into your notebook or language journal. Pick them apart, look up words you don't know, and try to figure out the other grammatical constructions. You may not get everything 100% correct, but you'll definitely learn and practice in the process.

6. COME BACK TO IT

Just like vocabulary, grammar is best learned through repetition and review. Go back over your notes, go back to previous lessons and read over the grammar sections, listen to the audio, or check out the relevant section in the grammar summary. Even after you've completed lessons, it's never a bad idea to go back and keep the "old" grammar fresh.

HOW TO EXPAND YOUR LEARNING EXPERIENCE

Your experience with your new language should not be limited to this course alone. Like anything, learning a language will be more enjoyable if you're able to make it a part of your life in some way. And you'd be surprised to know how easily you can do that these days!

1. USE THE INTERNET

The internet is an absolutely amazing resource for people learning new languages. You're never more than a few clicks away from online newspapers, magazines, reference material, cultural sites, travel and tourism sites, images, sounds, and so much more. Develop your own list of favorite sites that match your needs and interests, whether it's business, cooking, fashion, film, kayaking, rock climbing, or . . . well, you get the picture. Use search engines creatively to find examples of vocabulary or grammar "in the wild." Find a favorite blog or periodical and take the time to work your way through an article or entry. Think of what you use the internet for in English, and look for similar sites in your target language.

2. CHECK OUT COMMUNITY RESOURCES

Depending on where you live, there may be plenty of practice opportunities in your own community. There may be a cultural organization or social club where people meet. There may be a local college or university with a department that hosts cultural events such as films or discussion groups. There may be a restaurant where you can go for a good meal and a chance to practice a bit of your target language. Of course, you can find a lot of this information online, and there are sites that allow groups of people to get organized and meet to pursue their interests.

3. FOREIGN FILMS

Films are a wonderful way to practice hearing and understanding a new language. With English subtitles, pause, and rewind, they're practically really long dialogues with pictures! Not to mention the cultural insight and experience they provide. And nowadays it's simple to rent foreign DVDs online or even access films online. So, if you're starting to learn a new language today, go online and rent yourself some movies that you can watch over the next few weeks and months.

4. Music

Even if you have a horrible singing voice, music is a great way to learn new vocabulary. After hearing a song just a few times, the lyrics somehow manage to plant themselves in the mind. And with the internet, it's often very easy to find the entire lyric sheet for a song online, print it out, and have it ready for whenever you're alone and feel like singing. . . .

5. Television

If you have access to television programming in the language you're studying, including of course anything you can find on the internet, take advantage of that! You'll most likely hear very natural and colloquial language, including idiomatic expressions and rapid speech, all of which will be a healthy challenge for your comprehension skills. But the visual cues, including body language and gestures, will help. Plus, you'll get to see how the language interacts with the culture, which is also a very important part of learning a language.

6. Food

A great way to learn a language is through the cuisine. What could be better than going out and trying new dishes at a restaurant with the intention of practicing your newly acquired language? Go to a restaurant, and if the names of the dishes are printed in the target language, try to decipher them. Then try to order in the target language, provided of course that your server speaks the language! At the very least you'll learn a few new vocabulary items, not to mention sample some wonderful new food.

Many Italian sounds are like English sounds, though the differences are enough that you need to familiarize yourself with them in order to make yourself understood properly in the Italian language. Some key things to remember:

1. Each vowel is pronounced clearly and crisply.

2. A single consonant is pronounced with the following vowel.

3. Some vowels bear an accent mark, sometimes used to show the accentuated syllable (**la città**—*the city*), and sometimes merely to distinguish words (**e**—*and,* **è**—*is*).

4. When a grave accent appears over the letter **e**, it gives it a more open pronunciation (**caffè**—*coffee*). An acute accent on the other hand, gives a more closed pronunciation (**perché**—*why*).

5. The apostrophe is used to mark elision, the omission of a vowel. For example, when the word **dove** (*where*) is combined with **è** (*is*), the **e** in **dove** is dropped: **Dov'è?** (*Where is?*).

The rest is a matter of listening and repeating, which you should do with each word in this section as you start to learn how the Italian language sounds.

I. COGNATES

Let's begin with a few cognates. These are words that are similar in both Italian and English and descend from the same root. Notice how Italian spelling and pronunciation differ from English.

agente	*agent*
animale	*animal*
attenzione	*attention*
attore	*actor*
azione	*action*

capitale	*capital*
caso	*case*
centrale	*central*
centro	*center*
cereale	*cereal*
certo	*certain*
chitarra	*guitar*
cioccolato	*chocolate*
colore	*color*
differente	*different*
difficile	*difficult*
dottore	*doctor*
esempio	*example*
familiare	*familiar*
festa	*feast*
generale	*general*
generoso	*generous*
importante	*important*
interessante	*interesting*
locale	*local*
materiale	*material*
nazione	*nation*
necessario	*necessary*
originale	*original*
personale	*personal*
possibile	*possible*
probabile	*probable*
radio	*radio*
regolare	*regular*
ristorante	*restaurant*
semplice	*simple*

simile	*similar*
solito	*usual*
tè	*tea*
teatro	*theater*
telefono	*telephone*
totale	*total*
treno	*train*
umore	*humor*
visita	*visit*

2. Vowels

Now that you've looked at the difference between Italian and English on a broad scale, let's get down to the specifics by looking at individual sounds, starting with Italian vowels.

LETTER	PRONUNCIATION	EXAMPLES
a	*ah* in *father*	a, amico, la, lago, pane, parlare
e	*e* in *bent*	era, essere, pera, padre, carne, treno, tre, estate, se
i	*i* in *police, machine, marine*	misura, sì, amica, oggi, piccolo, figlio
o	*o* in *no*	no, poi, ora, sono, corpo, con, otto, come, forma, voce
u	*oo* in *noon*	uno, una, tu, ultimo

There are also several diphthongs in Italian, vowel-and-vowel combinations which create a new sound.

LETTER	PRONUNCIATION	EXAMPLES
ai	*i* in *ripe*	guai
au	*ow* in *now*	auto
ei	*ay* in *say*	sei
eu	*play* + *Uno*	neutro
ia	*ya* in *yarn*	italiano
ie	*ye* in *yet*	miele
io	*yo* in *yodel*	campione
iu	*you*	fiume
oi	*oy* in *boy*	poi
ua	*wa* in *wand*	quando
ue	*we* in *wet*	questo
uo	*wa* in *war*	suono
ui	*wee* in *sweet*	guido

3. CONSONANTS

Next, let's take a look at Italian consonants. The consonants **b, d, f, k, l, m, n, p, q, t,** and **v** are all pronounced as they are in English. The rest differ slightly, as you'll see below.

LETTER	PRONUNCIATION	EXAMPLES
c	before **e** or **i**, *ch* in *church*	cena, cibo
	before **a, o,** and **u,** *k* in *bake*	caffè, conto, cupola

LETTER	PRONUNCIATION	EXAMPLES
g	before **e** or **i**, *j* in *joy*	**gente, gita**
	before **a, o,** or **u,** *g* in *gold*	**gala, gondola, gusto**
h	silent	**hotel**
r	trilled	**rumore**
s	generally, *s* in *set*	**pasta**
	between two vowels, or before **b, d, g, l, m, n, r,** or **v,** *z* in *zero*	**sbaglio**
z	generally, *ts* in *pits*	**zucchero, grazie**
	sometimes, *ds* in *toads*	**zingaro, zanzara**

4. Special Italian sounds

There are several sound combinations in Italian that appear quite often as exceptions to the above rules, so study them carefully.

CLUSTER	PRONUNCIATION	EXAMPLES
ch	before **e** or **i,** *c* in *can*	**amiche, chilo**
gh	*g* in *get*	**spaghetti, ghiotto**
	gh in *ghost*	**funghi**
gl	before a vowel + consonant, *gl* in *globe*	**globo, negligente**

CLUSTER	PRONUNCIATION	EXAMPLES
gli	*lli* in *scallion*	gli
glia	*lli* in *scallion* + *ah*	famiglia
glie	*lli* in *scallion* + *eh*	moglie
glio	*lli* in *scallion* + *oh*	aglio
gn	*ny* in *canyon*	Bologna
sc	before **e** or **i**, *sh* in *fish*	pesce, sci
	before **a**, **o**, or **u**, *sc* in *scout*	scala, disco
sch	before **e** or **i**, *sk* in *sky*	pesche, fischi

Unit 1
Introducing yourself and others

Ciao! In Unit 1 you will learn how to introduce yourself and others, how to say where you are from, and how to ask other people for basic information about themselves.

─────────────── Lesson 1 (Words) ───────────────

WORD LIST 1

Come sta? *(fml.)*	*How are you?*
Come stai? *(infml.)*	*How are you?*
io	*I*
Lei *(fml.)*	*you*
uomo	*man*
donna	*woman*
professore	*professor (male)*
professoressa	*professor (female)*
libro	*book*
americano/a	*American (m./f.)*
italiano/a	*Italian (m./f.)*
inglese	*English*

NUTS & BOLTS 1
PERSONAL PRONOUNS IN THE SINGULAR

Notice that there are two ways of asking *How are you?* One is formal, to be used with strangers, in business interactions, and with anyone you want to address with respect, especially if they are older than you or if you are not well acquainted with them. The other is informal, to be used with family, friends, and people whom you know better and are more familiar with, and in general among young people even if they have never met before. Italian even has different forms of the pronoun *you* to show this distinction. Let's take a look at all of the subject pronouns in Italian. We'll start with the singular pronouns.

io	*I*
tu *(infml.)*	*you*
lui	*he*
lei	*she*
Lei *(fml.)*	*you*

As you can see, there are two forms of *you* in the table above. The **tu** form is the familiar or informal form, and **Lei** (always written with a capital "L") is the formal or polite form. Please notice that the formal *you* is the same as the word for *she*. You'll be able to distinguish the different meanings through context and verb endings.

PRACTICE 1
Which Italian pronoun would you use in each of the following situations?

1. Talking to your best friend Claudio.

2. Asking directions from an older stranger you see on the street.

3. Talking about your cousin Roberto.

4. Talking about yourself.

5. Talking about your teacher, professoressa Cocchi.

WORD LIST 2
buongiorno	*good morning*
buonasera	*good evening*
ciao *(infml.)*	*hello, goodbye*
arrivederla *(fml.),*	*goodbye*
arrivederci *(infml.)*	

piacere	*nice to meet you*
perché	*why, because*
casa	*house, home*
ufficio	*office*
lavoro	*work*
vacanza	*vacation, holiday*
stanco/a	*tired (m./f.)*
ragazzo	*young man, boy*
ragazza	*young woman, girl*

NOTES

The word **ciao** is always informal and only used with people you would also address with **tu**.

NUTS & BOLTS 2
PERSONAL PRONOUNS IN THE PLURAL

Now let's look at the subject pronouns that refer to more than one person.

noi	*we*
voi *(infml.)*	*you (all)*
loro	*they*
Loro *(fml.)*	*you (all)*

The singular pronoun **Lei** is more commonly used than the formal plural pronoun **Loro,** which is used in extremely formal situations and is practically disappearing from spoken Italian. Normally, you would use **voi** instead of **Loro** when addressing two or more people you would individually address using **Lei**.

PRACTICE 2
Replace each of the following nouns with the correct pronoun.

1. Carlo e Maria
2. Tu e Giorgio
3. Il professore e io
4. Tu, io e Marcella
5. La professoressa
6. Tu, Franco e Daniela

> ### Tip!
> There are quite a few different ways to memorize new vocabulary, so it's a good idea to try a few out to see what works for you. Reading a word in a list isn't going to be enough for you to actually remember it, though. Write down your new vocabulary in a notebook, then try written or spoken repetition to make it sink in. (You can use the recordings for that, too.) You could also make flash cards, with the Italian on one side and the English on the other. Start going from Italian into English and once you've mastered that, go from English into Italian, which will be harder. You could also label things in your home or office. Experiment and explore, but whatever you do, try to make vocabulary learning as active as possible!

ANSWERS:
PRACTICE 1: 1. tu; 2. Lei; 3. lui; 4. io; 5. lei.

PRACTICE 2 : 1. loro; 2. voi; 3. noi; 4. noi; 5. lei; 6.voi.

Lesson 2 (Phrases)

PHRASE LIST 1

sono americano/a	*I'm American (m./f.)*
di Verona	*from Verona*

a Bologna	*in/to Bologna*
all'università	*at/to the university*
è	*it is, he is, she is*
sono	*I am, they are*
e	*and*
o	*or*
sono uno studente/ una studentessa	*I'm a student (m./f.)*
sono uno professor/ una professoressa	*I'm a professor (m./f.)*

NUTS & BOLTS 1
THE VERB ESSERE IN THE SINGULAR

Now let's look at one of the most important verbs in Italian, **essere** *(to be)*. The form **essere** is called the infinitive and it corresponds to the basic *to* form in English. When you change the verb into different forms to match different subjects, as in English *I speak* but *she speaks*, it's called conjugation. Here's the singular conjugation of **essere** *(to be)*.

io sono	*I am*
tu sei *(infml.)*	*you are*
lui è	*he is*
lei è	*she is*
Lei è *(fml.)*	*you are*

It is very common in Italian to drop the subject pronoun, since the conjugated form of the verb—being different for every subject—makes it clear who is performing the action or who you are talking about.

Io sono americano./Sono americano.

I'm an American.

Sei uno studente.

You're a student.

La professoressa è di Roma o di Verona?

Is the professor from Rome or from Verona?

PRACTICE 1

Complete the following sentences with the correct form of the verb **essere**.

1. Signora Giusti, Lei ____ italiana?

2. Io ____ stanco oggi

3. Marco non ____ uno studente

4. Tu ____ di Roma?

5. Rossella ____una professoressa?

PHRASE LIST 2

sono stanco/a	*I'm tired (m./f.)*
ma	*but*
in ufficio	*in the office*
a casa	*at home*
in vacanza	*on vacation*
ho molto lavoro	*I've a lot of work to do, I'm swamped with work*
siete fortunati	*you're lucky*
è vero	*it's true*
è tardi	*it's late*

NUTS & BOLTS 2

THE VERB ESSERE IN THE PLURAL

Now let's look at the plural conjugation of **essere** *(to be)*.

noi siamo	*we are*
voi siete *(infml.)*	*you (pl.) are*
loro sono	*they are*
Loro sono *(fml.)*	*you (pl.) are*

As mentioned in Lesson 1, the plural formal form **Loro** is used very rarely nowadays; from now on, it will be omitted from the conjugations provided in this course.

Siamo a casa in vacanza.	*We're at home on vacation. We're spending our vacation at home.*
Siete fortunati!	*You're lucky!*
Stanno bene.	*They're well.*

PRACTICE 2
Choose the correct form of the verb in the following sentences.

1. Noi siamo/siete a Bologna per lavoro.

2. Loro sono/siamo di Londra.

3. Signori Rossi, siamo/sono italiani Loro?

4. Voi sono/siete studenti all'università?

5. Lui sono/è stanco oggi.

Tip!
Reading and pronouncing Italian is not very difficult. The most important trick to learn is the correct way to pronounce vowels. First of all, all vowels in Italian are pronounced clearly, not run together as they sometimes are in English. Secondly, the vowels are always pronounced the same way. An **a** always sounds like *ah* as in *father*, **e** always sounds like *eh* as in *pet*, **i** is pronounced *ee* as in *week*, **o** sounds like *oh* as in *hope*, and **u** is pronounced *oo* as in *tool*.

However, when a vowel is accented, as in the verb form **è,** make sure to pronounce that vowel as more open than you would when there is no accent. Listen to how **è** *(it's)* is pronounced when compared to **e** *(and)* and you will easily learn the difference.

ANSWERS
PRACTICE 1: 1. è; 2. sono; 3. è; 4. sei; 5. è.

PRACTICE 2: 1. siamo; 2. sono; 3. sono; 4. siete; 5. è.

—————— Lesson 3 (Sentences) ——————

SENTENCE GROUP 1
Di dove sei?

Where are you from? (infml.)

Di dov'è?

Where are you (fml.) from?, Where is he/she from?

Sono americano/a.

I'm American.

Non sono inglese.

I'm not English.

Siamo di Chicago.

We're from Chicago.

Mi chiamo Giovanna Barbato.

My name is Giovanna Barbato.

Sono uno studente/una studentessa universitario.

I'm a student at the university. I'm a college student.

(Lui) è in Italia per lavoro.

He's in Italy on business.

NUTS & BOLTS 1
NEGATIVE CONSTRUCTION
The negative construction in Italian is very simple. All you need to do to make a sentence negative is add **non** *(not)* in front of the verb.

Io sono americano, non sono inglese.
I'm American, I'm not English.
Lui è uno studente, non è un professore.
He's a student, he's not a professor.
Noi siamo di New York, non siamo di Miami.
We're from New York, we're not from Miami.

PRACTICE 1
Change the following positive sentences into negative sentences using **non**.

1. Mi chiamo Francesco Giannini.

2. Loro sono di Milano.

3. Noi siamo a Roma per lavoro.

4. Lei è una professoressa.

5. Lui è stanco.

SENTENCE GROUP 2
Sono stanco/a.
I'm tired.
Ho molto lavoro.
I have a lot of work (to do).
Siete fortunati.
You're lucky.
Siamo in vacanza.
We're on vacation.
Sono a Roma.
They are in Rome. I am in Rome.
Siete in Italia.
You are in Italy.
Sono a casa.
I'm at home. They are at home.

Sei in ufficio.
You're in the office.

NUTS & BOLTS 2
Prepositions a and in
The prepositions **a** and **in** both mean *in, at,* and *to* but are not interchangeable. The preposition **in** is always used before a country, while **a** is used before a city.

Noi siamo a Roma, in Italia.
We are in Rome, in Italy.

In addition, different places will use either **a** or **in,** sometimes according to the sound that follows it, but often for no obvious reason. For instance, Italians use **in** in front of **ufficio,** but **a** in front of **casa,** and they always say **in vacanza** when they're neither at work or at home, but on vacation instead.

PRACTICE 2
Insert either the preposition **in** or **a** appropriately.

1. Noi siamo _____ Roma.

2. Io sono _____ vacanza.

3. Il professore non è _____ ufficio.

4. I signori Giannini sono _____ casa.

5. Verona è _____ Italia.

Tip!
As you might have already realized, prepositions in Italian are very idiomatic and therefore it's not always easy to decide which preposition to use. The best way to learn them is to remember prepositions as phrases. Note the prepositions and which nouns they go with each time they come up in expressions you read or hear. Eventually they will come to you more easily.

ANSWERS:

PRACTICE 1: 1. Io non mi chiamo Francesco Giannini. 2. Loro non sono di Milano. 3. Noi non siamo a Roma per lavoro. 4. Lei non è una professoressa. 5. Lui non è stanco.

PRACTICE 2: 1. a; 2. in; 3. in; 4. a; 5. in.

─────────── Lesson 4 (Conversations) ───────────

CONVERSATION 1

Mark Smith runs into Professor Cocchi at the University of Bologna.

Mark Smith:	**Buongiorno signora, come sta?**
Professoressa Cocchi:	**Bene grazie e Lei?**
Mark Smith:	**Molto bene. (Io) mi chiamo Mark Smith, sono uno studente qui all'università.**
Professoressa Cocchi:	**Piacere, mi chiamo Mariella Cocchi. Lei è inglese?**
Mark Smith:	**No, non sono inglese, sono americano di Chicago.**
Professoressa Cocchi:	**Ah, è una bella città. Perchè è a Bologna?**
Mark Smith:	**Sono a Bologna per scrivere un libro. Lei Signora di dov'è?**
Professoressa Cocchi:	**Sono di Verona, ma sono a Bologna per lavoro.**

Mark Smith:	*Good day, Ma'am, How are you?*
Professor Cocchi:	*Fine, thanks, and you?*
Mark Smith:	*Very well. My name is Mark Smith. I'm a student here at the university.*
Professor Cocchi:	*Pleased to meet you, my name is Mariella Cocchi. Are you English?*
Mark Smith:	*No, I'm not English; I'm American, from Chicago.*

Professor Cocchi:	*Ah, it's a beautiful city. Why are you in Bologna?*
Mark Smith:	*I'm in Bologna to write a book. Where are you from, Ma'am?*
Professor Cocchi:	*I'm from Verona, but I'm in Bologna for work.*

NOTES

Note that Mark and **professoressa Cocchi** typically drop **io** in the dialogue: **sono uno studente, sono di Verona** and so on. As mentioned in Lesson 2, subject pronouns are rarely used, as the verb itself will tell you the subject.

Also note that Italians introduced themselves using the idiomatic expression **mi chiamo,** literally translated as *I call myself.* **Mi chiamo** is a reflexive verb, we will see how these work in a later Unit. For now, just practice introducing yourself with **mi chiamo** followed by your name.

NUTS & BOLTS 1
GENDER

In Italian, every noun has a gender—either masculine or feminine. For nouns with natural gender, this is easy—**uomo** *(man)*, **ragazzo** *(boy)*, and **professore** *(male professor)* are all masculine, while **donna** *(woman)*, **ragazza** *(girl)*, and **professoressa** *(female professor)* are all feminine.

Object nouns, like **un libro** *(a book)* and **una città** *(a city)*, also have a gender, which is indicated by the final vowel of the word. As a general rule, most nouns that end in **-a** are feminine and most nouns that end in **-o** are masculine.

Some nouns, however, end in **-e,** as in **giornale** *(newspaper)*; with these nouns the gender is harder to tell, as the final vowel **-e** is typical of both feminine and masculine words. Here's a bit of help: nouns that end in **-ione,** such as **stazione** *(station)*, **televisione** *(television)*, etc, are mostly feminine; nouns that end in **-ore,** such as

signore *(gentleman),* **dottore** *(doctor),* etc., are always masculine. For other nouns ending in **-e,** though, the best thing to do is simply memorize the gender of each new noun ending in **-e** that you learn. In the vocabulary lists, the gender of words will be shown with an article (see Nuts & Bolts 2 in this lesson), or with *(m.)* or *(f.)* Let's look at the gender of some of the nouns you've learned so far.

MASCULINE		FEMININE	
uomo	*man*	**donna**	*woman*
professore	*male professor*	**professoressa**	*female professor*
libro	*book*	**casa**	*house*
ufficio	*office*	**sera**	*evening*
lavoro	*work*	**vacanza**	*vacation*
ragazzo	*boy*	**ragazza**	*girl*

PRACTICE 1
Indicate whether the following nouns are feminine or masculine.

1. studente

2. vacanza

3. professore

4. casa

5. ragazzo

6. lavoro

CONVERSATION 2

Roberto and Daniela, two friends, meet on the street.

Roberto: Ciao, Daniela, come stai?
Daniela: Bene, grazie, e tu?
Roberto: Abbastanza bene, ma sono stanco.
Daniela: Perchè sei stanco?
Roberto: Perchè ho molto lavoro in ufficio. E tu?
Daniela: No, io non ho molto lavoro. Gianni e io siamo a casa in vacanza.
Roberto: Siete fortunati!
Daniela: Si, è vero.
Roberto: È tardi. Ciao, Daniela.
Daniela: Arrivederci.

Roberto: *Hello, Daniela, how are you?*
Daniela: *Well, thank you. And you?*
Roberto: *Fairly well, but I'm tired.*
Daniela: *Why are you tired?*
Roberto: *Because I have a lot of work at the office. And you?*
Daniela: *No, I don't have much work. Gianni and I are at home on vacation.*
Roberto: *You're lucky!*
Daniela: *Yes, it's true.*
Roberto: *It's late. Bye, Daniela.*
Daniela: *Bye.*

NOTES

Ho is the **io** form of the verb **avere** *(to have),* which you will learn in the next Unit. Note that the letter **h** is always silent in Italian.

The word **abbastanza,** which normally means *enough,* here means *fairly.*

NUTS & BOLTS 2
INDEFINITE ARTICLES

Now that you know that Italian words have a gender, you need to learn that every word referring to a noun—an article or an adjective, for example—will also have the same gender as the noun to which they refer. In Conversation 1 you saw two nouns, one preceded by **uno (uno studente),** and another by **un (un libro). Un** and **uno** are the masculine indefinite articles, equivalent to the English *a* or *an.* We use **un** in front of any masculine word, except those words beginning with **s** + consonant **(studente,** *student)*; **z (zaino,** *backpack)*; **ps (psicologo,** *psychologist)*; and **gn (gnomo,** *gnome)*, in front of which we use **uno.** There is also a feminine indefinite article, **una,** which is spelled **un'** in front of a noun beginning with a vowel.

MASCULINE		
un	**un libro** *(a book)*	in front of a consonant or vowel
uno	**uno studente** *(a male student)*	in front of *s* + consonant, *z, ps, gn*
FEMININE		
una	**una casa** *(a house)*	in front of a consonant
un'	**un'amica** *(a female friend)*	in front of a vowel

PRACTICE 2
Place the correct indefinite article in front of the following nouns.

1. _____ uomo

2. _____ donna

3. _____ professore

4. _____ professoressa

5. _____ ufficio

6. _____ lavoro

7. _____ vacanza

8. _____ studente

9. _____ aria

10. _____ zaino

Tip!

The University of Bologna where Mark Smith studies is the oldest university in the western world, founded ca. 1088. To find out more about the history of the university and its curricula and services today, visit the following website, available both in Italian and in English: **www.unibo.it**

ANSWERS:

PRACTICE 1: 1. m; 2. f; 3. m; 4. f; 5. m; 6. m.

PRACTICE 2: 1. un; 2. una; 3. un; 4. una; 5. un; 6. un; 7. una; 8. uno; 9. un'; 10. uno.

UNIT 1 ESSENTIALS

Mi chiamo Mark Smith.	*My name is Mark Smith.*
Di dov'è? *(fml./infml.)*	*Where are you from? Where is he/she from?*
Di dove sei? *(infml.)*	*Where are you from?*
Sono americano.	*I'm American.*
Sono uno studente.	*I'm a student.*
Sono di Chicago.	*I'm from Chicago. They're from Chicago.*
Non sono inglese.	*I'm not English.*
Sono a casa.	*I'm at home. They're at home.*
Sei in ufficio.	*You're in the office.*
Siete fortunati.	*(All of) you are lucky.*
Sono in vacanza.	*I'm on vacation. They're on vacation.*
È vero.	*It's true. Correct.*

UNIT 2
Around the city and around the home

Now that you know how to introduce yourself, and meet other people, you're ready to learn how to talk to other people about your (or any other) city, and describe your house. Let's begin by learning some important words for describing cities.

---------------- Lesson 5 (Words) ----------------

WORD LIST 1

città	*city*
paese *(m.)*	*town, country*
museo	*museum*
edificio	*building*
centro	*center, downtown*
mostra	*exhibit*
biblioteca	*library*
libreria	*bookstore, bookshelves (in a house or office)*
ristorante *(m.)*	*restaurant*
parco	*park*
albero	*tree*
aria	*air*
vista	*view*
chiesa	*church*

NUTS & BOLTS 1
PLURAL OF NOUNS

As you learned in Unit 1, nouns that end in **-a** are generally feminine, and nouns that end in **-o** are generally masculine. (There are also very few masculine nouns ending in **-a**.) Nouns that end in **-e** can be either feminine or masculine. So, if we talk about a

church, we'll say **una chiesa,** and if we talk about a *tree,* we'll say
un albero. If we want to speak about more than one object, however, we need to form the plural of these nouns.

A feminine noun that ends in -a will change the final -a into an -e.

chiesa *(church)*	**chiese** *(churches)*

A noun that ends in -o will change the final -o into an -i. Simi-
larly, masculine nouns ending in -a will also change the final -a
into an -i.

albero *(tree)*	**alberi** *(trees)*
programma *(program)*	**programmi** *(programs)*

A noun that ends in -e, whether it's feminine or masculine, will
change the final -e into an -i.

ristorante *(restaurant)*	**ristoranti** *(restaurants)*

Please note that a noun ending with an accented vowel, such as
città, will not change in the plural.

città *(city)*	**città** *(cities)*

Also, a noun ending in -io will not end in a double i, but instead
ends in one i, unless the i carries the stress.

edificio *(building)*	**edifici** *(buildings)*
zio *(uncle)*	**zii** *(uncles)*

PRACTICE 1
Give the plural of the following nouns.

1. paese

2. mostra

3. città

4. museo

5. negozio

6. vista

7. ristorante

8. caffè

WORD LIST 2

appartamento	*apartment*
via	*street*
stanza	*room*
camera *(fml.)*	*room, chamber, cabinet*
soggiorno	*living room*
cucina	*kitchen*
bagno	*bathroom*
letto	*bed*
camera da letto	*bedroom*
armadio	*armoire, closet*
tavolo	*table*
divano	*sofa, couch*
televisione *(f.)*	*television*
televisore *(m.)*	*television*

NUTS & BOLTS 2
NUMBERS 0–10
Let's look at the numbers 0 through 10 in Italian.

zero	*zero*
uno	*one*
due	*two*
tre	*three*
quattro	*four*
cinque	*five*
sei	*six*
sette	*seven*
otto	*eight*
nove	*nine*
dieci	*ten*

PRACTICE 2
Change the following nouns according to the model of the example: **un letto. 2 ➔ due letti.**

1. un tavolo.   3 _____

2. una cucina.   7 _____

3. una televisione.   5 _____

4. una stanza.   9 _____

5. un divano.   4 _____

6. un soggiorno.   6 _____

7. una casa.   8 _____

8. un appartamento.   10 _____

Culture note

In this unit we'll learn how to speak about the house, so we should first say a few words about where Italians live. Individual houses are very rare in Italian cities, which are usually very old and densely populated. For this reason, most Italians who live in urban areas live in apartments. Apartments, however, come in all shapes and sizes, and Italian apartments can be as spacious as houses.

ANSWERS:

PRACTICE 1: 1. paesi; **2.** mostre; **3.** città; **4.** musei; **5.** negozi; **6.** viste; **7.** ristoranti; **8.** caffè.

PRACTICE 2: 1. tre tavoli; **2.** sette cucine; **3.** cinque televisioni; **4.** nove stanze; **5.** quattro divani; **6.** sei soggiorni; **7.** otto case; **8.** dieci appartamenti.

——————————— Lesson 6 (Phrases) ———————————

PHRASE LIST 1

Che bello!	*How beautiful!*
bene	*well*
c'è	*there is*
ci sono	*there are*
in questo periodo	*in this period, currently*
abbastanza	*enough*
perfetto	*perfect*
non c'è	*there isn't*
lì vicino	*near there*
vicino a	*near to*
in centro	*to/in the city, in the center of town, downtown*

NUTS & BOLTS 1
THERE IS . . . THERE ARE . . .

The phrases **c'è** and **ci sono** correspond to the English *there is* and *there are,* and are used to describe what is present or exists in a particular place. **C'è** is used with a singular noun, while **ci sono** is used with plural nouns.

C'è una mostra su Leonardo.
There is an exhibit about Leonardo.

Non ci sono molti alberi in centro.
There aren't many trees in the center of town.

PRACTICE 1
Complete the following sentences with either **c'è** or **ci sono.**

1. Al museo degli Uffizi _____ molti quadri.

2. _____ molti studenti in questa classe.

3. _____ una cucina grande in questa casa

4. Nel mio appartamento _____ due camere da letto.

5. Non _____ un parco in città.

6. _____ una televisione nella camera da letto.

PHRASE LIST 2

Dov'è . . . ?	*Where is . . . ?*
Dove sono . . . ?	*Where are . . . ?*
abbiamo	*We have*
non ho	*I don't have*
abito	*I live*
Com'è?	*How is . . . ?*
Come sono?	*How are . . . ?*
studiamo	*we study*
in un appartamento	*in an apartment*
in via Mazzini 13	*in/at Mazzini Street, number 13*

NUTS & BOLTS 2
Numbers 11–20
Now let's learn the numbers 11 through 20 in Italian.

undici	*eleven*
dodici	*twelve*
tredici	*thirteen*
quattordici	*fourteen*
quindici	*fifteen*
sedici	*sixteen*
diciassette	*seventeen*
diciotto	*eighteen*
diciannove	*nineteen*
venti	*twenty*

PRACTICE 2
Change the following nouns following the example: **una casa.**
2 _____ → **due case.**

1. un quadro   12 _quadri_
2. una mostra   15 _mostre_
3. un caffè   17 _caffè_
4. una cucina   11 _cucine_
5. un museo   13 _musei_
6. una chiesa   14 _chiese_
7. un paese   18 _paesi_
8. un edificio   16 _edifici_
9. una televisione   19 _televisioni_

Tip!

The numbers from 11 to 19 are the most difficult to learn. You will need to practice them a lot. You can find hints in these words: notice that the number **dieci** *(ten)* appears in different form in these numbers as the suffix **(-dici)**, indicating these are the *teens*. The best way to practice is by counting. Make sure to count objects around your house; try to find objects of which you have at least ten. Solve some math problems, count your change all in Italian! You'll be surprised how well they start to stick in your mind.

ANSWERS:

PRACTICE 1: 1. ci sono; **2.** ci sono; **3.** c'è; **4.** ci sono; **5.** c'è; **6.** c'è.

PRACTICE 2: 1. dodici quadri; **2.** quindici mostre; **3.** diciassette caffè; **4.** undici cucine; **5.** tredici musei; **6.** quattordici chiese; **7.** diciotto paesi; **8.** sedici edifici; **9.** diciannove televisioni.

―――――――― Lesson 7 (Sentences) ――――――――

SENTENCE GROUP 1

Oggi visitiamo il museo degli Uffizi.

Today, we'll visit the Uffizi museum.

C'è una mostra su Leonardo.

There's an exhibit on Leonardo.

Abbiamo abbastanza tempo?

Do we have enough time?

Sì, abbiamo quattro ore.

Yes, we have four hours.

Non c'è tempo per la biblioteca.

There's no time for the library.

Mangiamo con Gianni.

We're eating with Gianni.

C'è un parco vicino al museo?

Is there a park by the museum?

Non ci sono molti alberi.

There aren't many trees.

A Fiesole l'aria è pulita.

Fiesole has clean air. (lit., In Fiesole the air is clean.)

NUTS & BOLTS 1

THE VERB AVERE

Another very important verb in Italian is the verb **avere** *(to have).* Just like **essere, avere** is an irregular verb. Unlike regular verbs, which conjugate according to patterns common to other verbs, irregular verbs have forms that are unique, and thus they must be memorized individually.

io ho	*I have*
tu hai	*you have*
lui ha	*he has*
lei ha	*she has*
Lei ha *(fml.)*	*you have*
noi abbiamo	*we have*
voi avete	*you (all) have*
loro hanno	*they have*

Forming questions from these verbs is simple. Consider the following two sentences.

Abbiamo abbastanza tempo?

Do we have enough time?

Sì, abbiamo quattro ore.

Yes, we have four hours.

As you can see, the question and the answer have exactly the same structure, which makes asking questions in Italian very easy! Here's another example.

Lui ha un appartamento grande.
He has a large apartment.
Lui ha un appartamento grande?
Does he have a large apartment?

If a question and a statement look exactly the same, how do we distinguish them? In written form, the question is followed by a question mark, while in speech the distinction is made by raised intonation at the end of the sentence, which is part of what gives Italian the sing-song quality we associate with the language. Placing the subject at the very end of the question is another way to differentiate a question from a statement.

Ha un appartamento grande, lui?
Does he have a large apartment?

The above structure, though it is very common, is not always necessary, as Italians often leave out the subject altogether.

Ha un appartamento grande?
Does (he/she) have a large apartment?

Remember that the interrogative structure is the same no matter what verb you're using.

PRACTICE 1
Unscramble the following sentences.

1. piccola/loro/una/càsa/hanno/?

2. appuntamento/voi/al/un/avete/museo/.

3. ha/un/interessante/libro/lei/?

4. professoressa/di/tu/una/italiano/hai/simpatica/.

5. abbiamo/tempo/abbastanza/noi/?

6. signora/ha/scusi/molto/oggi/lavoro/Lei/?

SENTENCE GROUP 2

Dov'è la tua casa?

Where is your house?

Abito in un appartamento.

I live in an apartment.

Quante stanze ci sono?

How many rooms are there? How many rooms does it comprise?

C'è il soggiorno e la cucina.

There are the living room and the kitchen.

C'è anche lo studio.

There's also a study.

Com'è la tua camera da letto?

How's your bedroom?

È bella e spaziosa.

It's beautiful and spacious.

C'è lo stereo e la televisione.

There's a stereo and a television.

NUTS & BOLTS 2

DEFINITE ARTICLES

Now let's look at the singular forms of the definite article (equivalent to *the*) in Italian. As you can see from the sentences above, there are different ways to express *the* in Italian. There are two masculine singular definite articles, **il** and **lo**. We use **il** in front of masculine nouns beginning with a consonant, except those masculine words beginning with **s** + consonant (**stereo**, *stereo*); **z** (**zaino**, *backpack*); **ps** (**psicologo**, *psychologist*); and **gn** (**gnomo**, *gnome*), in front of which we use **lo**. **Lo** is also used in front of masculine nouns beginning with a vowel, but in this case, the **o** is always dropped and **lo** becomes **l'**: **l'appartamento**. The feminine article is **la (la cucina)**, which becomes **l'** when it appears before a noun beginning with a vowel: **l'aria**.

MASCULINE		
il	**il soggiorno** *(the living room)*	in front of a consonant
lo	**lo stereo** *(the stereo)*	in front of s + consonant, **z, ps, gn**
l'	**l'appartamento** *(the apartment)*	in front of a vowel
FEMININE		
la	**la cucina** *(the kitchen)*	in front of a consonant
l'	**l'aria** *(the air)*	in front of a vowel

PRACTICE 2
Complete with the appropriate singular definite article:

1. _____ casa

2. _____ ufficio

3. _____ camera da letto

4. _____ studio

5. _____ televisione

6. _____ museo

7. _____ armadio

8. _____ divano

Culture note

The Museo degli Uffizi holds, among other works of art, an extraordinary collection of Medieval and Renaissance masterpieces, including works by Giotto, Simone Martini, Botticelli, Leonardo, Michelangelo, Raffaello, and many other world renowned painters. You can take a virtual tour of this and other Florentine museums by visiting the website **www.polomuseale.firenze.it**, where you will be able to discover many world famous works of art.

ANSWERS

PRACTICE 1: 1. Loro hanno una casa piccola?/Hanno una casa piccola loro? **2.** Voi avete un appuntamento al museo. **3.** Lei ha un libro interessante?/Ha un libro interessante Lei? **4.** Tu hai una professoressa di italiano simpatica. **5.** Noi abbiamo abbastanza tempo?/Abbiamo abbastanza tempo noi? **6.** Scusi signora, Lei ha molto lavoro oggi?/Scusi signora, ha molto lavoro Lei oggi?

PRACTICE 2: 1. la; **2.** l'; **3.** la; **4.** lo; **5.** la; **6.** il; **7.** l'; **8.** il.

──────── Lesson 8 (Conversations) ────────

CONVERSATION 1

Stephanie: Che bello essere a Firenze! È una città fantastica e sono fortunata che tu sei la mia guida!

Guido: Bene, oggi visitiamo il museo degli Uffizi. È in un edificio rinascimentale in centro. Ci sono quadri di Botticelli, Leonardo da Vinci, Michelangelo, Raffaello e Tiziano, tutti gli artisti importanti del Rinascimento. Inoltre in questo periodo c'è anche una mostra su Leonardo.

Stephanie: Perfetto! Abbiamo abbastanza tempo?

Guido: Sì, abbiamo quattro ore.

Stephanie: E la biblioteca?

Guido: Non c'è tempo per la biblioteca. Pranziamo con Gianni. Il ristorante è in una strada lì vicino.

Stephanie: C'è un parco vicino al museo?

Guido: No, non ci sono molti alberi in centro. Ma domani visitiamo Fiesole, un paese vicino a Firenze. A Fiesole l'aria è pulita e la vista, le chiese, gli alberi e i prati sono bellissimi.

Stephanie: *How beautiful to be in Florence! It's a fantastic city, and I'm fortunate you're my guide!*

Guido: *Well, today we'll visit the Uffizi Gallery. It's in a Renaissance building in the center of town. There are paintings by Botticelli, Leonardo da Vinci, Michelangelo, Raphael and Titian, all the important Renaissance artists. And in this period, there's also an exhibit on Leonardo.*

Stephanie: *Great! Do we have enough time?*

Guido: *Yes, we have four hours.*

Stephanie: *And the library?*

Guido: *There's no time for the library. We're eating with Gianni. The restaurant is in a street nearby.*

Stephanie: *Is there a park near the museum?*

Guido: *No, there aren't many trees in the center of town. But tomorrow, we'll visit Fiesole, a town near Florence. In Fiesole the air is clean, and the view, the churches, the trees and the meadows are very beautiful.*

NOTES

Again, please note the use of the proposition **a** and **in** in certain expressions: Italians use the preposition **in** to indicate where things are in a city: **in centro** *(in the center of town);* **in un edificio** *(in a building);* **in una strada** *(in a street);* and with actual addresses: **in via Mazzini** *(in Mazzini street).* However, they often use the preposition **a** to indicate where things are located with respect to other objects: **vicino a** *(near);* **davanti a** *(in front of);* **di fronte a** *(facing),* etc.

Pranzare is a regular **-are** verb meaning *to dine.*

Inoltre can mean either *besides* or *in addition to.*

NUTS & BOLTS 1
Regular -are verbs in the present tense

Now that you've learned two irregular verbs, **essere** and **avere,** let's learn some regular verb patterns. Every Italian verb belongs to one of three verb groups: verbs whose infinitive ends in **-are,** such as **abitare** *(to live);* verbs whose infinitive ends in **-ere,** such as **ricevere** *(to receive);* and verbs whose infinitive ends in **-ire,** such as **dormire** *(to sleep).* Each group has its own conjugation pattern which will allow you to conjugate any regular verb belonging to that group. Let's begin with **-are** verbs. The **-are** group is the largest (most verbs belong to this group), as well as the more regular (there are only four irregular **-are** verbs, which we'll learn in a later lesson). To conjugate a regular **-are** verb, for example **abitare,** drop the ending **-are** and add to the stem of the verb **abit-** the appropriate subject ending.

io abit-o	*I live*
tu abit-i	*you live*
lui abit-a	*he lives*
lei abit-a	*she lives*
Lei abit-a	*you live (fml.)*
noi abit-iamo	*we live*
voi abit-ate	*you (pl.) live*
loro abit-ano	*they live*

Here's a list of common Italian **-are** verbs.

abitare	*to live*
arrivare	*to arrive*
ascoltare	*to listen (to)*
aspettare	*to wait (for)*
ballare	*to dance*
cantare	*to sing*
chiamare	*to call, to telephone*
comprare	*to buy*
giocare (a)	*to play (a game, a sport)*
parlare	*to speak*
suonare	*to play (an instrument), to ring (a bell)*
(ri)tornare	*to return, to go back*

Again, remember that any regular **-are** verb will follow exactly the pattern above.

Verbs ending in **-care** and **-gare,** such as **giocare** and **pagare,** add an **h** between the stem of the verb, and the **tu** ending, **-i,** and the **noi** ending, **-iamo.**

Noi giochiamo a tennis.
We play tennis.
Tu non paghi mai il conto.
You never pay the bill.

PRACTICE 1
Complete the following sentences with the correct form of the verbs given in parentheses.

1. Maria _____ (abitare) in centro.

2. Giovanni e Roberto _____ (mangiare) in un ristorante italiano.

3. Io _____ (visitare) il museo degli Uffizi.

4. Noi _____ (lavorare) in un ufficio in centro.

5. Tu e Giulia _____ (giocare) a tennis.

6. Rossella, tu _____ (parlare) italiano?

7. Tu ed io _____ (aspettare) l'autobus.

8. Enrico _____ (ritornare) in Italia ogni anno.

CONVERSATION 2

Lorenzo: Mirella, dov'è la tua casa?

Mirella: Abito in un appartamento in via Mazzini 13. L'appartamento è molto grande.

Lorenzo: Quante stanze ci sono?

Mirella: C'è il soggiorno e la cucina, ci sono due bagni, tre camere da letto e c'è anche lo studio che condivido con mio fratello.

Lorenzo: Com'è la tua camera da letto?

Mirella: È bella e spaziosa. Ci sono due letti, un armadio, un tavolo e quattro librerie. C'è anche un piccolo divano, lo stereo e la televisione.

Lorenzo: È veramente molto grande!

Mirella: Sì, sono fortunata!

Lorenzo: *Mirella, where's your house?*

Mirella: *I live in an apartment, at 13 Mazzini Street. The apartment is quite big.*

Lorenzo: *How many rooms are there?*

> *Mirella:* There are the living room and the kitchen, there are two bathrooms and three bedrooms, and there's also a study room my brother and I share.
>
> *Lorenzo:* How is your bedroom?
>
> *Mirella:* It's beautiful and spacious. There are two beds, a closet, a table and four bookshelves. There are also a small couch, a stereo, and a television.
>
> *Lorenzo:* It's really very big!
>
> *Mirella:* Yes, I'm lucky!

NOTES

Condividere is a regular **-ere** verb meaning *to share*. You'll learn more about **-ere** verbs in Lesson 12.

NUTS & BOLTS 2
PLURAL FORMS OF THE DEFINITE ARTICLE

Let's learn the plural forms of the Italian definite article. For the masculine, the plural of **il** is **i**; and the plural of **lo** and **l'** is **gli**. The feminine **la** and **l'** both pluralize in **le**.

MASCULINE		
i	i soggiorni *(the living rooms)*	in front of consonants
gli	gli studi *(the studies)*	in front of s + consonant, z, ps, gn, and vowels
	gli appartamenti *(the apartments)*	
FEMININE		
le	le cucine *(the kitchens)*	in front of consonants and vowels
	le amiche *(the female friends)*	

PRACTICE 2
Complete with the appropriate plural definite article:

1. _____ case

2. _____ uffici

3. _____ camere da letto

4. _____ studi

5. _____ televisioni

6. _____ musei

7. _____ armadi

8. _____ divani

Tip!

Italians count the floors in their buildings differently than Americans do. What Americans call the first floor is always called **pian terreno** or **piano terra** (lit., *ground floor*) in Italy, and what Americans call the second floor is **primo piano** (*first floor*). The thirteenth floor isn't skipped the way it is in some American buildings, as according to Italian tradition the number 13 (**tredici**) brings good luck rather than bad luck. The penthouse is called **attico** and the basement is called **seminterrato** or **sottano**. When you go to visit somebody in Italy, make sure you ring the correct bell according to the Italian floor-counting criteria.

ANSWERS
PRACTICE 1: 1. abita; 2. mangiano; 3. visito; 4. lavoriamo; 5. giocate; 6. parli; 7. aspettiamo; 8. ritorna.

PRACTICE 2: 1. le; 2. gli; 3. le; 4. gli; 5. le; 6. i; 7. gli; 8. i.

UNIT 2 ESSENTIALS

Oggi visitiamo il museo degli Uffizi.	*Today, we visit the Uffizi museum.*
C'è una mostra su Leonardo.	*There's an exhibit on Leonardo.*
Non ci sono molti alberi in centro.	*There aren't many trees in the city.*
Le chiese, gli alberi, i prati sono belli.	*The churches, the trees, and the meadows are beautiful.*
Abbiamo tempo.	*We have time.*
Non abbiamo una casa.	*We don't have a house.*
Abito in un appartamento in centro.	*I live in an apartment in the center of town/in the city.*
C'è il soggiorno, la cucina e lo studio.	*There are a living room, a kitchen, and a study.*
Ci sono due letti e quattro librerie.	*There are two beds and four bookshelves.*
Io e mio fratello studiamo nello studio.	*My brother and I study in the study.*

UNIT 3
Everyday life

In this unit you will learn how to describe your everyday life, from work **(il lavoro)** to free time **(il tempo libero),** if you're **fortunato** or **fortunata** *(lucky)* to have any! You will learn more verbs, including some irregular ones, and, among other things, how to describe things and people using **gli aggettivi** *(adjectives).* So, let's get to work! We're going to be **occupati** *(busy)!*

────────────── Lesson 9 (Words) ──────────────

WORD LIST 1

la settimana	*the week*
il giorno	*the day*
lunedì	*Monday*
martedì	*Tuesday*
mercoledì	*Wednesday*
giovedì	*Thursday*
venerdì	*Friday*
sabato	*Saturday*
domenica	*Sunday*
il lavoro	*work*
la moda	*fashion*

NUTS & BOLTS 1
DAYS OF THE WEEK AND RECURRENCE

In this lesson, you'll be dealing with **i giorni della settimana** *(the days of the week).* Notice that in Italian the names of weekdays are not capitalized. Also, remember that all the names of weekdays are masculine, with the exception of **domenica,** which is feminine. Another important rule to remember: in Italian, when talking about what's happening on a specific day, you don't use a preposition.

Non lavoro lunedì.
I'm not working on Monday (next Monday).

When talking about something that always happens on a specific day of the week, place the definite article in front of the day of the week.

Non lavoro il lunedì.
I don't work on Mondays (every Monday).

PRACTICE 1
Translate the following sentences into Italian:

1. I won't work on Monday because I'm on vacation.
2. On Wednesdays we eat at the restaurant.
3. On Tuesday they call Maria.
4. He'll visit Florence on Thursday.
5. On Sundays there is an exhibit.

WORD LIST 2

terribile	*terrible*
bello/bella	*beautiful*
nervoso/nervosa	*nervous*
malato/malata	*sick*
piccolo/piccola	*small*
grande	*big*
carino/carina	*cute, pretty*

brutto/brutta	*ugly*
rumoroso/rumorosa	*noisy*
pièno/piena	*full*
silenzioso/silenziosa	*silent*
solo/sola	*lonely*
depresso/depressa	*depressed*
felice	*happy*
vero/vera	*true*
falso/falsa	*false*
molto	*a lot, many; very*
tanto	*a lot, many; very*

NUTS & BOLTS 2
ADJECTIVE AGREEMENT

You have already learned that nouns and definite articles in Italian have a gender (masculine or feminine) and a number (singular or plural). The same is true for adjectives, which have to agree in gender and number with the noun they modify. Adjectives are usually placed after the noun. There are two groups of adjectives: adjectives whose singular masculine form ends in -o (such as **piccolo**) with four possible endings (-o, -a, -i, -e), and adjectives whose singular masculine form ends in -e (such as **felice**) with two possible endings (-e, -i).

	Singular	Plural
Masculine	**piccolo**	**piccoli**
Feminine	**piccola**	**piccole**
Masculine/Feminine	**felice**	**felici**

Un bambino piccolo.

A small child (male).

Una bambina piccola.

A small child (female).

I bambini piccoli.

The small children (male, or both male and female).

Le bambine piccole.

The small children (female).

Un bambino felice.

A happy child (male).

Una bambina felice.

A happy child (female).

I bambini felici.

The happy children (male, or both male and female).

Le bambine felici.

The happy children (female).

Notice that when we talk about a mixed gender group, both the noun and the adjective will take the masculine plural ending **-i**.

Molto and **tanto** in Italian can be used both as adverbs and adjectives. When we use them as adverbs, they both mean *very* and they are invariable (**molto fortunata, molto fortunati**). When we use them as adjectives, they both mean *a lot* or *many* and like the other adjectives agree in gender and number to the nouns they modify (**molta pasta, molti bambini**).

PRACTICE 2

Complete the following sentences with the appropriate form of the adjective given in parentheses.

1. È una professoressa _____. (simpatico)

2. I dottori sono molto _____. (occupato)

3. Noi abbiamo una casa _____. (rumoroso)

4. È una bambina molto _____. (grande)

5. Silvia e Ilaria sono _____ per il colloquio di lavoro. (nervoso)

6. Mario è molto _____. (malato)

Tip!

If you look at an Italian calendar, you will notice that the week in Italy begins on **lunedì** *(Monday)*, not on **domenica** *(Sunday)*. After all, **domenica** is one of the days of the week "end", not the week "beginning"!

ANSWERS

PRACTICE 1: 1. Lunedì non lavoro perché sono in vacanza. **2.** Il mercoledì mangiamo al ristorante. **3.** Martedì chiamano Maria. **4.** Giovedì visita Firenze. **5.** La domenica c'è una mostra.

PRACTICE 2: 1. simpatica; **2.** occupati; **3.** rumorosa; **4.** grande; **5.** nervose; **6.** malato.

Lesson 10 (Phrases)

PHRASE LIST 1

fai	*you do, you make*
faccio	*I do, I make*
andiamo	*we go*
magari	*I wish, perhaps*
mi dispiace	*I'm sorry*
ho bisogno di	*I need*
ho fame	*I'm hungry*
ho fretta	*I'm in a hurry*
un colloquio di lavoro	*a job interview*
lavoro part-time	*part-time job*
non credo	*I don't think so*
purtroppo	*unfortunately*

NUTS & BOLTS 1
IRREGULAR -ARE VERBS IN THE PRESENT TENSE

As mentioned in Unit 2, there are only four irregular -are verbs: **andare** *(to go)*, **dare** *(to give)*, **fare** *(to do, to make)*, **stare** *(to stay)*. These conjugations must be memorized, as these verbs are not conjugated like other regular -are verbs.

ANDARE	to go	DARE	to give
io vado	I go	io do	I give
tu vai	you go	tu dai	you give
lui va	he goes	lui dà	he gives
lei va	she goes	lei dà	she gives
Lei va	you (fml.) go	Lei dà	you (fml.) give
noi andiamo	we go	noi diamo	we give
voi andate	you (pl.) go	voi date	you (pl.) give
loro vanno	they go	loro danno	they give

Quando vai al supermercato?

When do you go to the supermarket?

Susanna dà una festa il sabato.

Susanna gives a party on Saturdays. Susanna throws parties on Saturdays.

FARE	to do, to make	STARE	to stay
io faccio	I do/make	io sto	I stay
tu fai	you do/make	tu stai	you stay
lui fa	he does/makes	lui sta	he stays

FARE	to do, to make	STARE	to stay
lei fa	she does/makes	lei sta	she stays
Lei fa	you (fml.) do/make	Lei sta	you (fml.) stay
noi facciamo	we do/make	noi stiamo	we stay
voi fate	you (pl.) do/make	voi state	you (pl.) stay
loro fanno	they do/make	loro stanno	they stay

Note that **stare,** in addition to its literal meaning *to stay,* is used idiomatically to mean *to be feeling,* as you saw in previous dialogues.

Che lavoro fai?
What (job) do you do?
Giovanna, come stai?
Giovanna, how are you?

PRACTICE 1
Complete the following sentences with the correct form of either **andare, dare, fare,** or **stare.**

1. Loro _____ al cinema il sabato.

2. Il professore _____ un libro ai suoi studenti.

3. Maria, come _____?

4. _____ bene, grazie, e tu?

5. Voi _____ un lavoro molto interessante.

6. Noi _____ in ufficio alle 8:30.

7. Questa sera tu _____ al ristorante o _____ a casa?

PHRASE LIST 2

alle sette	*at seven*
mille cose	*tons of things, a million things (lit., a thousand things)*
cinquantaquattro	*fifty-four*
una giornata piena	*a full day, a busy day*
un momento	*a moment, wait a second*
di mattina	*in the morning*
di pomeriggio	*in the afternoon*
di sera	*in the evening*
di notte	*at night*
ho ragione	*I'm right*
ho torto	*I'm wrong*
fare spese	*to shop*

NUTS & BOLTS 2
NUMBERS 20 AND ABOVE

Now that you've learned the most difficult numbers, you're ready to tackle all other cardinal numbers in Italian. Let's now look at numbers 20 and above.

venti	*twenty*
trenta	*thirty*
quaranta	*forty*
cinquanta	*fifty*
sessanta	*sixty*
settanta	*seventy*
ottanta	*eighty*

novanta	*ninety*
cento	*one hundred*
mille	*one thousand*
milione/i	*million*
miliardo/i	*billion*

To form all other numbers, you just need to add numbers **uno,
due, tre,** etc., up through **nove,** as in **cinquantaquattro** *(fifty-
four)*. Note that you need to drop the final vowel of numbers
venti through **novanta** when you add the numbers **uno** and **otto,**
as in **ventuno, ventotto.** When adding the number **tre** to those
numbers, **-tré** requires a written accent, as in **quarantatré.**

The numbers *one hundred* and *one thousand* are expressed respectively with **cento** and **mille** (without translating the English *one*).
Note that **mille** has an irregular plural: **mila,** as in **duemila.**

The numbers **milione** and **miliardo** require the preposition **di** in
front of a noun, as in **un milione di dollari.**

PRACTICE 2
Write out the following numbers:

1. 68   _____
2. 281   _____
3. 3,726   _____
4. 43,263   _____
5. 875,974   _____
6. 3,268,957   _____

ANSWERS

PRACTICE 1: 1. vanno; 2. dà; 3. stai; 4. sto; 5. fate; 6. andiamo; 7. vai, stai.

PRACTICE 2: 1. sessantotto; 2. duecentottantuno;
3. tremilasettecentoventisei;
4. quarantatremiladuecentosessantatré;
5. ottocentosettantacinquemilanovecentosettantaquattro;
6. tremilioniduecentosessantottomilanovecentocinquantasette.

─────────── Lesson 11 (Sentences) ───────────

SENTENCE GROUP 1

Come stai?

How are you?

Che cosa fai?

What do you do? (What are you doing?)

Che lavoro fai?

What kind of work do you do?

Quante ore lavori?

How many hours do you work?

Dove lavori?

Where do you work?

Perché hai fretta?

Why are you in a hurry?

Chi va al supermercato oggi?

Who's going to the supermarket today?

Di che cosa ha bisogno il direttore?

What does the director need?

Quando andiamo al ristorante?

When are we going to the restaurant?

Quanto costa un caffè in Italia?

How much does a (cup of) coffee cost in Italy?

Quale ristorante preferisci?

Which restaurant do you prefer?

NUTS & BOLTS 1

INTERROGATIVES

As you can see in the sentences above, some questions begin with interrogatives, also known as question words. In these types of questions, when the subject is expressed, it is usually placed at the end of the sentence.

Quando arriva Marco?

When does Marco arrive?

Most interrogative words are invariable. **Quale** and **quanto,** however, are adjectives, and as such they agree in gender and number with the noun they modify.

Quali riviste leggi?

Which magazines do you read?

Quanti libri hai?

How many books do you have?

When you need to use a preposition in a sentence beginning with the question word **chi,** the preposition always precedes the question word and is never placed at the end of the sentence.

Con chi vai al cinema?

Who are you going to the movies with?

A chi dai il giornale?

Who are you giving the newspaper to?

PRACTICE 1

Ask the questions for which the following sentences are answers:

1. Sto bene, grazie.   _____?

2. Ho solo una macchina. _____?

3. Preferisco Venezia.   _____?

4. Andiamo al cinema alle 8. _____?

5. Ha bisogno di denaro.   _____?

6. Studiano a Perugia.   _____?

7. Oggi non lavoro perché sto male.   _____?

8. Andiamo al ristorante con Luisa.   _____?

SENTENCE GROUP 2

Hanno molta fame.

They're very hungry.

Il direttore non ha bisogno di aiuto.

The director doesn't need any help.

Purtroppo ho fretta.

Unfortunately, I'm in a hurry.

Lei ha torto.

She's wrong.

Noi abbiamo ragione.

We're right.

Gisella fa la giornalista.

Gisella is a journalist.

Facciamo la spesa al supermercato.
We go grocery shopping at the supermarket.

NUTS & BOLTS 2
IDIOMATIC EXPRESSIONS USING AVERE AND FARE

Avere and **fare** are two very idiomatic verbs. **Avere** is used in many expressions that require *to be* in English, such as **avere fame** *(to be hungry)*. **Fare** is often used in expressions that require *to take* in English, such as **fare una fotografia** *(to take a picture)*. Here is a list of the most common idiomatic expressions that use **avere**.

avere fame	*to be hungry*
avere sete	*to be thirsty*
avere caldo	*to be hot*
avere freddo	*to be cold*
avere ragione	*to be right*
avere torto	*to be wrong*
avere fretta	*to be in a hurry*
avere sonno	*to be sleepy*
avere bisogno di	*to need*
avere voglia di	*to feel like*
avere paura di	*to be afraid of*

In addition, **avere** is used to express age in Italian.

"Quanti anni hai?" "Ho ventitré anni".
"How old are you?" "I am twenty-three."

Now let's look at idiomatic expression using **fare**.

fare la spesa	*to do/go grocery shopping*
fare spese	*to shop*
fare la doccia	*to take a shower*
fare il bagno	*to take a bath*
fare colazione	*to have breakfast*
fare una domanda	*to ask a question*
fare una fotografia	*to take a picture*
fare una passeggiata	*to take a walk*
fare una pausa	*to take a break*
fare un viaggio	*to take a trip*

PRACTICE 2
Complete with the correct form of either **fare** or **avere**.

1. Francesca _____ una passeggiata nel parco.

2. Enrico _____ trentacinque anni.

3. Io _____ una fotografia del monumento.

4. I bambini _____ sempre fame!

5. Renzo e Lucia _____ bisogno di soldi.

6. Noi _____ un viaggio in Italia.

7. Voi _____ ragione, questo ristorante è eccellente.

8. Alle dieci Teresa _____ un pausa per un caffè.

Tip!

Remember that every language is made up of many idiomatic expressions, expressions that have a different meaning than the individual words of which they are composed. For instance, when in American English we want to wish someone good luck in accomplishing a specific task, we often say: *break a leg!* The equivalent expression in Italian is **in bocca al lupo** (literally *in the mouth of the wolf*). The answer to this expression is **crepi il lupo**, which broadly means *thank you*, but literally means *may the wolf die*. Poor wolf, but lucky for you.

ANSWERS

PRACTICE 1: 1. Come stai? **2.** Quante macchine hai? **3.** Quale città preferisci? **4.** Quando andate al cinema? **5.** Di che cosa ha bisogno? **6.** Dove studiano? **7.** Perché non lavori oggi? **8.** Con chi andate al ristorante?

PRACTICE 2: 1. fa; **2.** ha; **3.** faccio; **4.** hanno; **5.** hanno; **6.** facciamo; **7.** avete; **8.** fa.

———————— Lesson 12 (Conversations) ————————

CONVERSATION 1

Renzo: Ciao Mariella, come stai?
Mariella: Sto molto bene, grazie. Ho un nuovo lavoro.
Renzo: Davvero? Che cosa fai?
Mariella: Lavoro part-time per una rivista di moda.
Renzo: Fai la giornalista?
Mariella: Magari! Faccio un po' di tutto: rispondo al telefono, scrivo lettere a macchina, mando fax, metto in ordine, qualche volta servo anche il caffè al direttore.
Renzo: Quante ore lavori alla settimana?
Mariella: Lavoro il lunedì e il mercoledì dalle nove alle due e il venerdì dalle nove a mezzogiorno.
Renzo: Sono in cerca di lavoro. Per caso il tuo direttore ha bisogno di aiuto il martedì e il giovedì?

Mariella: Non credo, mi dispiace. Ho molta fame, andiamo a mangiare qualcosa?

Renzo: Purtroppo vado di fretta, ho un colloquio di lavoro fra mezz'ora.

Mariella: Peccato! Ciao, Renzo, ti chiamo presto e in bocca al lupo!

Renzo: Crepi il lupo!

Renzo: Hi, Mariella, how are you?

Mariella: I'm very well, thank you. I have a new job.

Renzo: Really? What do you do?

Mariella: I work part time for a fashion magazine.

Renzo: Are you a journalist?

Mariella: I wish! I do a bit of everything: I answer the phone, type letters, send faxes, I put things away, and sometimes I even serve coffee to the director.

Renzo: How many hours a week do you work?

Mariella: I work Mondays and Wednesdays, from nine to two, and on Fridays from nine to twelve.

Renzo: I'm looking for a job. Does your director, by any chance, need help on Tuesdays and Thursdays?

Mariella: I don't believe so, I'm sorry. I'm really hungry, should we go and have something to eat?

Renzo: Unfortunately I'm in a hurry, I have a job interview in half an hour.

Mariella: Too bad! Good-bye, Renzo, I'll call you soon, and good luck!

Renzo: Thanks!

NOTES

When talking about professions, you have two different ways of expressing what a person does. You can either use the idiomatic expression: **fare** + definite article + profession, as in **Fai la giornalista?,** or you can use the more literal expression: **essere** + (indefinite article) + profession, as in **No, non sono (una) giornalista.** Note that the indefinite article can be omitted.

NUTS & BOLTS 1
REGULAR -ERE AND -IRE VERBS IN THE PRESENT TENSE

We'll now learn how to conjugate the other two regular verb groups, the **-ere** and **-ire** groups.

Just as with **-are** verbs, to conjugate regular -ere and -ire verbs, such as **scrivere** *(to write)* and **dormire** *(to sleep)*, we'll start with their infinitive forms. The first thing we need to do is drop the infinitive endings **-ere** and **-ire.** We are left with the stem of the verbs, **scriv-** and **dorm-**, to which we will add the appropriate subject endings. Here are the present tense verb endings.

-ere verbs		-ire verbs	
io	-o	io	-o
tu	-i	tu	-i
lui	-e	lui	-e
lei	-e	lei	-e
Lei/noi	-e/-iamo	Lei/noi	-e/-iamo
voi	-ete	voi	-ite
loro	-ono	loro	-ono

Here's how it works with **scrivere** and **dormire.**

io scriv-o	*I write*	io dorm-o	*I sleep*
tu scriv-i	*you write*	tu dorm-i	*you sleep*
lui scriv-e	*he writes*	lui dorm-e	*he sleeps*
lei scriv-e	*she writes*	lei dorm-e	*she sleeps*

Lei scriv-e	*you (fml.) write*	**Lei dorm-e**	*you (fml.) sleep*
noi scriv-iamo	*we write*	**noi dorm-iamo**	*we sleep*
voi scriv-ete	*you (pl.) write*	**voi dorm-ite**	*you (pl.) sleep*
loro scriv-ono	*they write*	**loro dorm-ono**	*they sleep*

Note that the conjugations of **-ere** and **-ire** verbs are almost identical, except for the **voi** subject ending.

Other regular **-ere** and **-ire** verbs are listed in the following chart.

-ere verbs		**-ire** verbs	
chiedere	*to ask*	**aprire**	*to open*
chiudere	*to close*	**offrire**	*to offer*
correre	*to run*	**partire**	*to leave*
credere	*to believe*	**seguire**	*to follow*
leggere	*to read*	**sentire**	*to hear*
mettere	*to put*	**servire**	*to serve*
perdere	*to lose*		
prendere	*to take*		
ricevere	*to receive*		
rispondere (a)	*to answer (to)*		
vedere	*to see*		
vivere	*to live*		

PRACTICE 1
Complete the following sentences with the correct form of the verbs given in parentheses.

1. Loro _____ (vivere) in un appartamento elegante.

2. La signora _____ (servire) un caffè molto buono.

3. Noi _____ (rispondere) alla telefonata.

4. Voi _____ (ricevere) molte lettere.

5. Il treno _____ (partire) alle due.

6. Io _____ (aprire) la finestra perché ho caldo.

7. Marisa _____ (chiudere) la porta.

8. Tu e Giovanni _____ (leggere) il giornale tutti i giorni.

CONVERSATION 2

Marco: Ciao Daniela, andiamo in centro domani a fare spese?

Daniela: Magari! Ho una giornata terribile e sono già nervosa! Alle sette preparo la colazione e quando tutti hanno finito di mangiare pulisco la cucina. Poi accompagno i bambini a scuola e vado al supermercato a fare la spesa . . . Ho mille cose da fare!

Marco: Un momento, non capisco. Perché non porta i bambini a scuola Mario?

Daniela: Perché deve essere in ospedale alle sette e mezza per visitare un paziente molto malato.

Marco: E dopo il supermercato?

Daniela: I bambini hanno invitato due amici a giocare. Così di pomeriggio ci saranno quattro bambini piccoli, adorabili, ma rumorosi, in casa! Di mattina faccio anche una torta per il compleanno di Mario. Compie cinquantaquattro anni! Come vedi ho una giornata piena!

Marco: Giusto, io sono solo e depresso e tu non sei una vera amica!

Daniela: Mi dispiace, Marco, ma hai torto! Sono solo un'amica occupata!

Marco: Hai ragione, scusami! Ho davvero esagerato!

Marco: Hello, Daniela, are we going shopping in the city, tomorrow?

Daniela: I wish! I've a terrible day and I'm already nervous! At 7, I'm going to prepare breakfast, and when everyone is finished eating, I'll clean the kitchen. Then I'll take the kids to school, and I'll go to the supermarket to buy food . . . I have a million things (lit., a thousand things) to do.

Marco: Wait a second, I don't understand. Why isn't Mario taking the kids to school?

Daniela: Because he has to be at the hospital at 7:30 to see a very sick patient.

Marco: And after the supermarket?

Daniela: The kids have invited two friends over to play. So at two in the afternoon, there are going to be four small children, nice but noisy, in the house! In the morning, I'm also going to make a cake for Mario's birthday. He's going to be fifty-four . . . as you can see I have a full day!

Marco: Yes, and I'm lonely and depressed, and you're not a true friend!

Daniela: I'm sorry, Marco, you're wrong! I'm just a busy friend!

Marco: You're right, I'm sorry! I'm being unreasonable!

Notes

In Italian when we have two verbs, the first of which governs the second, the second verb is always in the infinitive mode: **Desidero andare al cinema** *(I want to go to the movies)*. Certain verbs, however, require either the preposition **a** or **di** in front of the infinitive:

Finiscono di mangiare.
They finish eating.
Andiamo a fare spese.
We go shopping.

When you encounter such constructions, you should make an effort to memorize which preposition, if any, a verb requires in front of an infinitive.

NUTS & BOLTS 2
REGULAR -ISC- VERBS IN THE PRESENT TENSE
A large number of **-ire** verbs follow a slightly different, yet still regular pattern. These verbs are known as "**isc**" verbs, as they insert **-isc-** between the regular stem and the regular ending of the verb, in the **io, tu, lui/lei,** and **loro** subjects.

Here's how it works with the verb **capire** *(to understand):*

io cap-isc-o	*I understand*
tu cap-isc-i	*you understand*
lui cap-isc-e	*he understands*
lei cap-isc-c	*she understands*
Lei cap-isc-c	*you (fml.) understand*
noi cap-iamo	*we understand*
voi cap-ite	*you (pl.) understand*
loro cap-isc-ono	*they understand*

In general, verbs that have only one consonant before the ending **-ire** (**preferire**—*to prefer*, **finire**—*to finish*, **pulire**—*to clean*), will conjugate using the **-isc-** conjugation; if they have two consonants before **-ire** (**partire, offrire, aprire**), they will conjugate regularly.

PRACTICE 2

Complete the following sentences with the correct forms of the **-ire** verbs in parentheses.

1. A che ora _____ (partire) Susanna?

2. Tu _____ (pulire) la casa tutti i giorni.

3. Noi _____ (preferire) mangiare a casa.

4. Io non _____ (capire) il professore.

5. Quando _____ (servire) il caffè loro?

6. Il negozio _____ (aprire) alle 9.

7. Giovanna _____ (finire) di lavorare alle 6.

8. Lui _____ (seguire) sempre i miei consigli.

Tip!

Now that you've learned the verb **partire,** and the expression **fare un viaggio,** you might be tempted to organize a trip in Italy. A great way to travel within Italy is by train, and you might want to check out the official site of the **Ferrovie dello Stato** (the national railway system) at **www.trenitalia.it**, where you can find out schedules, prices, and news related to traveling by train in Italy and Europe.

ANSWERS

PRACTICE 1: 1. vivono; **2.** serve; **3.** rispondiamo; **4.** ricevete; **5.** parte; **6.** apro; **7.** chiude; **8.** leggete.

PRACTICE 2: 1. parte; **2.** pulisci; **3.** preferiamo; **4.** capisco; **5.** servono; **6.** apre; **7.** finisce; **8.** segue.

UNIT 3 ESSENTIALS

Il lunedì rispondo alle lettere.	*On Mondays, I answer letters.*
Martedì vado a fare la spesa.	*Next Tuesday, I'm going grocery shopping.*
Marinella è nervosa.	*Marinella is nervous.*
Giulia e Silvana sono carine.	*Giulia and Silvana are cute.*
Quanti milioni di persone vivono a New York?	*How many million people live in New York?*
Che lavoro fai?	*What do you do?*
Faccio il meccanico.	*I'm a mechanic.*
Hai fame?	*Are you hungry?*
No, ho sete.	*No, I'm thirsty.*
Loro finiscono di lavorare alle otto.	*They finish working at eight.*
Voi leggete molte riviste.	*You read a lot of magazines.*

UNIT 4
Talking about other people

In this unit you will learn how to speak about your favorite people and things, **i tuoi amici** (*your friends*), **la tua famiglia** (*your family*), and anything else that belongs to you or to them. You will thus learn **gli aggettivi e i pronomi possessivi,** possessive adjectives and pronouns. You will also learn more irregular verbs, and **le preposizioni,** prepositions, those tiny little words without which it's impossible to express our thoughts. Let's begin by learning a few useful words.

─────────────── Lesson 13 (Words) ───────────────

WORD LIST 1

amico	*(male) friend*
amica	*(female) friend*
viene	*he/she comes*
dici	*you say*
possiamo	*we can*
voglio	*I want*
sai	*you know*
coppia	*couple*
chiaro	*clear*
insieme	*together*
solo	*only, lonely, alone*
posto	*place*

NUTS & BOLTS 1
PREPOSITIONS
Let's take a look at Italian prepositions.

di	of, from
a	at, to, in
da	from
in	at, to, in
con	with
su	on, about
per	for
tra/fra *(either spelling)*	between, among

Il libro è su un tavolo in soggiorno.
The book is on a table in the living room.
Vado al cinema con Luisa.
I go to the movies with Luisa.
Lavoro per tre ore.
I (will) work for three hours.

In Unit 1 you learned **a** and **in,** and you know that translating prepositions literally is very difficult, given that they are very idiomatic in every language. The translations given above thus convey only the most literal meaning of each preposition. Let's practice now with these prepositions, and don't forget to review what you've learned about prepositions in the previous units!

PRACTICE 1
Complete each sentence with the appropriate preposition.

1. Noi andiamo _____ Italia d'estate.

2. Lui fa una passeggiata _____ Maria.

3. Io lavoro _____ il Dottor Romagnoli.

4. Loro vanno _____ Roma _____ studiare italiano.

5. Il treno arriva _____ Milano alle 7:30.

6. Voi finite _____ studiare all 5:00.

WORD LIST 2

famiglia	*family*
padre	*father*
madre	*mother*
genitori	*parents*
parenti	*relatives*
fratello	*brother*
sorella	*sister*
fratelli/sorelle	*siblings*
moglie	*wife*
marito	*husband*
figlio	*son*
figlia	*daughter*
cugino/cugina	*cousin*
zia	*aunt*
zio	*uncle*
conoscere	*to know, to meet (for the first time), to get/be acquainted*
sapere	*to know (a fact), to know how*

NUTS & BOLTS 2

CONOSCERE AND SAPERE *(TO KNOW)*

In Italian, there are two separate verbs used to express *to know:* **conoscere** and **sapere**. They have slightly different meanings and are not interchangeable.

Conoscere means to be familiar or acquainted with a person, thing, or place.

Conosci mia cugina?
Do you know my cousin?

Io non conosco bene Roma.
I don't know Rome well.

Sapere is an irregular verb, and it's conjugated as follows:

io so	*I know*
tu sai	*you know*
lui sa	*he knows*
lei sa	*she knows*
Lei sa	*you (fml.) know*
noi sappiamo	*we know*
voi sapete	*you (pl.) know*
loro sanno	*they know*

Sapere means *to know a fact* or *to know how to do something*. When **sapere** is used with the latter meaning, it is always followed by a verb in the infinitive form.

Sai che domani arriva mio fratello da Firenze?
Do you know that tomorrow my brother is arriving from Florence?

Il bambino sa suonare il piano molto bene.
The child can (knows how to) play the piano very well.

PRACTICE 2
Choose either **sapere** or **conoscere** and conjugate it in the sentence appropriately.

1. Noi conosciamo/sappiamo un buon ristorante.

2. Lui conosce/sa cucinare molto bene.

3. Voi conoscete/sapete mio padre?

4. Io conosco/so che lui non risponde mai al telefono.

5. Tu conosci/sai suonare la chitarra?

6. Io non conosco/so parlare cinese.

Culture note

Italian is a language rich in proverbs, those sayings that convey accepted popular wisdom. Many proverbs refer to the family, such as: **Tra moglie e marito non mettere il dito.** It translates literally as *don't put your finger between wife and husband,* meaning *don't interfere in marital affairs.* The equivalent to the English *you can't have your cake and eat it too* is much more salacious in Italian: **Non puoi avere la botte piena e la moglie ubriaca,** or *you can't have the wine cask full, and your wife drunk.*

ANSWERS

PRACTICE 1: 1. in; **2.** con; **3.** per; **4.** a, a; **5.** da, a; **6.** di.

PRACTICE 2: 1. conosciamo; **2.** sa; **3.** conoscete; **4.** so; **5.** sai; **6.** so.

────────────── Lesson 14 (Phrases) ──────────────

PHRASE LIST 1

Di chi è?	*Whose is it?*
È di . . .	*It belongs to/it is . . .*
l'amico di Claudia	*Claudia's friend*
Ma come!	*How's it possible! How can this be!*
venire a trovare	*to come visit*
andare a trovare	*to go visit*
fare un giro	*to go for a walk, to go for a ride*
tutti gli anni	*every year*
in/d'estate	*in the summer*
in/d'autunno	*in the fall*
in/d'inverno	*in the winter*
in/di primavera	*in the spring*

NUTS & BOLTS 1
THE PREPOSITION DI

The preposition **di** *(of)* is used to express possession in Italian. Note the difference in structure between the Italian and the English in the following sentence.

Lorenzo è l'amico di Claudia.
Lorenzo is Claudia's friend.

Sono le sorelle di Michele.
They are Michele's sisters.

Di chi sono quelle riviste?
Whose magazines are those?

Please note that the preposition **di** is more commonly used in the expressions **d'estate** *(in the summer),* and **d'inverno** *(in the winter),* while with **primavera** *(spring)* we more often use the preposition **in. Autunno** *(fall)* can take either **in** (**in autunno**) or **di** (**d'autunno**) with equal frequency.

PRACTICE 1
Translate the following sentences into Italian.

1. Whose book is it?

2. It's Giorgio's book.

3. Mirella's sister is cute.

4. Paola's brother is nervous.

5. Alessandro's house is noisy.

6. In the summer, I'm going to Giulia's house.

PHRASE LIST 2

posso	*I can*
vuoi	*you want*

ti voglio bene	*I care about you, I love you*
siamo in sette	*there're seven of us*
eccetto la mia	*except for mine*
mi chiamo	*my name is*
si chiama	*his/her name is*
si chiamano	*their names are*
è sposato/è sposata	*he/she is married*
neanche	*not even*

NUTS & BOLTS 2

MODAL VERBS: DOVERE, POTERE, AND VOLERE

We are now going to learn three important irregular verbs of the -ere group: the modal verbs **dovere** *(must, to have to);* **potere** *(can, to be able to);* and **volere** *(to want).* When these verbs are followed by another verb, the second verb will be in the infinitive form.

DOVERE	*must, to have to*
io devo	*I must*
tu devi	*you must*
lui deve	*he must*
lei deve	*she must*
Lei deve	*you (fml.) must*
noi dobbiamo	*we must*
voi dovete	*you (pl.) must*
loro devono	*they must*

POTERE	can, to be able to
io posso	I can
tu puoi	you can
lui può	he can
lei può	she can
Lei può	you (fml.) can
noi possiamo	we can
voi potete	you (pl.) can
loro possono	they can

VOLERE	to want
io voglio	I want
tu vuoi	you want
lui vuole	he wants
lei vuole	she wants
Lei vuole	you (fml.) want
noi vogliamo	we want
voi volete	you (pl.) want
loro vogliono	they want

Oggi Luigi deve studiare per un esame.

Today, Luigi must study for an exam.

Potete venire a cena a casa mia domani sera?

Can you come to my house for dinner tomorrow night?

Noi vogliamo andare a trovare i nostri amici.

We want to go visit our friends.

PRACTICE 1

Insert the correct form of the verb in parentheses:

1. Loro _____ (volere) comprare una macchina nuova.

2. Tu _____ (dovere) preparare la cena.

3. Io non _____ (potere) venire con te a fare spese.

4. Sofia _____ (volere) cercare un nuovo lavoro.

5. Tu e Caterina _____ (dovere) leggere il giornale.

6. Tu ed io _____ (potere) guardare la TV.

Tip!

There are words in Italian for *stepmother* (**la matrigna**), *stepfather* (**il patrigno**), *stepbrother* (**il fratellastro**), *stepsister* (**la sorellastra**), *stepson* (**il figliastro**), and *stepdaughter* (**la figliastra**). However, they have historically negative connotations (there was no divorce in Italy until relatively recently) and are avoided as much as possible. Thus, instead of **matrigna** and **patrigno**, **la moglie di mio padre** (*my father's wife*) and **il marito di mia madre** (*my mother's husband*) are preferred. Simply **fratello** and **sorella** are used instead of **fratellastro** and **sorellastra**; and **il figlio/la figlia di mio marito** (or **di mia moglie**), or **adottivo/a** meaning *my husband's son/daughter* (or *my wife's son/daughter*) are used instead of **figliastro** and **figliastra**.

ANSWERS

PRACTICE 1: 1. Di chi è il libro?; 2. È il libro di Giorgio; 3. La sorella di Mirella è carina; 4. Il fratello di Paola è nervoso; 5. La casa di Alessandro è rumorosa; 6. D'estate vado a casa di Giulia.

PRACTICE 2: 1. vogliono; 2. devi; 3. posso; 4. vuole; 5. dovete; 6. possiamo.

—————————— Lesson 15 (Sentences) ——————————

SENTENCE GROUP 1

Di chi è quella Ferrari rossa?

Whose red Ferrari is it?

È di Lorenzo, l'amico di Claudia.

It's Lorenzo's, Claudia's friend.

Claudia è la mia amica.

Claudia is my friend.

Lei dice che è solo un amico.

She says (that) he's just a friend.

Sembrano una coppia.

They look like a couple.

La sua macchina è bellissima.

His car is very beautiful.

Possiamo fare un giro?

Can we (all) go for a ride?

Ci sono solo due posti.

It's a two-seater (car). (lit., There are only two seats.)

NUTS & BOLTS 1

IRREGULAR -ERE AND -IRE VERBS

In addition to the irregular **-ere** verbs we have already learned, **sapere, dovere, potere,** and **volere,** the verb **bere** *(to drink)* has an irregular conjugation.

BERE	to drink
io bevo	*I drink*
tu bevi	*you drink*
lui beve	*he drinks*
lei beve	*she drinks*
Lei beve	*you (fml.) drink*
noi beviamo	*we drink*
voi bevete	*you (pl.) drink*
loro bevono	*they drink*

Please notice that, if you imagine that the infinitive is **bevere,** rather than **bere,** then the verbs is conjugated regularly.

Now we'll learn three important irregular verbs of the **-ire** group: **dire** *(to say, to tell),* **uscire** *(to go out),* and **venire** *(to come).*

DIRE	to say, to tell
io dico	*I say/I tell*
tu dici	*you say/tell*
lui dice	*he says/tells*
lei dice	*she says/tells*
Lci dicc	*you (fml.) say/tell*
noi diciamo	*we say/tell*

DIRE	to say, to tell
voi dite	*you (pl.) say/tell*
loro dicono	*they say/tell*

USCIRE	to go out
io esco	*I go out*
tu esci	*you go out*
lui esce	*he goes out*
lei esce	*she goes out*
Lei esce	*you (fml.) go out*
noi usciamo	*we go out*
voi uscite	*you (pl.) go out*
loro escono	*they go out*

VENIRE	to come
io vengo	*I come*
tu vieni	*you come*
lui viene	*he comes*
lei viene	*she comes*
Lei viene	*you (fml.) come*
noi veniamo	*we come*

VENIRE	to come
voi venite	*you (pl.) come*
loro vengono	*they come*

Tu dici molte bugie.
You tell many lies.
Loro escono spesso.
They go out often.
Lui viene a trovarci raramente.
He rarely comes to visit us.

PRACTICE 1
Complete with the correct forms of either **dire, uscire,** or **venire.**

1. Quando noi _____ con loro, di solito andiamo al cinema.

2. Mio cugino _____ a trovare la sua famiglia di primavera.

3. Loro non _____ mai che cosa fanno.

4. La mattina io _____ alle 7:00 per andare in ufficio.

5. (Tu) _____ a casa mia stasera? Ho una sorpresa!

6. Voglio _____ a Mario dove vado domani.

7. Vuoi _____ domani sera? Ho voglia di andare a teatro.

SENTENCE GROUP 2
Posso conoscere la tua famiglia?
Can I meet your family?
La mia famiglia è molto numerosa.
My family is very big.
Mi parli di tuo padre e (di) tua madre?
Would you tell me about your father and mother?

Non so niente dei tuoi fratelli.

I don't know anything about your siblings.

Siamo in sette.

There are seven of us.

Non esistono più famiglie così grandi.

Such big families no longer exist.

I miei fratelli si chiamano Marco e Giulio.

My brothers' names are Marco and Giulio.

Sua moglie si chiama Manuela.

His wife's name is Manuela.

I loro bambini si chiamano Andrea e Fabrizio.

Their children's names are Andrea and Fabrizio.

NUTS & BOLTS 2

PREPOSITIONS FOLLOWED BY DEFINITE ARTICLES

In Lesson 13 of this unit you learned the Italian prepositions. When followed by a definite article, the prepositions **di, a, da, in,** and **su** contract with the article and form a single word. In this process, the following spelling changes occur:

a) the preposition **in > ne,**

b) the preposition **di > de,**

c) the article **il** drops the **i,**

d) every article beginning with **l** doubles the **l.**

	IL	LO	LA	L'	I	GLI	LE
DI	del	dello	della	dell'	dei	degli	delle
A	al	allo	alla	all'	ai	agli	alle
DA	dal	dallo	dalla	dall'	dai	dagli	dalle
IN	nel	nello	nella	nell'	nei	negli	nelle
SU	sul	sullo	sulla	sull'	sui	sugli	sulle

di + l' → dell'
È la macchina dell'amico di Claudia.
It's Claudia's friend's car.

in + la → nella
La famiglia cena nella sala da pranzo.
The family is having dinner in the dining room.

a + il → al
Ho fatto la spesa al mercato.
I bought groceries at the market.

su +gli → sugli
I libri sono sugli scaffali.
The books are on the shelves.

PRACTICE 2
Merge the given preposition with the appropriate definite article in the following sentences.

1. La macchina di Filippo è (in) _____ garage.

2. Gli amici di Rodolfo vanno (a) _____ cinema stasera.

3. Gli studenti rispondono (a) _____ domande (di) _____ professore.

4. Marco ritorna (da) _____ ufficio alle 7:00.

5. Ci sono molti libri (su) _____ tavolo.

6. I figli (di) _____ amica di Giuseppe sono molto bravi a scuola.

Language link

Do you or does anyone you love have an Italian surname? Would you like to find out where the majority of people with that surname live in Italy? Then visit **http://gens.labo.net**, where you will find information about Italian names and their meaning, as well as information about Italian regions.

ANSWERS

PRACTICE 1: 1. usciamo; **2.** va; **3.** dicono; **4.** esco; **5.** vieni; **6.** dire; uscire.

PRACTICE 2: 1. nel; **2.** al; **3.** alle, del; **4.** dall'; **5.** sul; **6.** dell'.

——————— Lesson 16 (Conversations) ———————

CONVERSATION 1

Stefano: Cristina, di chi è quella Ferrari rossa parcheggiata davanti al tuo ufficio?

Cristina: È di Lorenzo, l'amico di Claudia.

Stefano: Scusa ma chi è Claudia?

Cristina: Ma come, non ricordi? Claudia è la mia amica di Palermo. Viene a trovarmi tutti gli anni d'estate. E quest'anno è con Lorenzo, il suo amico, o forse il suo ragazzo.

Stefano: Perché dici "forse il suo ragazzo"? Non lo sai se è il suo ragazzo o no?

Cristina: Non è chiaro. Claudia dice che è solo un amico, ma quando sono insieme sembrano una coppia.

Stefano: Beh, non è importante se Lorenzo è il suo amico o il suo ragazzo, ma la sua macchina è bellissima. Possiamo andare tutti insieme a fare un giro sulla Ferrari?

Cristina: La tua idea è interessante, ma nella Ferrari ci sono solo due posti.

Stefano: Cristina, who does that red Ferrari parked in front of your office belong to?

Cristina: It's Lorenzo's, Claudia's friend.

Stefano: Excuse me, and who is Claudia?

Cristina: What! You don't remember? Claudia is that friend of mine from Palermo. She comes to visit me every year in the summer. And this year she's with Lorenzo, her friend, or perhaps her boyfriend.

Stefano: Why do you say "perhaps her boyfriend"? Don't you know if he's her boyfriend or not?

Cristina: It's not clear. Claudia says that he's just a friend, but when they're together they look like a couple.

Stefano: Well, it's not important if Lorenzo is her friend or her boyfriend, but his car is very beautiful. Can we go all together and take a ride in the Ferrari?

Cristina: Your idea is interesting, but there're only two seats in a Ferrari.

Notes

Ma come! (*How come!/How can it be!*) is a very common exclamation in Italian, which shows surprise and disappointment at someone's perceived failings.

Andare (or **venire**) **a trovare** is an idiomatic expression that means *to go (or come) and visit someone.*

Lo so, and **non lo so,** translate to English as *I know* and *I don't know it.*

NUTS & BOLTS 1
POSSESSIVE ADJECTIVES

Let's take a look at Italian possessive adjectives, words equivalent to *my, his, her,* etc. in English.

	SINGULAR MASCULINE	SINGULAR FEMININE	PLURAL MASCULINE	PLURAL FEMININE
my	il mio	la mia	i miei	le mie
your (infml.)	il tuo	la tua	i tuoi	le tue
*his/her/its your (fml.)**	il suo	la sua	i suoi	le sue
our	il nostro	la nostra	i nostri	le nostre
your (pl.)	il vostro	la vostra	i vostri	le vostre
their	il loro	la loro	i loro	le loro

* When *your* is used in the formal form it is written with a capital S-: il Suo, la Sua, i Suoi, le Sue.

Italian possessive adjectives agree in gender and number with what is possessed and not the possessor (except for **loro** which is invariable). Note that because of this, there is no difference in Italian between *his* or *her*.

Possessive adjectives are always preceded by the definite article, and less often by the indefinite **article (un mio amico**–*a friend of mine*). As an exception, the definite article does not precede the possessive adjectives before singular nouns denoting members of the family **(suo padre, mia sorella, vostro zio).**

Differently from the other Italian adjectives, the possesive adjectives are always used in front of the noun they modify, except when we need to express a special emphasis, as in exclamations **(Mamma mia!)** or poetic expressions and songs **(O sole mio!)** Also in these cases the article will not be used.

Claudia è la mia amica.
Claudia is my friend.
La sua macchina è bellissima.
His/her car is very beautiful.
Il suo amico è simpatico.
His/her friend is nice.
Mi puoi parlare di tuo padre?
Can you speak to me about your father?
Mia sorella si chiama Franca.
My sister's name is Franca.

Note that the definite article is used in front of plural nouns denoting members of the family.

I miei fratelli abitano a Torino.
My brothers (siblings) live in Torino.

PRACTICE 1
Translate the possessive adjective given in parentheses. Insert the definite article when appropriate.

1. (My) _____ amica Cristina viene a trovarmi domani.

2. (Their) _____ casa è bellissima.

3. (His) _____ cugine abitano a Toronto.

4. (His) _____ sorella non è sposata.

5. (Her) _____ figli studiano in una scuola privata.

6. (Your) _____ lavoro è interessante, ma stressante.

7. (Our) _____ vicini di casa sono inglesi.

8. (Your pl.) _____ genitori arrivano domani

CONVERSATION 2

Luca: Mi presenti la tua famiglia?

Elisabetta: Sei sicuro che vuoi?

Luca: Perché no? Ti voglio bene e voglio conoscerli tutti.

Elisabetta: Va bene, ma lo sai, la mia famiglia è molto numerosa.

Luca: Mi hai raccontato molto di tuo padre e tua madre, ma non so quasi niente dei tuoi fratelli.

Elisabetta: Beh, sai che siamo in sette, quattro femmine e tre maschi.

Luca: Lo so, è davvero difficile immaginare una famiglia così numerosa. Non esistono più famiglie con tanti figli!

Elisabetta: Eccetto la mia! Allora, i miei fratelli si chiamano Marco, Giulio e Francesco. Mio fratello Francesco è sposato. Sua moglie si chiama Manuela, e loro non hanno bambini. Le mie sorelle si chiamano Carla, Rossella e Silvana. Rossella è sposata, e suo marito si chiama Giovanni. Loro hanno due bambini che si chiamano Andrea e Fabrizio. Carla è fidanzata e il suo fidanzato si chiama . . .

Luca: Basta così! Non ricordo già più neanche un nome!

Luca: *Can I meet your family?*

Elisabetta: *Are you sure you want to?*

Luca: *Why not? I care about you, and I want to meet all of them.*

Elisabetta: *All right, but you know, my family is very large.*

Luca: *You told me a lot about your father and mother, but I know almost nothing about your siblings.*

Elisabetta: *Well, you know we're seven, four girls and three boys.*

Luca: *I know, and it's really difficult to imagine such a large family. Families with many children no longer exist.*

> *Elisabetta:* *Except for mine. So, my brothers' names are Marco,*
> *Giulio, and Francesco. My brother Francesco is*
> *married. His wife's name is Manuela, and they don't*
> *have any children. My sisters' names are Carla,*
> *Rossella, and Silvana. Rossella is married, and her*
> *husband's name is Giovanni. They have two children*
> *whose names are Andrea and Fabrizio. Carla is*
> *engaged and her fiancé's name is . . .*
> *Luca:* *That's enough! I can't remember any names as it is!*

NOTES

The expression **ti voglio bene** is literally translated as *I want goodness for you.* It is used to express love toward members of the family or friends and lovers, whereas the expression **ti amo** would only be used between lovers.

Note that we use the article in front of **il suo fidanzato** because he is not a family member yet.

The expression **mi hai raccontato** . . . *(you told me about . . .)* is in the past tense, which we will learn in the next unit.

NUTS & BOLTS 2
POSSESSIVE PRONOUNS

The Italian possessive pronouns have exactly the same forms as the possessive adjectives, and they are always preceded by the definite articles, even with singular nouns indicating members of the family.

Mia sorella fa l'insegnante e la tua fa l'impiegata.

My sister is a teacher and yours is an office employee.

La sua casa è grande, ma la loro è piccola.

His/her house is big, but theirs is small.

I miei parenti vivono in Italia, ma i suoi vivono in Argentina.

My relatives live in Italy, but his/hers live in Argentina.

PRACTICE 2

Translate the following sentences into Italian.

1. My brother works every day, and yours works part-time.

2. His mother teaches, and mine doesn't work.

3. Their house is old, but ours is new.

4. Her job is stressful, buy yours is easy.

5. I know your (pl.) sister; do you know mine?

Language link

Although the contemporary Italian family does not look anything like the large patriarchal family of the past, one thing has not changed: food is still the center of the Italian family life. If you want to learn more about Italian food, here's a good website where you can find authentic recipes, cooking lessons, information about regional food in Italy, and a complete glossary to guide you in the labyrinth of Italian food:

www.lacucinaitaliana.it

ANSWERS

PRACTICE 1: 1. la mia; **2.** la loro; **3.** le sue; **4.** sua; **5.** i suoi; **6.** il tuo; **7.** i nostri; **8.** i vostri.

PRACTICE 2: 1. Mio fratello lavora tutti i giorni e il tuo lavora part-time; **2.** Sua madre fa l'insegnante e la mia non lavora; **3.** La loro casa è vecchia, ma la nostra è nuova; **4.** Il suo lavoro è stressante, ma il tuo è facile; **5.** Conosco vostra sorella; conoscete la mia (or le mie)?

UNIT 4 ESSENTIALS

Di chi è la macchina rossa?	*Whose red car is it?*
È di Lorenzo, l'amico di Claudia.	*It's Lorenzo's, Claudia's friend.*
Conosci Silvia?	*Do you know Silvia?*
Non so se è il suo ragazzo.	*I don't know if he's her boyfriend.*

Possiamo andare a fare un giro?	*Can we go for a ride?*
Loro vogliono comprare una macchina nuova.	*They want to buy a new car.*
Io devo lavorare molto domani.	*I must work a lot tomorrow.*
Lui dice molte bugie.	*He tells many lies.*
Viene a trovare tua zia domani?	*Is he coming to visit your aunt tomorrow?*
Esci con Giulietta stasera?	*Are you going out with Giulietta tonight?*
La cugina della tua amica è carina.	*Your friend's cousin is cute.*
Nella mia camera da letto c'è una TV.	*In my bedroom there's a TV.*
Mia sorella parla italiano bene.	*My sister speaks Italian well.*
I nostri fratelli arrivano domani.	*Our brothers arrive tomorrow.*

Unit 5
Food

Did you check out the cooking website we mentioned in the last unit? Did it put you in the mood to learn more about Italian food? We hope so, because in Unit 5 we're going to learn vocabulary related to food and restaurants, so you'll be ready to read those Italian menus when you go out to eat. We are also going to learn how to speak about the past, and to describe everything that is beautiful and good in our lives. Let's begin then!

────────── Lesson 17 (Words) ──────────

WORD LIST 1

supermercato	*supermarket*
frigorifero	*refrigerator*
vuoto	*empty*
roba	*stuff*
gelato	*ice cream*
vino	*wine*
birra	*beer*
carne *(f.)*	*meat*
fettina	*thin slice*
vitello	*veal*
ricetta	*recipe*
piatto	*plate, dish*
comprare	*to buy*
cucinare	*to cook*
ospite	*guest (male and female)*

NUTS & BOLTS 1

ADJECTIVES BUONO AND BELLO

The adjectives **buono** *(good)* and **bello** *(beautiful, nice)* usually precede the noun and work differently from typical adjectives. In the singular, the **-no** ending of **buono** changes in the same pattern as the indefinite article **un/uno/una/un'**: **un buon gelato, un buono studente, una buona ricetta, una buon'amica.** The plural forms are always **buoni** and **buone.**

The **-lo** ending of **bello** changes in the same pattern as the definite articles. Let's see how this works with **che bello,** which is often used to mean *What a beautiful . . .* when referring to food.

il piatto	**Che bel piatto!**	*What a beautiful dish!*
lo spezzatino	**Che bello spezzatino!**	*What a nice stew!*
la minestra	**Che bella minestra!**	*What a nice soup!*
l'arancia	**Che bell'arancia!**	*What a nice orange!*
l'ossobuco	**Che bell'ossobuco!**	*What a nice ossobuco!*
i panini	**Che bei panini!**	*What nice sandwiches!*
gli zucchini	**Che begli zucchini!**	*What nice zucchini!*
gli ananas	**Che begli ananas!**	*What nice pineapples!*
le fragole	**Che belle fragole!**	*What nice strawberries!*

Loro preparano sempre un bel pranzo.

They always prepare a nice lunch.

Che begli spaghetti ci sono sulla tavola!

What nice spaghetti there is on the table!

PRACTICE 1
Choose the correct form of the adjective.

1. Mangiano spesso in un (bello/bel/bell') ristorante francese.
2. Nel negozio vendono dei (belli/bei/begli) avocadi.
3. Che (belli/belle/bell') carote!
4. È un (buono/buona/buon) cappuccino.
5. Sono dei (buoni/buone/buon) tortellini.
6. Voglio comprare un (bello/bella/bell') arrosto.

WORD LIST 2

ieri	*yesterday*
sera	*evening*
trattoria	*family style restaurant*
primo	*first course*
secondo	*second course*
contorno	*side dish (vegetables)*
arrosto	*roast*
frutta	*fruit*
ordinare	*to order*
conto	*bill*
pieno	*full*
soddisfatto	*satisfied*
colazione	*breakfast*
pranzo	*lunch*
cena	*dinner*

NUTS & BOLTS 2
DEMONSTRATIVE ADJECTIVES QUESTO AND QUELLO
Questo *(this)* and **quello** *(that)* are demonstrative adjectives that always precede the noun. **Questo** has four different forms: **questo, questa** *(this)*, and **questi, queste** *(these)*. Just as with **bello**, however, the endings of **quello** change in the same pattern as the definite article.

quel formaggio	*that cheese*
quello spezzatino	*that stew*
quella cipolla	*that onion*
quell' avocado	*that avocado*
quell'insalata	*that salad*
quei gamberetti	*those shrimps*
quegli ananas	*those pineapple*
quegli spaghetti	*those spaghetti (noodles)*
quelle mele	*those apples*

Quanto costa quel pollo?
How much does that chicken cost?
Quei broccoli sono molto freschi.
That broccoli is very fresh. (lit., Those broccoli are very fresh.)

PRACTICE 2
Complete with the correct forms of **quello**.

1. _____ trattoria è buona e non è cara.

2. Come sono _____ tortellini?

3. Quanto costa _____ gelato?

4. Come cucini _____ aragosta?

5. _____ spaghetti sono molto buoni.

Language link

Hungry for a nice **spezzatino**? Or perhaps some **ossobuco**? If you look up "recipe for spezzatino" or "recipe for ossobuco" on the internet, you will be surprised how many recipes you'll find! The choice is yours. **Buon appetito!**

ANSWERS

PRACTICE 1: 1. bel; 2. begli; 3. belle; 4. buon; 5. buoni; 6. bell'.

PRACTICE 2: 1. Quella; 2. quei; 3. quel; 4. quell'; 5. quegli.

—————— Lesson 18 (Phrases) ——————

PHRASE LIST 1

del gelato	*some ice cream*
della birra	*some beer*
degli spaghetti	*some spaghetti*
d'accordo	*all right*
se insisti	*if you insist*
che tipo di pasta?	*what kind of pasta?*
due giorni fa	*two days ago*
un sacco di roba	*a bunch/lot of stuff*
meglio	*better/the best*
stasera (questa sera)	*tonight*

NUTS & BOLTS 1

EXPRESSING *SOME* OR *ANY*

The preposition **di** + article is used idiomatically to express the partitive *some* or *any*.

Per favore, compra del latte e della pasta.

Please, buy some milk and some pasta.

Ieri ho mangiato delle penne alla vodka.

Yesterday, I ate (some) penne with vodka sauce (penne alla vodka).

Qualche and **alcuni/e** also express the partitive in Italian. **Qualche** can only be used with nouns in the singular form, although it always has a plural meaning. **Alcuni/e** is only used with nouns in the plural form.

Ho bisogno di alcune braciole di maiale.

I need some pork chops.

Puoi sbucciare qualche mela, per favore?

Can you please peel some apples?

PRACTICE 1

Choose the appropriate partitive.

1. Loro mangiano della/qualche/alcune mele tutti i giorni.

2. Stasera cucinano delle/qualche/alcune bistecche.

3. Domani invitiamo degli/qualche/alcuni amico a cena.

4. Hai comprato del/qualche/alcuni caffè?

5. In questa città ci sono dei/qualche/alcuni ristoranti buoni.

PHRASE LIST 2

ieri sera	*last night*
davvero	*really*
lasagne alla bolognese	*lasagna Bolognese style*
spaghetti alla carbonara	*spaghetti carbonara style*
per primo	*as first course*
di secondo	*as second course*
di contorno	*as side dish*
per finire	*to end, to finish*
un conto salato	*an expensive bill, a large bill*
ho ordinato	*I ordered*
ho mangiato	*I ate*

NUTS & BOLTS 2

TELLING TIME

There are two interchangeable ways to ask what time it is in Italian: **Che ora è?** and **Che ore sono?** The answer, according to the time we are asked, is:

È mezzogiorno.
It's noon. (12:00 p.m.)
È mezzanotte.
It's midnight. (12:00 a.m.)

Notice that there is no article in front of the time in the above two cases. The article does appear before **una** as **l'.**

È l'una.
It's one o'clock. (1:00)

For the rest of the hours we use the article **le.** **Le** refers to the word **ore** (*hours*) even though it is omitted: **sono le (ore) due.**

Sono le due.
It's two o'clock.
Sono le tre.
It's three o'clock.
Sono le quattro.
It's four o'clock.

Minutes are expressed after the hour and are introduced by **e:** for instance, **sono le tre e dieci** *(it's 3:10).* *It's 3:15* can be expressed by either: **sono le tre e quindici,** or **sono le tre e un quarto** (more commonly used). *It's 3:30* can be expressed by either: **sono le tre e trenta,** or **sono le tre e mezza** (more commonly used). *It's 3:45* can be expressed by either **sono le tre e quarantacinque, sono le tre e tre quarti, manca un quarto alle quattro,** or **sono le quattro meno un quarto** (more commonly used).

To indicate a.m. or p.m., Italians use **di mattina** *(in the morning),* **di pomeriggio** *(in the afternoon),* **di sera** *(in the evening),* and **di notte** *(at night)* whenever is not clear by the context.

Finally, to indicate that an action occurs at a certain time, the preposition **a** is used and contracts with the article.

A che ora pranzate?
At what time do you have lunch?
Pranziamo sempre alle due.
We always have lunch at 2:00 p.m.

PRACTICE 2
Express the time in Italian:

1. It's 8:15 _____

2. It's 9:25 _____

3. It's 10:30 _____

4. It's 11:45 _____

5. It's 12 p.m. _____

6. It's 12 a.m. _____

7. It's 1:20 _____

Culture note

While in America there are no well-defined times for meals, Italians always follow a very strict schedule. Breakfast typically takes place between 7:00 and 9:00. Lunch is between 1:00 and 2:00, and dinner between 7:30 and 8:30. In southern Italy lunch and dinner are usually later. Restaurants will close between lunch and dinner, but if you get hungry during those hours, you can always go to a café to have **uno spuntino** (*a snack*).

ANSWERS
PRACTICE 1: 1. alcune; **2.** delle; **3.** qualche; **4.** del; **5.** dei.

PRACTICE 2: 1. Sono le otto e un quarto; **2.** Sono le nove e venticinque; **3.** Sono le dieci e trenta (sono le dieci e mezza);

4. Sono le undici e quarantacinque (sono le undici e tre quarti; sono le dodici meno un quarto); **5.** Sono le dodici (è mezzogiorno); **6.** Sono le ventiquattro (è mezzanotte); **7.** È l'una e venti.

───────────── Lesson 19 (Sentences) ─────────────

SENTENCE GROUP 1

Puoi andare al supermercato a fare la spesa?

Can you go grocery shopping at the supermarket?

Di che cosa abbiamo bisogno?

What do we need?

Ho fatto la spesa due giorni fa.

I went grocery shopping two days ago.

Ho comprato un sacco di roba.

I bought a lot of stuff.

Hai portato a casa solo del gelato.

You brought home only ice cream. All you brought home is ice cream.

Compra delle fettine di vitello.

Buy some thin veal slices.

Abbiamo già mangiato carne ieri.

We already ate meat yesterday.

È il piatto che so cucinare meglio.

It's the dish that I know how to cook the best.

NUTS & BOLTS 1
THE PRESENT PERFECT

The present perfect **(passato prossimo)** is used to indicate a completed action in the past. **Ho mangiato,** for example, translates into English as *I have eaten, I ate,* or *I did eat.* With the majority of verbs, this tense is formed with the present tense of the auxiliary verbs **avere,** followed by the past participle of the main verb. Regular past participles are formed by dropping the infinitive ending (**-are, -ere,** or **-ire**), and replacing it respectively with **-ato, -uto,** or

-ito (i.e., **mangiare** → **mangiato; ricevere** → **ricevuto; dormire** →
dormito.) Here is the **passato prossimo** of these verbs.

MANGIARE	to eat
io ho mangiato	*I ate/have eaten*
tu hai mangiato	*you ate/have eaten*
lui ha mangiato	*he ate/has eaten*
lei ha mangiato	*she ate/has eaten*
noi abbiamo mangiato	*we ate/have eaten*
voi avete mangiato	*you (pl.) ate/have eaten*
loro hanno mangiato	*they ate/have eaten*

RICEVERE	to receive
io ho ricevuto	*I received/have received*
tu hai ricevuto	*you received/have received*
lui ha ricevuto	*he received/has received*
lei ha ricevuto	*she received/has received*
noi abbiamo ricevuto	*we received/have received*
voi avete ricevuto	*you (pl.) received/have received*
loro hanno ricevuto	*they received/have received*

DORMIRE	to sleep
ho dormito	I slept/have slept
tu hai dormito	you slept/have slept
lui ha dormito	he slept/has slept
lei ha dormito	she slept/has slept
noi abbiamo dormito	we slept/have slept
voi avete dormito	you (pl.) slept/have slept
loro hanno dormito	they slept/have slept

Ieri abbiamo comprato delle mele.
Yesterday we bought some apples.
Loro hanno servito un caffè molto buono.
They served (us/you/etc.) a very good coffee.

Very few verbs in the **-are** and **-ire** groups have irregular past participles. Many verbs in the **-ere** group, however, do have irregular past participles. Here are some of the most common irregular past participles.

INFINITIVE	PAST PARTICIPLE	
fare	fatto	*to do, to make*
chiedere	chiesto	*to ask*
chiudere	chiuso	*to close*
correre	corso	*to run*
leggere	letto	*to read*

INFINITIVE	PAST PARTICIPLE	
mettere	messo	*to put*
perdere	perso	*to lose*
prendere	preso	*to take, to have*
rispondere	risposto	*to answer*
scrivere	scritto	*to write*
vedere	visto	*to see*
aprire	aperto	*to open*
dire	detto	*to say, to tell*

Che cosa hai preso di primo?

What did you have as a first course?

Il cameriere ha risposto a tutte le nostre domande.

The waiter answered all our questions.

Hai messo le posate in tavola?

Did you put the silverware on the table?

Common time expressions used in the past include: **ieri** *(yesterday)*, **fa** *(ago)*, and the adjective **scorso/a** *(last)*.

Ieri il bambino ha detto una bugia.

Yesterday, the child told a lie.

Abbiamo comprato la nostra casa sei anni fa.

We bought our house six years ago.

L'anno scorso hanno aperto un ristorante italiano vicino a casa mia.

Last year, they opened an Italian restaurant near my house.

The adverbs of time **sempre** *(always)*, **mai** *(never, ever)*, **già** *(already)*, and **ancora** *(yet)* are inserted between the auxiliary and the past participle. **Mai** means *never* when it is used by itself in exclamations (**mai!**) and in negative sentences, otherwise, it means *ever*. **Ancora,** when used in positive sentences, means *again* or *still*.

Non ho ancora fatto la spesa.
I haven't shopped for groceries yet.
Abbiamo già finito di cenare.
We have already finished having dinner.
Hai mai mangiato in questo ristorante?
Have you ever eaten in this restaurant?

PRACTICE 1
Complete the following sentences with the correct form of the past tense.

1. Ieri lui _____ (portare) la sua ragazza al ristorante.

2. La settimana scorsa noi _____ (vedere) un film interessante.

3. Tra anni fa io _____ (lavorare) in America per sei mesi.

4. (Voi) _____ (mettere) i piatti in tavola?

5. Lei non _____ (leggere) quel libro di Eco.

6. Tu _____ (scrivere) una lettera ai tuoi cugini?

7. Loro _____ (cucinare) un'ottima cena.

8. Ieri Marco ed io _____ (studiare) insieme.

SENTENCE GROUP 2
Ieri sera siamo andati a mangiare in un buon ristorante.
Last night, we went to eat in a good restaurant.
Che cosa avete mangiato?
What did you eat?
Maria ha ordinato dell'arrosto.
Maria ordered some roast.

Ci hanno portato delle verdure alla griglia.

They brought us some grilled vegetables.

Avete preso della frutta?

Did you have any fruit?

Sì abbiamo ordinato delle mele.

Yes, we ordered some apples.

Siete stati soddisfatti?

Were you satisfied?

È stata una bella cena.

It was a nice dinner.

NUTS & BOLTS 2

THE PRESENT PERFECT WITH ESSERE + PAST PARTICIPLE

While the majority of verbs form the **passato prossimo** with the auxiliary **avere,** some verbs use the present tense of **essere** + past participle. When a verb is conjugated with **avere,** the past participle remains unchanged, unless the verb is preceded by a direct object pronoun (see Lesson 20 in this unit). When a verb is conjugated with **essere,** however, the past participle agrees in gender and number with the subject of the verb.

io sono andato/a	*I went*
tu sei andato/a	*you went*
lui è andato	*he went*
lei è andata	*she went*
noi siamo andati/e	*we went*
voi siete andati/e	*you (pl.) went*
loro sono andati/e	*they went*

Verbs conjugated with essere include: verbs indicating movement from a place to another, such as **andare** *(to go),* **venire** *(to come),* uscire *(to go out)*, entrare *(to come in)*, arrivare *(to arrive)*, partire *(to leave)*, ritornare *(to return)*, etc., as well as verbs that indicate absence of movement, such as stare *(to stay)*, restare *(to stay)*, rimanere *(to remain)*, etc.

Il treno è arrivato con mezz'ora di ritardo.
The train arrived half an hour late.
Un mese fa siamo andati in Italia.
A month ago we went to Italy.

Other verbs that are conjugated with essere are those verbs indicating a physical or psychological change of state, such as nascere *(to be born)*, morire *(to die)*, ingrassare *(to gain weight)*, dimagrire *(to lose weight)*, invecchiare *(to grow old)*, succedere *(to happen)*, etc.

Quando sono andato in Italia sono ingrassato un chilo.
When I went to Italy, I gained a kilo.
Suo padre è invecchiato molto.
His/her father aged a lot.

Note that essere is conjugated with essere in the past, and that essere and stare share the same past participle, stato. Also note that the following verbs have an irregular past participle.

INFINITIVE	PAST PARTICIPLE	
rimanere	rimasto	*to remain*
morire	morto	*to die*
nascere	nato	*to be born*
succedere	successo	*to happen*
venire	venuto	*to come*

La festa è stata molto bella.

It was a very nice party.

L'anno scorso i miei amici italiani sono venuti a trovarmi.

Last year, my Italian friends came to see me.

I miei genitori sono nati in Germania.

My parents were born in Germany.

In compound tenses, the modal verbs **dovere, potere,** and **volere** use the auxiliary normally used by the infinitive that follows them. However, in modern spoken Italian, **avere** is often used in all cases.

Ieri siamo dovuti andare a lavorare presto.

Yesterday, we had to go to work early.

La settimana scorsa abbiamo dovuto pulire la casa.

Last week, we had to clean the house.

PRACTICE 2

Complete the following sentences with the correct form of the past tense. Pay attention to the auxiliary **avere** or **essere.**

1. Quando _____ (arrivare) Marta?

2. Ieri sera noi _____ (uscire) e _____ (vedere) una bella commedia.

3. L'anno scorso le ragazze _____ (andare) a Roma e _____ (visitare) il Colosseo.

4. Un mese fa io _____ (ritornare) in Italia perché mio padre _____ (compiere) 80 anni.

5. Ieri Luisa _____ (rimanere) a casa.

6. La settimana scorsa noi _____ (potere) uscire con gli amici.

7. L'anno scorso loro _____ (dovere) visitare i nostri parenti.

ANSWERS

PRACTICE 1: 1. ha portato; **2.** abbiamo visto; **3.** ho lavorato; **4.** avete messo; **5.** ha letto; **6.** hai scritto; **7.** hanno cucinato; **8.** abbiamo studiato.

PRACTICE 2: 1. è arrivata; **2.** siamo usciti, abbiamo visto; **3.** sono andate; hanno visitato; **4.** sono ritornato/a, ha compiuto; **5.** è rimasta; **6.** siamo potuti; **7.** hanno dovuto.

—————— Lesson 20 (Conversations) ——————

CONVERSATION 1

Alessia: Giorgio, puoi andare al supermercato a fare la spesa?

Giorgio: D'accordo, di che cosa abbiamo bisogno?

Alessia: Di tutto! Il frigorifero è vuoto!

Giorgio: Ma come! Ho fatto la spesa due giorni fa e ho comprato un sacco di roba.

Alessia: No, hai portato a casa solo del gelato, del vino e della birra!

Giorgio: Non è vero, ma se insisti . . . Allora, che tipo di pasta devo prendere?

Alessia: Compra degli spaghetti e delle penne.

Giorgio: E che carne vuoi?

Alessia: Compra delle fettine di vitello per fare delle scaloppine.

Giorgio: Ma le abbiamo già mangiate ieri!

Alessia: Sì, ma abbiamo ospiti stasera ed è il piatto che so cucinare meglio!

Alessia: Giorgio, can you go to the supermarket and buy food?

Giorgio: All right, what do we need?

Alessia:	Everything! The refrigerator is empty!
Giorgio:	What do you mean! I bought groceries two days ago and I bought a lot of stuff.
Alessia:	No, you only brought home ice cream, wine, and beer.
Giorgio:	It's not true, but if you insist . . . So, what kind of pasta do I have to get?
Alessia:	Buy some spaghetti and some penne.
Giorgio:	And which meat do you want?
Alessia:	Buy some thin slices of veal to make scaloppine.
Giorgio:	But we ate them yesterday!
Alessia:	Yes, but we've guests tonight, and it's the dish that I can cook the best!

NUTS & BOLTS 1
DIRECT OBJECT PRONOUNS

A direct object indicates the direct recipient(s) of the action of the verb. It is not introduced by a preposition, and it answers the question *what?* or *whom?* For example, in the sentence **Stefania compra il pane tutti i giorni** *(Stefania buys bread every day)*, **il pane** is the direct object. In Italian, just as in English, a direct object noun can be replaced by a direct object pronoun. But in Italian, this pronoun is generally placed immediately before the verb. Let's take a look at the Italian direct object pronouns.

mi	me
ti	you
lo	him, it
la	her, it
La *(fml.)*	you
ci	us
vi *(pl.)*	you
li *(m.)*	them
le *(f.)*	them

"Mangi spesso la pasta?" "Sì, la mangio tutti i giorni".

"Do you eat pasta often?" "Yes, I eat it every day."

"Vedi Paolo stasera?" "No, lo vedo domani".

"Are you seeing Paolo tonight?" "No, I'll see him tomorrow."

Ci chiamano una volta alla settimana.

They call us once a week.

When the verb is in the infinitive form, the object pronoun is attached to the end of the infinitive, after dropping its final -e. However, with the modal verbs **potere, dovere** or **volere,** the object pronoun can be placed either before the conjugated modal verb or attached to the infinitive.

"Perché mangi la verdura?" "Perché è importante mangiarne".

"Why do you eat vegetables?" "Because it's important to eat them."

Quando posso invitarti a cena? Quando ti posso invitare a cena?

When can I invite you (over) for dinner?

Note that the following verbs take a noun or a pronoun after a preposition in English, but in Italian they take the noun as a direct object or its pronoun without a preposition: **ascoltare** *(to listen to);* **aspettare** *(to wait for);* **cercare** *(to look for);* **guardare** *(to look at);* and **pagare** *(to pay for).*

"Ascolti molto la musica?" "Sì, l'ascolto sempre".

"Do you listen to music a lot?" "Yes, I listen to it all the time."

Lui è sempre in ritardo e io lo devo sempre aspettare.

He's always late, and I always have to wait for him.

PRACTICE I

Answer the following questions using the appropriate pronouns.

1. Mangi spesso la carne? Sì, _____.

2. Ci porti al ristorante domani? Sì, _____.

3. Vuoi ordinare il dolce? No, _____.

4. Mi permetti di pagare il conto? No, _____.

5. Mi chiami più tardi? Sì, _____.

6. Per favore, cucini gli spaghetti? Sì, _____.

CONVERSATION 2

Fabio: Ieri sera Maria ed io siamo andati a mangiare in un buon ristorante italiano.

Lucia: Davvero? Cosa avete mangiato?

Fabio: Per primo io ho mangiato delle buone lasagne alla bolognese e Maria degli spaghetti alla carbonara.

Lucia: E di secondo?

Fabio: Maria ha ordinato dell'arrosto di vitello ed io ho preso della carne alla brace. E di contorno ci hanno portato delle verdure alla griglia.

Lucia: E per finire avete preso della frutta?

Fabio: Sì, l'abbiamo ordinata, ma non l'abbiamo mangiata perché eravamo troppo pieni.

Lucia: Siete rimasti soddisfatti?

Fabio: Sì, è stata una bella cena, ma abbiamo pagato anche un bel conto salato!

Fabio: *Last night, Maria and I went to eat in a good Italian restaurant.*

Lucia: *Really? What did you eat?*

Fabio: *As a first course I ate some good lasagna Bolognese, and Maria had some spaghetti carbonara.*

Lucia: *And as a second course?*

Fabio: *Maria ordered some veal roast, and I had some grilled meat. And as a side dish we were served grilled vegetables.*

Lucia: *And to finish, did you have any fruit?*

Fabio: *Yes, we ordered some, but we didn't eat it because we were too full.*

> Lucia: *Were you satisfied with your meal?*
> Fabio: *Yes, it was a nice dinner, but we paid a nice big bill as well!*

NOTES

In Italian the preposition **a** + article is used idiomatically to express how, or in what style, a food is cooked. Note the four examples in the dialogue above: **lasagne alla bolognese, spaghetti alla carbonara,** and **carne alla brace,** and **verdure alla griglia.** Also note that **lasagne,** like every kind of pasta, is plural in Italian.

NUTS & BOLTS 2

DIRECT OBJECT PRONOUNS IN THE PRESENT PERFECT

When direct object pronouns are used in a sentence in the **passato prossimo,** they are placed right in front of the verb **avere,** and the past participle agrees in gender and number with the pronoun. The pronouns **lo** and **la** drop the final vowel in front of the present forms of **avere.**

"Daniela, hai finito la frutta?" "Sì, l'ho finita".
"Daniela, did you finish your fruit?" "Yes, I did."
Abbiamo ordinato due gelati, ma non li abbiamo mangiati.
We ordered two ice creams, but we didn't eat them.

PRACTICE

Answer the following questions using the appropriate direct object pronouns. Pay attention to the past participle.

1. Hai visto Teresa ieri? Sì, _____.

2. Avete comprato le pere? No, _____.

3. Giuseppe ha mangiato i fusilli? Sì, _____.

4. Loro hanno cucinato le braciole di maiale? Sì, _____.

5. Franca ha apparecchiato la tavola? No, _____.

6. Hai pulito gli zucchini? Sì, _____.

Culture note

As you saw in the dialogue, an Italian meal consists of different courses. It begins with an **antipasto**, which could be **affettati misti** *(mixed cold cuts)*, **prosciutto e melone** *(prosciutto and melon)*, or many other options. The **primo** *(first course)* consists of **pasta, risotto,** or **minestra** *(soup)*. The **secondo** is a dish of meat or fish, accompanied by the **contorno** of vegetables (ordered separately). **L'insalata** *(salad)* is served as **contorno** or after the **secondo,** never at the beginning of the meal. Finally, the meal ends with **il dolce,** which may consist of just plain fruit.

ANSWERS

PRACTICE 1: 1. Sì, la mangio spesso; **2.** Sì, vi porto al ristorante domani; **3.** No, non lo voglio ordinare, (No, non voglio ordinarlo); **4.** No, non puoi pagarlo, (No, non lo puoi pagare); **5.** Sì, ti chiamo più tardi; **6.** Sì, li cucino.

PRACTICE 2: 1. Sì, l'ho vista; **2.** No, non le abbiamo comprate; **3.** Sì, li ha mangiati; **4.** Sì, le hanno cucinate; **5.** No, non l'ha apparecchiata; **6.** Sì, li ho puliti.

UNIT 5 ESSENTIALS

È un buon ristorante italiano.	*It's a good Italian restaurant.*
Ho fatto la spesa due giorni fa.	*I bought groceries two days ago.*
Hai portato del gelato e della birra.	*You brought ice cream and beer.*
Compra degli spaghetti e delle penne.	*Buy some spaghetti and some penne.*
Ho mangiato delle lasagne alla bolognese.	*I ate lasagna Bolognese style.*
Avete preso della frutta?	*Did you have some fruit?*
L'abbiamo ordinata, ma non l'abbiamo mangiata.	*We ordered it, but we didn't eat it.*
Siete stati soddisfatti?	*Were you satisfied?*
È stata una bella cena.	*It was a nice dinner.*
Abbiamo pagato un bel conto salato!	*We paid a huge bill!*

Unit 6
Shopping

Ready to buy those dream shoes? I hope so, because in this unit you will learn everything you need to have a wonderful shopping experience in Italy!

─────────── Lesson 21 (Words) ───────────

WORD LIST 1

negozio d'abbigliamento	*clothing store*
giacca	*jacket*
pantaloni	*pants*
abito	*suit*
camicia	*shirt*
cravatta	*tie*
vestito	*dress*
scarpa	*shoe*
borsa	*purse*
cappello	*hat*
bianco	*white*
rosso	*red*
nero	*black*
grigio	*gray*
giallo	*yellow*

NUTS & BOLTS 1
THE GERUND

As we have already learned, in Italian the present indicative can be used to express a habitual action in the present: **pranzo sempre all'una** *(I always have lunch at one)*, but also an action in progress: **in questo momento guardo la TV** *(I'm watching TV right now)*. An action in progress, however, can also be expressed with the progressive form, which is constructed with the present tense of the verb **stare** + gerund, and is the equivalent of the English *to be doing something*. The Italian gerund is formed by adding **-ando** to the stem of verbs belonging to the first conjugation, and **-endo** to the stem of verbs belonging to the second and third conjugation: **parl-ando, scriv-endo; dorm-endo.** Thus the sentence **in questo momento guardo la TV** can also be expressed with **(in questo momento) sto guardando la TV.** There are a few irregular gerunds: **bere → bevendo, dire → dicendo,** and **fare → facendo.**

Cosa stai facendo qui
What are you doing here?
Sto cercando un paio di scarpe eleganti.
I'm looking for an elegant pair of shoes. I'm looking for a pair of dress shoes.
Stanno leggendo il giornale.
They're reading the paper.

PRACTICE 1
Restate the following sentences in the present progressive.

Example: **Q: Maria parla con Teresa → A: Maria sta parlando con Teresa.**

1. Noi compriamo una casa nuova.

2. Tu scrivi una lettera.

3. Loro giocano a tennis.

4. Io lavoro molto.

5. Voi imparate l'italiano.

6. Lei segue un corso di storia dell'arte.

WORLD LIST 2

camicetta	*blouse*
camicia	*shirt*

maglione	*sweater*
maglioncino	*light sweater*
gonna	*skirt*
convinto/a	*convinced (m./f.)*
indossare	*to wear*
mese *(m.)*	*month*
gennaio	*January*
febbraio	*February*
marzo	*March*
aprile	*April*
maggio	*May*
giugno	*June*
luglio	*July*
agosto	*August*
settembre	*September*
ottobre	*October*
novembre	*November*
dicembre	*December*

NUTS & BOLTS 2
INDIRECT OBJECT PRONOUNS

An indirect object indicates the indirect recipient(s) of the action of the verb. As a noun, it is introduced by the preposition **a,** and it answers the question **to whom?** or **for whom?** In the sentence **Maria scrive una lettera a sua madre** *(Maria writes a letter to her mother),* **a sua madre** is the indirect object (while **una lettera** is the direct object). An indirect object noun can be replaced by an indirect object pronoun, which does not need the preposition **a,** and is generally placed immediately before the verb. While a direct object pronoun can refer to both a thing or a person, an indirect object pronoun can only refer to a person. When indirect object pronouns are used in the **passato prossimo,** the ending of the verb's participle is unaffected by the pronouns. Let's take a look at the Italian indirect object pronouns.

mi	*to me*
ti	*to you*
gli	*to him*
le	*to her*
Le *(fml.)*	*to you*
ci	*to us*
vi *(pl.)*	*to you*
gli	*to them*

The rules governing the position of the indirect object pronoun are exactly the same as those for the direct object pronoun (see Unit 5, Lesson 20).

Certain verbs, such as **telefonare** *(to telephone)*, **insegnare** *(to teach)*, **interessare** *(to interest)*, **rispondere** *(to answer)*, **mandare** *(to send)*, and **spedire** *(to send)*, take an indirect object pronoun in Italian, but a direct object pronoun in English.

"Hai parlato al direttore?" "Sì, gli ho parlato".

"Did you speak to the director?" "Yes, I spoke to him."

Perché non ci telefonate stasera?

Why don't you call us tonight?

"Hai risposto a Silvana?" "No, non le ho ancora risposto".

"Did you answer Silvana?" "No, I didn't answer her yet."

La prossima settimana è il compleanno di Giulio e devo mandargli un regalo.

Next week is Giulio's birthday and I have to send him a gift.

PRACTICE 2

Answer the following questions replacing the underlined words with the appropriate pronouns:

1. Hai scritto a tua cugina? Sì, _____

2. Avete telefonato a Roberto? No, _____

3. Hai parlato ai tuoi amici? Sì, _____

4. Vi hanno spedito il pacco? No, _____

5. Hai raccontato la favola alle bambine? Sì, _____

Tip!

If you are going on a shopping spree in Italy, make sure you really like or need what you buy, because it is almost impossible to return any merchandise after you walk out of a store. Very few stores will give you a store credit, but none will return your money!

ANSWERS

PRACTICE 1: 1. Noi stiamo comprando una casa nuova; **2.** Tu stai scrivendo una lettera; **3.** Loro stanno giocando a tennis; **4.** Io sto lavorando molto; **5.** Voi state imparando l'italiano; **6.** Lei sta seguendo un corso di storia dell'arte.

PRACTICE 2: 1. Sì, le ho scritto; **2.** No, non gli abbiamo telefonato; **3.** Sì, gli ho parlato; **4.** No, non ci hanno spedito il pacco; **5.** Sì, gli ho raccontato la favola.

—————————— Lesson 22 (Phrases) ——————————

PHRASE LIST 1

si sposa	*he/she is getting married*
si mette	*he/she wears/puts on*
si chiama	*his/her name is . . .*
a proposito di	*speaking of*
Che sorpresa!	*What a surprise!*

da Bang Bang	*at Bang Bang's*
mi sembra bello	*it seems nice to me*
Come mi sta?	*How do I look? (lit., How is it on me?)*
di velluto a coste	*made out of corduroy*
di pelle	*made out of leather*

NUTS & BOLTS 1
REFLEXIVE VERBS

Reflexive verbs, whose infinitives are recognizable by their -si ending, are verbs in which the action refers back to the subject (as in *I enjoy myself*). You have already learned the verb **chiamarsi** *(to be named)*. Italian uses reflexive verbs more often than English, which prefers prepositional sentences (i.e., *to wake up, to get up,* etc.) to express the same idea. Reflexive verbs are conjugated just like non reflexive verbs, but are preceded by the reflexive pronoun as follows:

ALZARSI *(to get up)*	METTERSI *(to put on)*	DIVERTIRSI *(to enjoy oneself)*	PULIRSI *(to clean oneself)*
io mi alzo	io mi metto	io mi diverto	io mi pulisco
tu ti alzi	tu ti metti	tu ti diverti	tu ti pulisci
lui si alza	lui si mette	lui si diverte	lui si pulisce
lei si alza	lei si mette	lei si diverte	lei si pulisce
noi ci alziamo	noi ci mettiamo	noi ci divertiamo	noi ci puliamo
voi vi alzate	voi vi mettete	voi vi divertite	voi vi pulite
loro si alzano	loro si mettono	loro si divertono	loro si puliscono

Review the following list of some common reflexive verbs.

| addormentarsi | *to fall asleep* |
| annoiarsi | *to get bored* |

fermarsi	*to stop*
lavarsi	*to wash up*
preoccuparsi	*to worry*
prepararsi	*to get ready*
sentirsi	*to feel*
svegliarsi	*to wake up*
vestirsi	*to get dressed*

Perché ti preoccupi sempre così tanto?

Why do you always worry so much?

A che ora vi svegliate la mattina?

At what time do you wake up in the morning?

Quando lo vedo mi fermo sempre per salutarlo.

When I see him, I always stop to say hi.

In the past **(passato prossimo)** reflexive verbs are always conjugated with **essere**.

Claudia, ti sei divertita ieri sera alla festa?

Claudia, did you enjoy yourself at the party last night?

Ieri ci siamo alzati molto tardi.

Yesterday, we got up very late.

PRACTICE 1
Complete the following sentences with the present or past tenses of the verbs in parentheses, depending on sense.

1. Tutte le mattine lui _____ (svegliarsi) alle 6:30.

2. Ieri io _____ (annoiarsi) molto a teatro.

3. Oggi noi non _____ (sentirsi) molto bene.

4. Ieri sera tu _____ (addormentarsi) davanti alla TV.

5. Voi _____ (lavarsi) sempre prima di andare a letto.

6. La settimana scorsa loro _____ (mettersi) un vestito da sera per andare alla festa.

PHRASE LIST 2

posso esserLe utile *(fml.)*	*How can I help you? (lit., Can I be useful to you?)/Can I assist you?*
di seta	*made out of silk*
di cachemire	*made out of cashmere*
Le faccio vedere *(fml.)*	*I'll show you*
Le piace? *(fml.)*	*Do you like it?*
mi piace	*I like it*
le mezze stagioni	*half seasons (spring and fall)*
ci penso	*I'll think about it*
fra qualche giorno	*in a few days*
chiedere un consiglio	*to ask for advice*

NUTS & BOLTS 2

EXPRESSING LIKES AND DISLIKES

Although **piacere** and *to like* have the same meaning, they have very different structures. The verb **piacere** can be literally translated as *to be pleasing to* or *to appeal to*. So, when you want to express the English *Cristina likes this dress* into Italian, you need to rephrase it as *this dress is appealing to Cristina*. In this structure, what is liked *(the dress)* constitutes the subject of the sentence, while the person who likes *(Cristina)* is the indirect object. So the sentence would be rendered in Italian as **il vestito piace a Cristina.** If the subject of the sentence—what is being liked—is a plural noun, then the verb **piacere** will be in the plural form **piacciono.** Although the word order is flexible, the most typical construction is: indirect object + **piacere** + what is liked.

A Maria piace quella borsa.

Maria likes that purse.

Alla signora Panzacchi piacciono le scarpe rosse.

Mrs. Panzacchi likes red shoes.

Gli piacciono i vestiti di Armani.
He likes Armani suits.

If what is liked is an action expressed in the infinitive, the verb **piacere** will be in the third person singular.

Gli piace svegliarsi presto la mattina.
He likes to wake up early in the morning.
Non ci piace fare spese al centro commerciale.
We don't like shopping at the mall.

The verb **piacere** is conjugated with **essere** in the past. Like with all other verbs conjugated with **essere,** the past participle has to agree with the subject of the sentence, which with **piacere** is the entity that is liked.

Mi è piaciuta la festa di ieri sera.
I liked the party last night.
Gli sono piaciute le cravatte che gli hai comprato.
He liked the ties you bought for him.

The verb **dispiacere,** which has the same structure of **piacere,** means *to be sorry* or *to mind.* The negative form of **piacere** is used to express dislike.

Le dispiace farmi vedere quella giacca?
Would you mind showing me that jacket?
Non ci piace quella gonna.
We don't like that skirt.

PRACTICE 2
Form sentences following the example, and then replace the indirect object with a pronoun.

Giorgio/comprare vestiti → A Giorgio piace comprare vestiti → Gli piace comprare vestiti.

1. Luigi/la pasta.

2. I bambini/le favole.

3. Le ragazze/fare spese.

4. La signora Piccoli/i vestiti eleganti.

5. Noi/le vacanze.

6. Lui/imparare le lingue straniere.

Language link

Are you interested in fashion? Would you like to know what the latest trends are? Go to **www.google.it** and search for **moda autunno-inverno,** or **moda primavera-estate,** and you will find all you need to know about fashion for the coming season.

ANSWERS

PRACTICE 1: 1. si sveglia; **2.** mi sono annoiato/a; **3.** ci sentiamo; **4.** ti sei addormentato/a; **5.** vi lavate; **6.** si sono messi/messe.

PRACTICE 2: 1. A Luigi piace la pasta/gli piace la pasta; **2.** Ai bambini piacciono le favole/gli piacciono le favole; **3.** Alle ragazze piace fare spese/gli piace fare spese; **4.** Alla signora Piccoli piacciono i vestiti eleganti/le piacciono i vestiti eleganti; **5.** A noi piacciono le vacanze/ci piacciono le vacanze; **6.** A lui piace imparare le lingue/gli piace imparare le lingue.

———— Lesson 23 (Sentences) ————

SENTENCE GROUP 1

Sto cercando un vestito.

I'm looking for a dress.

Mia sorella si sposa il mese prossimo.

My sister is getting married next month.

Sto cominciando a preoccuparmi.

I'm beginning to worry.

Anche lui frequentava il nostro liceo.

He also used to attend our high school.

Era due anni avanti.

He was two years ahead (of us).

Aveva i capelli lunghi.

He had long hair.

Portava una giacca di pelle.

He used to wear a leather jacket.

Guidava una motocicletta rossa.

He used to drive a red motorbike.

NUTS & BOLTS 1
THE IMPERFECT TENSE

The imperfect is a simple (not compound) past tense used to describe habitual actions in the past (what we used to do), actions in progress in the past (what we were doing), and general circumstances in the past. The imperfect is formed by dropping the final **-re** of the infinitive, and by adding the following endings: **-vo, -vi, -va, -vamo, -vate, -vano.**

PARLARE	VEDERE	DORMIRE	FINIRE
io parlavo	io vedevo	io dormivo	io finivo
tu parlavi	tu vedevi	tu dormivi	tu finivi
lui parlava	lui vedeva	lui dormiva	lui finiva
lei parlava	lei vedeva	lei dormiva	lei finiva
noi parlavamo	noi vedevamo	noi dormivamo	noi finivamo
voi parlavate	voi vedevate	voi dormivate	voi finivate
loro parlavano	loro vedevano	loro dormivano	loro finivano

The verb **essere** is irregular in the imperfect: **ero, eri, era, eravamo, eravate, erano.**

The following verbs have irregular stems, but regular endings: **bere → beve-; dire → dice-; fare → face-.**

Quando ero giovane portavo sempre vestiti sportivi.
When I was young I always used to dress casual.
Che cosa cercavi ieri al centro commerciale?
What were you looking for at the mall yesterday?
Le modelle alla sfilata (di moda) erano troppo magre.
The models at the (fashion) show were too thin/skinny.

PRACTICE 1
Put the following sentences in the imperfect tense.

1. Facciamo spesso spese in quella boutique.

2. Quel vestito costa troppo.

3. Mi piace indossare scarpe comode.

4. Quella ragazza porta sempre gonne corte.

5. La signora Giordani è molto elegante.

6. Bevete sempre spumante.

7. Lui dice spesso bugie.

SENTENCE GROUP 2
Sto cercando una camicetta di seta.
I'm looking for a silk blouse.
Sta arrivando la primavera.
Spring is coming.
Le faccio vedere i maglioncini che abbiamo.
I'll show you the sweaters we have.

Le piace questo maglioncino?

Do you like this (light) sweater?

Ci devo pensare.

I'll think about it.

Tornerò fra qualche giorno.

I'll come back in a few days.

Forse fra qualche giorno non lo troverà più.

Perhaps, in a few days, you will not find it anymore.

Chiederò consiglio a mio marito.

I'll ask my husband for advice. / I'll discuss it with my husband.

NUTS & BOLTS 2
THE FUTURE TENSE

The future tense is formed by dropping the final **-e** from the infinitive, and adding the endings **-ò, -ai, -à, -emo, -ete, -anno**. In verbs of the first conjugation, the **-a** of the infinitive ending changes to **-e**:

PARLARE	RICEVERE	DORMIRE	FINIRE
io parlerò	io riceverò	io dormirò	io finirò
tu parlerai	tu riceverai	tu dormirai	tu finirai
lui parlerà	lui riceverà	lui dormirà	lui finirà
lei parlerà	lei riceverà	lei dormirà	lei finirà
noi parleremo	noi riceveremo	noi dormiremo	noi finiremo
voi parlerete	voi riceverete	voi dormirete	voi finirete
loro parleranno	loro riceveranno	loro dormiranno	loro finiranno

Several common verbs have irregular stems in the future. They are: **venire → verr-; volere → vorr-; bere → berr-**, etc. Other irregular stems are formed by dropping both vowels from the infinitive ending: **andare** → **andr-**; **avere** → **avr-**; **cadere** → **cadr-**; **dovere** → **dovr-**; **potere** → **potr-**; **sapere** → **sapr-**; **vedere** → **vedr-**. The future stem of essere is **sar-**.

La prossima settimana comprerò un vestito da sera.
Next week, I'll buy an evening gown.
L'estate prossima loro andranno in Europa.
Next summer, they will go to Europe.
Se verrete in campagna vedrete molti animali.
If you come to the country, you'll (be able to) see many animals.

Since Italians these days commonly use the present tense to talk about the future, when the future tense is used it has a bit of more emphatic and assertive quality than the present tense. In addition to indicating future actions, the future tense is used idiomatically to express the idea of probability of a present situation.

"Che taglia porta Maria?" "Porterà una quarantaquattro".
"What size does Maria wear?" "She probably wears a 44."
"Quanti anni ha Giulio?" "Avrà trentotto anni".
"How old is Giulio?" "He's probably 38."

PRACTICE 2
Change the following sentences from the present to the future.

1. Domani lei va a fare compere al centro commerciale.

2. Non so se domani volete andare in centro.

3. Per rilassarmi questo weekend leggo un libro nuovo.

4. Stasera non guardiamo la TV.

5. Loro arrivano domani.

6. Il bambino partecipa a una gara sportiva.

WOMEN'S CLOTHING SIZES*

Coats, Dresses, Suits, Skirts, Slacks

U.S.	4	6	8	10	12	14	16	18
Italy	36	38	40	42	44	46	48	50

Blouses, Sweaters

U.S.	30	32	34	36	38	40	42
Italy	38	40	42	44	46	48	50

Shoes

U.S.	5-5½	6	6½-7	7½	8	8½	9	9½-10
Italy	35	36	37	38	38½	39	40	41

MEN'S CLOTHING SIZES*

Suits, Coats

U.S.	34	36	38	40	42	44	46	48
Italy	44	46	48	50	52	54	56	58

Sweaters

U.S.	XS/36	S/38	M/40	L/42	XL/44
Italy	42/2	44/3	46-48/4	50/5	52-54/6

Shirts

U.S.	14	14½	15	15½	15¾	16	16½	17	17½	18
Italy	36	37	38	39	40	41	42	43	44	45

Socks

U.S.	9½	10	10½	11	11½	12
Italy	36-37	38-39	40-41	42-43	44-45	46

Shoes

U.S.	6½	7	7½	8	8½	9	9½	10	10½	11	11½
Italy	39	39½	40	41	42	42½	43	43½	44	44½	45

*It's a good idea to try on all clothing before buying because sizes vary and do not always correlate exactly with U.S. sizes. Also, it is less customary in Italy to return clothing purchased, except at large department stores in major cities.

ANSWERS

PRACTICE 1: 1. Facevamo spesso spese in quella boutique; **2.** Quel vestito costava troppo; **3.** Mi piaceva indossare scarpe comode; **4.** Quella ragazza portava sempre gonne corte; **5.** La signora Giordani era molto elegante; **6.** Bevevate sempre spumante; **7.** Lui diceva spesso bugie.

PRACTICE 2: 1. Domani lei andrà a fare spese al centro commerciale; **2.** Non so se domani vorrete andare in centro; **3.** Per rilassarmi questo weekend leggerò un libro nuovo; **4.** Stasera non guarderemo la TV; **5.** Loro arriveranno domani; **6.** Il bambino parteciperà a una gara sportiva.

––––––––––– Lesson 24 (Conversations) –––––––––––

CONVERSATION 1

Gianni: Ciao Lucia, che sorpresa! Che cosa stai facendo qui?

Lucia: Sto cercando un abito da cerimonia. Mia sorella si sposa il mese prossimo e devo andare al suo matrimonio.

Gianni: Che bello! Non conosco il suo fidanzato, come si chiama?

Lucia: Luca Zanetti, sei sicuro che non lo conosci? Anche lui frequentava il nostro liceo, ma era due anni avanti. Aveva i capelli molto lunghi, portava sempre una giacca di pelle nera, dei pantaloni di velluto a coste grigi e guidava una motocicletta rossa enorme. Adesso è diventato un medico famoso e si mette sempre abiti, camicie e cravatte di Armani!

Gianni: Sì, lo ricordo vagamente ... ma a proposito di vestiti, hai idea di cosa metterti per il matrimonio?

Lucia: Non lo so, sto cominciando a preoccuparmi perché non ho ancora trovato nulla. Sono andata da Bang Bang, da Alexander e da Carnini, in tutti i migliori negozi d'abbigliamento e non ho visto un vestito che mi piace!

Gianni: Guarda questo, Lucia, mi sembra molto bello!

Lucia: Hai ragione, lo provo. Hai tempo di guardare come mi sta?

Gianni: Certamente e poi ti accompagno a cercare gli accessori. Devi assolutamente coordinare scarpe, borsa e cappello per essere veramente elegante.

Gianni: *Hi Lucia, what a surprise! What are you doing here?*

Lucia: *I'm looking for a dress. My sister is getting married next month, and I must go to her wedding.*

Gianni: *How nice! I don't know her fiancé, what's his name?*

Lucia: *Luca Zanetti, are you sure you don't know him? He was also attending our high school, but he was two years ahead. He used to have very long hair, was always wearing a black leather jacket, a pair of gray corduroy pants, and was (always) driving an enormous red motorbike. Now he's become a famous doctor and always wears Armani suits, shirts, and ties!*

Gianni: *Yes, I vaguely remember him ... but speaking of clothes, do you know what you want to wear for the wedding?*

Lucia: *I don't know, I'm beginning to worry because I haven't found anything yet. I went to Bang Bang's, Alexander's, and Carnini's, all the best clothing stores, and I haven't seen a dress I like!*

Gianni:	Look at this one, Lucia, it seems very beautiful to me!
Lucia:	You're right. I'll try it. Do you have time to look at how it fits me?
Gianni:	Certainly, and then I'll take you to look for accessories. You absolutely must find the perfect shoes, purse, and hat to be truly elegant.

NOTES

Liceo. In Italy there are various types of high schools. Students who expect to continue studying at the university will attend a **liceo,** while other students may prefer to go to one of the professional schools, or **istituti tecnici,** where they will be trained for a technical job.

Una giacca di pelle. To express what material an object is made of, Italian uses the preposition **di** + material. Other examples are: **una camicia di lino** *(a linen shirt),* **un tavolo di legno** *(a wooden table),* etc.

Una motocicletta rossa. Remember that colors are adjectives, and as such in Italian they agree in gender and number with the noun they modify. A few exceptions are foreign words, such as **blu** and **beige,** and colors that refer to names of flowers: **viola** *(purple);* **rosa** *(pink);* **fucsia** *(fuchsia),* etc. These colors are invariable.

NUTS & BOLTS 1
THE PREPOSITION DA
The preposition **da** literally means *from.*

Gli studenti tornano da scuola alle tre.
Students come back from school at 3:00 p.m.
Il treno da Milano arriva a Roma alle dodici e trenta.
The train from Milan arrives in Rome at 12:30 p.m.

Da, however, is also used idiomatically to express at somebody's house; store; office; or place in general.

Stasera ceniamo da Giorgio.

Tonight, we are having dinner at Giorgio's.

Domani vado dal dottore.

Tomorrow, I'm going to the doctor's.

Compro i vestiti da Bang Bang.

I buy my clothes at Bang Bang's.

PRACTICE 1

Complete the following sentences using one of the following prepositions as appropriate: **di, a, da, in.**

1. Partiamo _____ New York alle 7:00 di sera e arriviamo _____ Roma, alle 9:00 di mattina.

2. Ogni anno andiamo _____ Italia per due mesi.

3. Perché non andiamo a mangiare _____ Tonino?

4. Domenica non saremo _____ casa perché andiamo _____ vacanza.

5. "_____ chi è questo libro?" "È _____ Mirella."

CONVERSATION 2

Commesso: Buongiorno signora, benvenuta da Carnini, posso esserLe utile?

Signora Ricci: Sì, grazie, sto cercando una camicetta di seta da indossare con questa gonna.

Commesso: La gonna è molto bella, ma è un po' sportiva. Ha pensato di indossarla con un maglioncino di cachemire invece che con una camicetta? Se vuole Le faccio vedere i maglioncini che abbiamo. Ecco, guardi, Le piace questo?

Signora Ricci: Sì, mi piace molto, ma ormai siamo in aprile e forse il cachemire fa un po' troppo caldo.

Commesso: Signora, quando i maglioncini sono arrivati, ho parlato al direttore del negozio e gli ho detto la stessa cosa, ma lui mi ha risposto che

sono di cachemire e seta, sono molto leggeri e
adatti per le mezze stagioni.

Signora Ricci: È molto bello, ma ho già molti maglioncini.
Ci penserò e se decido di comprarlo tornerò
fra qualche giorno.

Commesso: Signora, forse fra qualche giorno non lo
troverà più. Questo è l'ultimo che abbiamo.

Signora Ricci: Mi dispiace, ma non sono convinta.
Chiederò consiglio a mio marito, e tornerò
domani.

Salesperson: *Good day, Madam, welcome to Carnini's. Can I help
you?*

Signora Ricci: *Yes, thanks. I'm looking for a silk blouse to wear with
this skirt.*

Salesperson: *Your skirt is very beautiful, but a bit casual. Have you
thought about wearing it with a cashmere sweater
rather than a blouse? If you'd like, I can show you the
sweaters we have. Look, do you like this one?*

Signora Ricci: *Yes, I like it a lot, but we are already in April and
perhaps cashmere is a bit too warm.*

Salesperson: *Madam, I spoke to the store manager as soon as we got
the sweaters, and I told him the same thing, but he
answered that these silk and cashmere sweaters are very
light, perfect for spring or fall weather.*

Signora Ricci: *It's very beautiful, but I already have many sweaters.
I'll think about it and, if I decide to buy it, I will come
back in a few days.*

Salesperson: *Madam, perhaps in a few days you will not find it
anymore. This is the last one we have left.*

Signora Ricci: *I'm sorry, but I'm not sure. I will ask my husband for
advice, and I'll come back tomorrow.*

NOTES

Le faccio vedere i maglioncini. Fare vedere *(to show)* literally
means to make or let someone see something.

Ho pensato di indossare la gonna. The verb **pensare** is followed by the preposition **di** + infinitive to convey the idea of thinking about doing something. It is followed by the preposition **a** + (pro)noun when it means to think about something or someone, as in: **penso sempre ai miei figli** *(I always think about my children).*

NUTS & BOLTS 2
ADJECTIVE AND ADVERBS MOLTO, POCO, AND TROPPO

Remember that **molto** *(much, a lot)* can be used both as an adjective and as an adverb. As an adjective it modifies a noun, and it agrees with that noun in gender and number.

Ho comprato molte scarpe.
I bought many (pairs of) shoes.
Mangio sempre molta verdura.
I always eat a lot of vegetables.

As an adverb, it modifies a verb, an adjective, or another adverb and is always invariable.

Questa camicia è molto bella.
This shirt is very beautiful.
Lui gioca molto a tennis.
He plays tennis a lot.
Voi vestite molto elegantemente.
You dress very elegantly.

Poco *(few, little)* and **troppo** *(too much)* work exactly the same way.

Lei ha poche borse.
She has few purses.
Loro dormono troppo.
They sleep too much.

PRACTICE 2
Complete with the correct form of **molto**.

1. Compriamo _____ vestiti.

2. Loro leggono _____.

3. È una ragazza _____ intelligente.

4. Noi abbiamo _____ amiche.

5. Correte _____ velocemente.

6. Mangio _____ pasta.

> ### Culture note
> Although traditionally Italians have always shopped in small stores and boutiques, in recent years **centri commerciali** (*malls*), **supermercati** (*supermarkets*), and outlet stores have become ubiquitous, and Italians enjoy the longer hours, with an **orario continuato** (*open all day/not closed during lunch break*), and the cheaper prices offered by these stores.

ANSWERS
PRACTICE 1: 1. da, a; 2. in; 3. da; 4. a, in; 5. di, di.

PRACTICE 2: 1. molti; 2. molto; 3. molto; 4. molte; 5. molto; 6. molta.

UNIT 6 ESSENTIALS

Sto cercando una camicetta di seta.	*I'm looking for a silk blouse.*
Sto cominciando a preoccuparmi.	*I'm beginning to worry.*
Gli ho detto la stessa cosa.	*I told him the same thing./ That's what I told him.*
Le piace questo maglioncino?	*Do you like this (light) sweater?*
Mia sorella si sposa.	*My sister's getting married.*
Come si chiama il suo fidanzato?	*What's her fiancé's name?*
Aveva i capelli lunghi.	*He used to have long hair.*

Portava una giacca di pelle.	*He used to wear a leather jacket.*
Ci penserò.	*I'll think about it.*
Tornerò domani.	*I'll come back tomorrow.*
Faccio spese da Alexander.	*I shop at Alexander's.*
In primavera il cachemire fa troppo caldo.	*Cashmere is too warm for spring.*
Ho già molti maglioncini.	*I already have a lot of sweaters.*

Unit 7
Getting around Italy

If you intend to travel in Italy, there are amazing choices: the seaside, the Alps, beautiful alpine lakes, little towns built on rocky hills, beautiful cities rich in art and history, and more. Are you ready to learn how to explain what you want to a travel agent?

─────────────── Lesson 25 (Words) ───────────────

WORD LIST 1

mare *(m.)*	*sea, seaside*
spiaggia	*beach*
montagna	*mountains*
campagna	*country, countryside*
gita	*day trip, short trip*
nuvola	*cloud*
sole	*sun*
pioggia	*rain*
vento	*wind*
tuono	*thunder*
fulmine	*lightning*
neve	*snow*

NUTS & BOLTS 1
MORE ON USING THE PAST AND IMPERFECT TENSES

In Units 5 and 6 we studied the past tense and the imperfect, both used to speak of events that occurred in the past. However, while the past is a narrative tense, the imperfect is a descriptive tense. Thus, when we want to speak about a past action that occurred in a specific moment in time, no matter how long it lasted, we use the

passato, although when we want to describe the circumstances associated with a past action, we use the **imperfetto**. In other words, the **imperfetto** expresses the physical or psychological circumstances surrounding the action, which is expressed by the **passato.**

As we saw in Unit 6, the **imperfetto** is used to express a habitual action in the past, as well as a progressive action in the past.

Quando andavo in montagna facevo molte escursioni.
When I used to go to the mountains, I would hike a lot.
Mentre camminavo improvvisamente ha cominciato a piovere.
I was walking, when all of a sudden it started to rain.

In addition, the **imperfetto** is used to express age, time, weather, and physical or emotional state in the past.

Quando avevo dieci anni andavo sempre al lago.
When I was 10, I would always go to the lake.
Erano le undici e trenta quando finalmente siamo partiti.
It was 11:30 when we finally left.
Il sole splendeva e non c'era una nuvola in cielo.
The sun was shining, and there wasn't a single cloud in the sky.
Ero molto felice.
I was very happy.

PRACTICE 1
Complete the following sentences using either the past or the imperfect form of the verbs in parentheses as appropriate.

1. _____ (Essere) l'una quando il treno finalmente _____ (arrivare).

2. Voi non _____ (andare) al parco perché _____ (piovere) molto forte.

3. Loro _____ (mangiare) quando Enrico _____ (entrare) in casa.

4. Mentre lui _____ (dormire) Mariella _____ (leggere) un libro.

5. Noi _____ (avere) dieci anni quando _____ (venire) a vivere in America.

WORD LIST 2

viaggio	*trip*
isola	*island*
sardegna	*Sardinia*
sicilia	*Sicily*
storia	*story, history*
cultura	*culture*
tempio	*temple*
greco	*Greek*
arabo	*Arab*
barocco	*baroque*
selvaggio	*wild*
entrambi/entrambe	*both (of them)*

NUTS & BOLTS 2

MODAL VERBS SAPERE AND CONOSCERE IN THE PAST OR IMPERFECT

Modal verbs (**dovere, volere,** and **potere**) have slightly different meanings when used in the past or the imperfect. Generally, the past has a stronger meaning than the imperfect, as exemplified in the following sentences.

Dovevo andare a cena a casa di amici dei miei genitori.

I was supposed to go to dinner at my parents' friends' house. (I didn't necessarily go.)

Sono dovuto andare a casa di amici dei miei genitori.

I had to go to dinner at my parents' friends' house. (I did go.)

Volevo fare un viaggio in Sicilia.

I wanted to take a trip to Sicily. (I didn't necessarily go.)

Ho voluto fare un viaggio in Sicilia.

I wanted to take a trip to Sicily. (I did go.)

Potevo andare in montagna.

I could go to the mountains. (I had the means and opportunity, but I didn't necessarily go.)

Sono potuto/potuta andare in montagna.

I managed to go to the mountains.

Also, the verbs **sapere** and **conoscere** have a slightly different meaning when used in the past or the imperfect.

When used in the imperfect, **conoscere** means *to be familiar with*, while in the past it means *to meet (for the first time).*

Non conoscevo Giuseppe Nannini, ma l'ho conosciuto ieri sera.

I didn't know Giuseppe Nannini, but I met him last night.

Used in the imperfect **sapere** means *to be aware*, while in the past it means *to find out.*

Non sapevo che volevi andare in vacanza con Gigi.

I didn't know you wanted to go on vacation with Gigi.

Hanno saputo che lui è già partito.

They found out that he had already left.

PRACTICE 2

Complete the following sentences with either the past or the imperfect of the verbs in parentheses.

1. Lui ha vinto un milione di euro alla lotteria e _____ (potere) permettersi di fare un viaggio di un anno intorno al mondo.

2. Noi _____ (dovere) andare in Italia quest'estate, ma Mirko si è ammalato e così non andremo.

3. "Tu _____ (sapere) che Franco si è fidanzato?" Sì, l' _____ (sapere) la settimana scorsa.

4. Quando ho visto quel vestito, l' _____ (volere) comprare a tutti i costi!

5. Quando ha cominciato a piovere, loro _____ (dovere) interrompere la passeggiata.

Language link

If you want to see what **Nuraghi** look like, go to **www.google.it** and enter "**Nuraghi**" into the search field. Click on **Immagihi** to see some images.

ANSWERS

PRACTICE 1: 1. era, è arrivato; 2. siete andati/e, pioveva; 3. mangiavano, è entrato. 4. dormiva, leggeva; 5. avevamo, siamo venuti/e.

PRACTICE 2: 1. ha potuto; 2. dovevamo; 3. sapevi, ho saputo; 4. ho voluto; 5. hanno dovuto.

—————— Lesson 26 (Phrases) ——————

PHRASE LIST 1

ci va	*he/she goes there*
ne parla	*he/she speaks about it*
beato te!	*lucky you!*
sto per	*I'm about to*
raccogliere funghi	*to pick mushrooms*
più adatto	*more appropriate*
del solito	*than usual*
mai più	*never again*
al mare	*at the beach*
al lago	*at the lake*
in montagna	*to the mountains*
in campagna	*to the country*

NUTS & BOLTS 1
THE PRONOUN CI

You have already encountered the pronoun **ci** in different functions: as a direct object pronoun *(us)*, as an indirect object pronoun *(to us)*, and as a reflexive pronoun *(ourselves)*. You have also encountered it in the expression **c'è** and **ci sono**, where it expresses a location and has the meaning of *there*. With this function it replaces the preposition **a** (or **da, in** and **su**) + a place.

"Vai spesso in montagna?" "Sì, ci vado spesso".
"Do you often go to the mountains?" "Yes, I go there a lot/often."
"Vieni a casa mia stasera?" "Sì, ci vengo".
"Are you coming to my house tonight?" "Yes, I'm coming (there)."

Ci can also be used to replace a prepositional phrase introduced by **a, su,** or **in,** even if it doesn't refer to location.

"Pensi di fare una vacanza in Europa?" "Oh, sì, ci penso spesso!"
"Do you think about taking a vacation to Europe?" "Oh, yes, I often think about it.
"Credi a quello che ci ha raccontato Mario?" "No, non ci credo affatto".
"Do you believe what Mario told us?" "No, I don't believe it at all."

The pronoun **ne** means *of/about it* or *of/about them*. It is used to replace a partitive *some* construction, including one introduced by a number, or expression indicating quantity.

Non me ne hai mai parlato.
You never spoke to me about it.
"Puoi comprare delle riviste?" "Quante ne devo comprare?"
"Can you buy some magazines?" "How many (of them) shall I buy?"
"Quanti viaggi fai quest'anno?" "Ne faccio due".
"How many trips are you taking this year?" "I'm taking two (trips)."

Ne also replaces a noun or expression introduced by the preposition **di**.

"Hai bisogno di aiuto?" "No, non ne ho bisogno".
"Do you need help?" "No, I don't need any."

PRACTICE 1
Complete the following sentences with either **ci** or **ne**.

1. Se vuoi andare in Sicilia _____ possiamo andare insieme.

2. Non preoccuparti, _____ penso io!

3. Mi hanno offerto dei soldi, ma io non _____ ho bisogno.

4. Sapevo che non c'erano più mele e così _____ ho comprato un chilo.

5. Stasera andiamo in discoteca, _____ vieni anche tu?

6. "Vuoi ancora un po' di vino?" "No grazie, non _____ voglio più."

PHRASE LIST 2

fare un viaggio	*to take a trip, to go on a trip*
in macchina	*by car*
in treno	*by train*
in aereo	*by plane*
fare una foto	*to take a picture*
insieme a te	*(together) with you*
te ne voglio parlare	*I want to talk with you about it, I want to discuss it with you*
gliele do	*I give them to him/to her/to them*
posso mandarglicle	*I can send them to him/to her/to them*
in ogni caso	*in any event*
più culture	*more/different cultures*

		wilder
più selvaggio/selvaggia		*wilder*
testa o croce		*heads or tails*

NUTS & BOLTS 2
DOUBLE OBJECT PRONOUNS

So far you have learned to replace either a direct or an indirect object with a pronoun (see Units 5 and 6). However, sentences often contain both a direct and an indirect object as in **Mando una lettera a mio zio** *(I send a letter to my uncle)*, where **una lettera** is the direct object and **a mio zio** is the indirect object. Both objects can be replaced by a pronoun, called a double object pronoun.

	+lo	+la	+li	+le	+ne*
mi	me lo	me la	me li	me le	me ne
ti	te lo	te la	te li	te le	te ne
ci	ce lo	ce la	ce li	ce le	ce ne
vi	ve lo	ve la	ve li	ve le	ve ne
gli	glielo	gliela	glieli	gliele	gliene
le/Le	glielo	gliela	glieli	gliele	gliene

* **Ne** is included in this chart, even though is not a direct object pronoun, because it behaves the same as direct object pronouns.

As you can see from the chart, the indirect object pronoun always precedes the direct object pronoun. In addition, some spelling changes occur in the indirect object pronouns: when followed by a direct object pronoun, the indirect object pronoun ending **-i** changes to **-e.** Also, the indirect objects pronouns **gli, le, Le** change to **glie,** which is attached to the direct objects, forming a single word. Please note that in the double object pronouns there is no difference between *to her* and *to him.* The position of double object pronouns is the same as for single object pronouns.

Faccio un viaggio e volevo parlartene.

I'm taking a trip, and I wanted to talk to you about it/discuss it with you.

Ho sentito una barzelletta divertente e ve la voglio raccontare.

I want to tell you a funny joke I heard.

"Dove hai comprato questa borsa?" "Me l'ha regalata mia madre".

"Where did you buy this purse?" "My mother gave it to me as a present."

In compound tenses the past participle agrees in gender and number with the preceding direct object.

Giuseppe mi ha chiesto di fare delle foto e io gliele ho promesse.

Giuseppe asked me to take some pictures, and I promised him that I would.

PRACTICE 2
Complete the following sentence using a double object pronoun.

1. Hai parlato a Vittorio del viaggio? No, non _____ ho parlato.

2. Ti fa dei regali il tuo ragazzo? Sì _____ fa molti.

3. Vi siete ricordati di comprare il pane? Sì, _____ siamo ricordati.

4. Hai dato la rivista a tuo padre? No, non _____ ho ancora data.

5. Mi mandi quella lettera per favore? Sì, _____ mando domani.

6. Più tardi ti racconto una fiaba. _____ puoi raccontare subito?

Tip!
If you want to plan a trip to Sicily, you can find a lot of information at the following website. You can search the site both in English and in Italian, so why don't you try to practice the Italian you have learned so far?

www.regione.sicilia.it/turismo/web_turismo

ANSWERS
PRACTICE 1: 1. ci; **2.** ci; **3.** ne; **4.** ne; **5.** ci; **6.** ne.

PRACTICE 2: 1. gliene; 2. me ne; 3. ce ne; 4. gliel'; 5. te la; 6. me la.

--- Lesson 27 (Sentences) ---

SENTENCE GROUP 1

Sto per andare in vacanza.

I'm about to go on vacation.

Non ci andrò mai più.

I'll never go there again.

Non ne hai mai parlato.

You never talked about it.

Quando andavo in montagna facevo escursioni.

When I used to go to the mountains, I would hike.

Sembrava la giornata migliore di tutte.

It seemed like the ideal day.

Mentre camminavo il cielo si è riempito di nuvole.

While I was walking, the sky filled with clouds. (It got overcast as I was walking.)

Tuonava e un fulmine è caduto vicino a me.

It was thundering, and lightning struck near me.

Il mare non è così interessante come la montagna.

The beach is not as interesting as the mountains.

NUTS & BOLTS 1

COMPARATIVES OF EQUALITY

To express a comparative of equality *(as/so . . . as; as much/as many . . . as)* Italian uses either **così . . . come, tanto . . . quanto,** or **sia . . . che.** The first part of the comparison (**così** or **tanto**) is often omitted.

Il mare non è così interessante come la montagna.

The beach is not as interesting as the mountains.

La Sicilia è tanto bella quanto ricca di storia.

Sicily is as beautiful as it is rich in history.

When two nouns are compared, **tanto . . . quanto** must be used, and they must agree in gender and number with the nouns they modify.

Lui sembra avere tanti giorni di lavoro quante vacanze.

He seems to have as many working days as vacation days.

PRACTICE 1

Form complete sentences with the given expressions, using a comparative of equality. Don't forget to conjugate the verb.

1. Mario/avere/libri/CD.

2. Noi/essere/stanchi/felici!

3. Loro/mangiare/pasta/carne.

4. Voi/viaggiare/in Europa/in Asia.

5. La campagna/non essere/divertente/mare.

SENTENCE GROUP 2

Quando hai chiamato ero già uscita.

When you called, I had already gone out/left.

Sono dovuto/dovuta andare a cena a casa di amici dei miei genitori.

I had to go to dinner at my parents' friends' house.

Sia in Sicilia che in Sardegna ci sono spiagge bellissime.

There are beautiful beaches in both Sicily and Sardinia.

La Sicilia ha una storia più ricca della Sardegna.

Sicily has a richer history than Sardinia.

In Sicilia si sono alternate più culture che in Sardegna.

In Sicily there have been more cultures than in Sardinia.

La natura è più selvaggia in Sardegna che in Sicilia.
Nature is wilder in Sardinia than in Sicily.

I Nuraghi sono forse più antichi di qualsiasi monumento in Sicilia.
The Nuraghi are perhaps more ancient than any monument in Sicily.

Giuseppe mi ha chiesto di fare delle foto e io gliele ho promesse.
Giuseppe asked me to take some pictures and I promised him that I would.

NUTS & BOLTS 2
COMPARATIVES OF INEQUALITY

The comparison of inequality can be either of superiority *(more, -er . . . than)* or of inferiority *(less . . . than)*. They are expressed in Italian by **più** . . . and by **meno** . . . , respectively. *Than* can either be translated as **di** or **che**. **Di** is used in front of numbers, or when two entities are compared in terms of the same quality or action.

La Sicilia ha una storia più ricca della Sardegna.
Sicily has a richer history than Sardinia.

I treni sono meno cari degli aerei.
Trains are less expensive than planes.

Che is used when comparing two entities of the same quality (expressed by nouns, adjectives, verbs, or adverbs).

La natura è più selvaggia in Sardegna che in Sicilia.
Nature is wilder in Sardinia than in Sicily.

È più comodo viaggiare in macchina che in treno.
It's more comfortable to travel by car than by train.

PRACTICE 2

Complete the following sentences with either **di** or **che**. Don't forget to combine **di** with the article when necessary.

1. La campagna è più noiosa _____ il mare.

2. In Italia è più costoso viaggiare in macchina _____ in treno.

3. Noi viaggiamo meno _____ voi.

4. Il biglietto aereo costa più _____ 1.500 dollari.

5. Tu viaggi più in Europa _____ in Asia.

6. La Toscana ha più opere d'arte _____ le altre regioni d'Italia.

Language link

Not too many people outside of Italy travel to Sardinia, perhaps because it is isolated and inconvenient to reach. Sardinia, however, offers some of the cleanest and most beautiful beaches in Europe, and it's certainly worth the trip! If you want to find out more about Sardinia, this is a good website: **www.mondosardegna.net**

ANSWERS

PRACTICE 1: 1. Mario ha tanti libri quanti CD; **2.** Noi siamo tanto stanchi quanto felici; **3.** Loro mangiano tanta pasta quanta carne; **4.** Voi viaggiate (così) in Europa come in Asia. **5.** La campagna non è così divertente come il mare.

PRACTICE 2: 1. La campagna è più noiosa del mare; **2.** In Italia è più costoso viaggiare in macchina che in treno; **3.** Noi viaggiamo meno di voi; **4.** Il biglietto aereo costa più di 1.500 dollari; **5.** Tu viaggi più in Europa che in Asia; **6.** La Toscana ha più opere d'arte delle altre regioni d'Italia.

—————— Lesson 28 (Conversations) ——————

CONVERSATION 1

Gabriela: Ciao Paolo, come va?

Paolo: Molto bene, sto per andare finalmente in vacanza.

Gabriela: Beato te, vai di nuovo in montagna?

Paolo: No, non ci andrò mai più! Non sai cosa mi è successo l'anno scorso?

Gabriela: No, non ne hai mai parlato.

Paolo: Allora, sai che mi piace molto camminare e quando andavo in montagna ogni giorno facevo delle escursioni sulle montagne o passeggiavo nei boschi per raccogliere funghi. Un giorno l'anno scorso mi sono svegliato ed era una giornata bellissima, splendeva il sole e non c'era una nuvola in cielo. Ero molto felice perché volevo fare un'escursione più lunga del solito e questa sembrava la giornata ideale. Dopo circa tre ore, mentre camminavo, improvvisamente il cielo si è riempito di nuvole e ha cominciato a piovere. Tuonava e lampeggiava e un fulmine è caduto a due metri da me e ha distrutto un albero! In quel momento ho deciso di non andare mai più in montagna!

Gabriela: E allora dove vai in vacanza?

Paolo: Vado al mare! Non è così interessante come la montagna, ma non è nemmeno così pericoloso.

Gabriela: *Hello, Paolo, how's it going?*

Paolo: *Very well, I'm finally about to go on vacation.*

Gabriela: *Lucky you; are you going to the mountains again?*

Paolo: *No, I'll never go there again! Don't you know what happened to me last year?*

Gabriela: *No, you never told me about it.*

Paolo: *Well, you know I like to walk a lot, and when I used to go to the mountains every day, I would hike (on mountains) or go mushroom picking in the woods. One day last year, I woke up and it was a gorgeous day: the sun was shining and there wasn't a cloud in the sky. I was very happy because I wanted to take a longer hike than usual, and that seemed like the perfect day. After about three hours, while I was walking, all of a sudden the sky filled with clouds and it began to rain. There was thunder and lightning, and a lightning bolt struck and*

destroyed a tree two meters away from me. At that precise
moment, I decided never to go to the mountains again!

Gabriela: So, where are you going on vacation?

Paolo: I'm going to the seaside! It's not as interesting as the
mountains, but it's not as dangerous either.

NOTES

Stare per + infinitive translates the idiomatic expression *to be
about to:* **l'aereo sta per decollare** *(the plane is about to take off).*

The verb **fare** is used idiomatically to express weather conditions:
fa caldo/freddo *(it is hot/cold),* **fa bello/brutto** *(it's good/bad
[weather]).*

NUTS & BOLTS 1
SUPERLATIVES

There are two superlatives in Italian: the relative superlative
(more/less beautiful than), and the absolute superlative *(the most/
least beautiful).*

The relative superlative is formed by placing the appropriate definite article in front of the comparatives **più** or **meno,** or by using
noun + **più** or **meno.** Italian uses **di** or **fra/tra** to express the English *in* or *of* in superlative constructions.

Sembrava la giornata più adatta di tutte.
It seemed like the ideal day.
Cortina è la cittadina più famosa delle Dolomiti.
Cortina is the best-known town in the Dolomites.
L'aereo è il mezzo di trasporto più veloce di tutti.
Airplanes are the fastest means of transportation (of all).

The absolute superlative is formed by adding the appropriate
form of the suffix **-ssimo (-ssima, -ssimi, -ssime)** to the masculine
plural form of the adjective: **bello → belli → bellissimo/a/i/e;
felice → felici → felicissimo/a/i/e.**

Era una giornata bellissima.

It was a very beautiful (gorgeous) day.

Ho fatto un viaggio interessantissimo.

I went on a very interesting trip.

The absolute superlative can also be expressed by preceding an adjective with the adverb **molto**.

Ero molto felice.

I was very happy.

Abbiamo visto monumenti molto antichi.

We saw very ancient monuments.

PRACTICE 1

Rewrite the following sentences following the example:

Marco è un ragazzo gentile. → Marco è il ragazzo più gentile del mondo. → Marco è un ragazzo gentilissimo.

1. Loro sono ragazzi simpatici.

2. Questo è un viaggio lungo.

3. L'Eurostar è un treno veloce.

4. Questo è un libro noioso.

5. Questa è una modella bella.

CONVERSATION 2

Mario: Ciao Giulietta, ti ho chiamata ieri sera, ma non c'eri.

Giulietta: Sì, ho ricevuto il tuo messaggio; quando hai chiamato ero già uscita. Sono dovuta andare a cena a casa di amici dei miei genitori. Lì ho conosciuto Giuseppe Nannini, lo conosci?

Mario: No. Scusa se cambio discorso, ma volevo chiederti se vuoi fare un viaggio con me quest'estate.

Giulietta: Dove hai in progetto di andare?

Mario: Non lo so, pensavo di andare in Sicilia o in Sardegna, ma volevo parlartene e decidere insieme a te.

Giulietta: Sono due isole molto belle, simili e diverse allo stesso tempo, sarà una decisione difficile. Vuoi andare in treno o in aereo?

Mario: Come vuoi, non importa, ma prima dobbiamo decidere che cosa vogliamo fare, sia in Sicilia che in Sardegna ci sono spiagge bellissime, ma la Sicilia ha una storia più ricca della Sardegna. In Sicilia si sono alternate più culture che in Sardegna. Ci sono molti templi e teatri greci da visitare, molti edifici con influenze arabe e molte chiese barocche. La natura è più selvaggia in Sardegna che in Sicilia e in Sardegna ci sono i famosi Nuraghi, monumenti archeologici forse più antichi di qualsiasi monumento in Sicilia. In ogni caso, in Sicilia o in Sardegna dovrò fare molte foto: Giuseppe mi ha chiesto se posso mandargliele perché vuole usarle nella sua agenzia di viaggi e io gliele ho promesse.

Giulietta: Mi sembrano entrambi due posti meravigliosi, e non so proprio quale scegliere. Perché non facciamo testa o croce?

Mario: *Hi, Giulietta. I called you last night, but you were not there.*

Giulietta: *Yes, I got your message; when you called I had already left. I had to go to my parents' friends' house for dinner. There I met Giuseppe Nannini; do you know him?*

Mario:	No. Excuse me if I change the subject, but I wanted to ask you if you would like to take a trip with me this summer.
Giulietta:	Where were you thinking of going?
Mario:	I don't know. I was thinking of going to Sicily, or Sardinia, but I wanted to talk to you about it, and decide with you.
Giulietta:	They are two very beautiful islands, similar and different at the same time; it is going to be a difficult decision. Do you want to go by train or by plane?
Mario:	I'll leave that up to you, it doesn't matter to me; by first we must decide what we want to do. There are beautiful beaches in both Sicily and Sardinia. There have been more cultures in Sicily than in Sardinia. There are many Greek temples and theaters to visit, many buildings with Arab influences, and many Baroque churches. Nature is wilder in Sardinia than in Sicily, and in Sardinia there are the famous Nuraghi, archeological monuments perhaps more ancient than any monument in Sicily. In any event, I will have to take many pictures either in Sicily or in Sardinia because Giuseppe asked me if I can send him some as he wants to use them for his travel agency, and I promised him that I will.
Giulietta:	They both seem like wonderful places, I wouldn't know which one to choose. Why don't we flip a coin?

NOTES

Tempio *(temple)* has an irregular plural: **templi.**

Sia . . . che expresses the English *both . . . and.*

NUTS & BOLTS 2
THE PAST PERFECT

The **trapassato prossimo,** or past perfect (*had* + past participle), is used to express an action that happened before another action in the past. It is formed with the imperfect of the auxiliary verb **essere** or **avere** followed by the past participle of the main verb. The same agreement rules as in the **passato prossimo** apply to the **trapassato prossimo.**

io avevo viaggiato	*I had traveled*	io ero andato/a	*I had gone*
tu avevi viaggiato	*you had traveled*	tu eri andato/a	*you had gone*
lui aveva viaggiato	*he had traveled*	lui era andato	*he had gone*
lei aveva viaggiato	*she had traveled*	lei era andata	*she had gone*
noi avevamo viaggiato	*we had traveled*	noi eravamo andati/e	*we had gone*
voi avevate viaggiato	*you had traveled*	voi eravate andati/e	*you had gone*
loro avevano viaggiato	*they had traveled*	loro erano andati/e	*they had gone*

Quando hai chiamato ero già uscito.
When you called, I had already left.
Non siamo andati ad Assisi perché loro l'avevano già visitata.
We didn't go to Assisi because they had already been there.

PRACTICE 2
Translate the following sentences into Italian.

1. When we arrived at the station, the train had already left.

2. I didn't eat because I had already eaten.

3. When we called, they had already left (the house).

4. He didn't go to Venice because he had already been there.

5. She didn't come to the theater with us because she had already seen that comedy.

Language link

Are you uncertain about how to organize your trip to Italy? You should go to **www.enit.it,** the official site of the Italian State Tourist Board, where you will be able to find a lot of information and many useful links. **Buon viaggio!**

ANSWERS

PRACTICE 1: 1. (Loro) sono i ragazzi più simpatici del mondo. (Loro) sono ragazzi simpaticissimi; **2.** Questo è il viaggio più lungo del mondo. Questo è un viaggio lunghissimo; **3.** L'Eurostar è il treno più veloce del mondo. L'Eurostar è un treno velocissimo. **4.** Questo è il libro più noioso del mondo. Questo è un libro noiosissimo; **5.** Questa è la modella più bella del mondo. Questa è una modella bellissima.

PRACTICE 2: 1. Quando siamo arrivati alla stazione il treno era già partito; **2.** Non ho mangiato perché avevo già mangiato; **3.** Quando abbiamo chiamato (loro) erano già usciti; **4.** Non è andato a Venezia perché c'era già stato; **5.** Non è venuta a teatro con noi perché aveva già visto quella commedia.

UNIT 7 ESSENTIALS

Mi sono svegliato/a ed era una giornata bellissima.	*I woke up and it was a beautiful day.*
Lampeggiava e un fulmine mi è caduto vicino.	*It was lightning and a lightning bolt struck near me.*
Sono dovuto/a andare a cena fuori.	*I had to go out to dinner.*
Volevo fare un'escursione.	*I wanted to go hiking.*
Non ci andrò mai più.	*I'll never go there again.*
Non me ne hai mai parlato.	*You never mentioned it to me.*
Gliele ho promesse.	*I promised them to him.*

Il mare non è così interessante come la montagna.	*The seaside is not as interesting as the mountains.*
La natura è più selvaggia in Sardegna che in Sicilia.	*Nature is wilder in Sardinia than in Sicily.*
Il mare della Sardegna è il più bello del mondo.	*The sea in Sardinia is the most beautiful in the world.*
La Sardegna e la Sicilia sono due isole bellissime.	*Sardinia and Sicily are two very beautiful islands.*
Quando hai chiamato io ero già uscito/a.	*When you called, I had already left.*

Unit 8

Getting around town

Now that you are finally in Italy, you might want to reserve a room in a hotel, and start walking around all those beautiful cities. Here you are going to learn how to talk to a hotel receptionist, and also how to ask for directions so that you won't get lost. In any event, however, don't forget to bring your maps!

Lesson 29 (Words)

WORD LIST 1

colloquio	*interview*
trasferirsi	*to move, to transfer*
esperto	*expert*
finalista	*finalist (male or female)*
metro	*meter*
centimetro	*centimeter*
chilometro	*kilometer*
voltare	*to turn*
girare	*to turn*
destra	*right*
sinistra	*left*
lungo	*along*
avanti	*ahead*

NUTS & BOLTS 1

EXPRESSING DURATION OF AN ACTION

To express the duration of an action that began in the past and is still going on in the present, Italian uses the present tense + **da** + time expression.

Non ti vedo da molto tempo.

I haven't seen you in a long time.

Studiamo italiano da due mesi.

We have been studying Italian for two months.

Non vanno al cinema da Natale.

They haven't gone to the movies since Christmas.

To ask for how long an action has been going on, Italian uses **da quanto tempo** + present.

Da quanto tempo non vedi Maria?

How long has it been since you've seen Maria?

PRACTICE 1

Translate the following sentences into Italian.

1. I haven't seen him for a long time.

2. We have been traveling for two months.

3. He hasn't eaten since last night.

4. You haven't come to my house since December.

5. For how long have you been working in this store?

WORD LIST 2

controllare	*to check*
prenotare	*to reserve*
fiera	*trade fair*
affollato/a	*crowded*
disponibile	*available*
camera matrimoniale	*double room (one queen-size bed)*
camera doppia	*double room (two twin-size beds)*
camera singola	*single room (one twin bed)*
piano	*floor (of a building)*
asciugamano	*towel*
saponetta	*soap (bar)*

carta igienica	toilet paper
aria condizionata	air conditioning
valigia	suitcase

NUTS & BOLTS 2
DISJUNCTIVE PRONOUNS

Direct and indirect object pronouns also have emphatic forms, known as disjunctive pronouns.

DIRECT DISJUNCTIVE		INDIRECT DISJUNCTIVE	
me	*me*	a me	*to me*
te	*you*	a te	*to you*
lui	*him*	a lui	*to him*
lei	*her*	a lei	*to her*
Lei *(fml.)*	*you*	a Lei *(fml.)*	*to you*
noi	*us*	a noi	*to us*
voi *(pl.)*	*you*	a voi *(pl.)*	*to you*
loro	*them*	a loro	*to them*

They are used for emphasis immediately after a verb or in exclamations.

Hanno chiamato te, ma non hanno chiamato me!
They called you, but they didn't call me!
Non lo do a te, lo do a lui.
I'm not giving it to you, I'm giving it to him.

They are always used after the prepositions **per, con,** and **tra/fra.**

Perché non vieni con me a Napoli?
Why don't you come to Naples with me?
Il dottor Benaglia mi ha detto che lavori per lui.
Dr. Benaglia told me you work for him.

PRACTICE 2
Replace the underlined expression with a disjunctive pronoun.

1. Esci con <u>Mariella</u> stasera?

2. Noi lavoriamo per <u>il direttore</u> dell'albergo.

3. Quando hanno chiamato hanno chiesto di parlare con <u>Franco e Mariella</u>.

4. Vieni con <u>me e Giorgio</u> al mare?

5. Posso venire a cena da <u>te e Francesca</u>?

Culture note

Bologna is one of the best-kept secrets in Italy. Everybody traveling from northern to southern Italy goes through Bologna, but very few people stop there. Those who do, however, always think of Bologna as one of their favorite places in Italy. Bologna is known as **la grassa** *(the fat one)* for its renowned food, **la rossa** *(the red one)* for the color of its buildings and roofs, or, alternatively, for its leftist political leanings, **la dotta** *(the learned one)* for its famous university, and **la turrita** *(the towered one)* for the more than 100 towers that used to be in this city. Only a few of these towers are still standing, the most famous are the **Torre Asinelli** and the **Torre Garisenda,** which stand right next to each other right in the center of the city.

ANSWERS

PRACTICE 1: 1. Non lo vedo da molto tempo; **2.** Viaggiamo da due mesi; **3.** Non mangia da ieri sera; **4.** Non vieni a casa mia da dicembre; **5.** Da quanto tempo lavori in questo negozio?

PRACTICE 2: 1. Esci con lei stasera? **2.** Noi lavoriamo per lui; **3.** Quando hanno chiamato hanno chiesto di parlare con loro; **4.** Vieni con noi al mare? **5.** Posso venire a cena da voi?

─────────── Lesson 30 (Phrases) ───────────

PHRASE LIST 1

da una vita	*for a very long time, since always, since forever*
riuscire a	*to manage to, to be able to*
fammi vedere	*let me see*
va' avanti	*go ahead*
a destra	*to/on the right*
a sinistra	*to/on the left*
sono in ritardo	*I'm late*
è tardi	*it's late*
sono in anticipo	*I'm early*
è presto	*it's early*
fra tre quarti d'ora	*in forty-five minutes*

NUTS & BOLTS 1

THE INFORMAL IMPERATIVE

The imperative is used to give a command or to make a suggestion. The forms of the informal imperative in Italian are the same as those of the present tense, with the exception of the **tu** form of first conjugation verbs (**-are**), which ends in **-a** rather than **-i**. Thus verbs that are irregular in the present tense are also irregular in the imperative. Notice that an exclamation point normally follows an imperative in Italian.

	CANTARE	PRENDERE	DORMIRE	PULIRE
(tu)	canta	prendi	dormi	pulisci
(noi)	cantiamo	prendiamo	dormiamo	puliamo
(voi)	cantate	prendete	dormite	pulite

Gira a sinistra!
Turn left.
Cammina lungo via Zamboni!
Walk along Zamboni Street.
Prendiamo l'autobus!
Let's take the bus.

Andare, dare, fare, stare, and **dire** have an irregular **tu** imperative form: **va', da', fa', sta',** and **di'.** But their other imperative forms are regular: **andiamo, andate; diamo, date; facciamo, fate; stiamo, state; diciamo, dite.**

Va' avanti cento metri!
Go ahead for one hundred meters.
Sta' attento!
Pay attention!/Be careful!/Watch it!/Watch out!

Essere and **avere** have an irregular imperative form: **essere: sii, siamo, siate; avere: abbi, abbiamo, abbiate.**

Sii gentile!
Be kind!
Abbiate pazienza!
Be patient!

The negative imperative is formed by placing **non** in front of the imperative. However, the **tu** negative imperative is formed by **non** + infinitive.

Non fate rumore!
Don't make any noise.
Non usciamo stasera!
Let's not go out tonight.
Non mangiare troppi dolci!
Don't eat too many sweets.

The infinitive is often used when giving directions to the general public in signs, public notices, recipes, etc.

Mescolare bene tutti gli ingredienti.
Mix all ingredients thoroughly.
Non calpestare l'erba.
Do not step on the grass.

PRACTICE 1
In your opinion, these people must or mustn't do certain things. Tell them to do or not do these things, following the example: **I ragazzi devono studiare → studiate!**

1. Mario deve imparare l'italiano.

2. Mirella non deve mangiare troppi dolci.

3. Noi dobbiamo andare al museo.

4. I ragazzi devono prenotare l'albergo.

5. Giorgio deve fare le valige.

6. Le signore non devono spendere troppi soldi.

7. Franco non deve accettare quel lavoro.

8. Noi dobbiamo fare più sport.

PHRASE LIST 2
siamo pieni	*we're full*
avere bisogno di	*to need*

a partire da	*starting from*
per quale data?	*for which date/day?*
va meglio	*it's better*
lo stesso	*the same*
al secondo piano	*on/to the second floor*
in fretta	*in a hurry, quickly*
all'ultimo minuto	*at the last minute*
andiamoci	*let's go there*

NUTS & BOLTS 2
THE INFORMAL IMPERATIVE AND PRONOUNS

Direct and indirect object pronouns, reflexive pronouns, and **ci** when used as an adverb meaning *there* are all attached to the end of the informal imperative. With the negative imperative, the pronouns can either precede the imperative, or be attached to it.

Andiamoci!
Let's go there.
Parlagliene!
Speak with him about it.
Non mandarle questa lettera! (Non le mandare questa lettera!)
Don't send this letter to her.

Before attaching a pronoun to **va', da', fa', sta',** and **di',** remember to drop the apostrophe and to double the first consonant of the pronoun, with the exception of **gli,** which does not double the consonant.

Fammi vedere che ore sono!
Let me see what time it is.
Digli la verità!
Tell him/them the truth.
Vacci!
Go there.

PRACTICE 2
Replace the underlined object(s) with a pronoun or a double pronoun.

1. Da' il libro a tuo cugino!

2. Parlate a vostra madre!

3. Non mangiate tutta la pasta!

4. Dite la verità a noi!

5. Ordiniamo un caffè!

6. Va' in via Zamboni!

7. Mandiamo una lettera al nostro amico!

8. Non leggere quel giornale!

Culture note

The University of Bologna was founded in 1088 and is thus the most ancient university in the Western World. It was famous for its instruction in law and medicine, and is still one of the most prestigious public universities in Italy.

ANSWERS
PRACTICE 1: 1. Impara l'italiano! **2.** Non mangiare troppi dolci! **3.** Andiamo al museo! **4.** Prenotate l'albergo! **5.** Fa' le valige! **6.** Non spendete troppi soldi! **7.** Non accettare quel lavoro! **8.** Facciamo più sport!

PRACTICE 2: 1. Daglielo! **2.** Parlatele! **3.** Non mangiatela! (Non la mangiate)! **4.** Ditecela! **5.** Ordiniamolo! **6.** Vacci! **7.** Mandiamogliela! **8.** Non leggerlo! (Non lo leggere)!

——————————— Lesson 31 (Sentences) ———————————

SENTENCE GROUP 1
Abito qui da un anno.	*I have been living here for a year.*
Ho saputo che ti eri trasferito.	*I found out that you had moved.*

Avresti tempo di prendere un caffè?	*Would you have time for a coffee?*
Non vorrei arrivare in ritardo.	*I wouldn't want to arrive late.*
Mi faresti un favore?	*Would you do me a favor?*
Va' avanti cento metri.	*Go ahead for one hundred meters.*
Gira a sinistra e cammina lungo via Zamboni.	*Turn left and walk along Zamboni street.*
Fammi vedere che ore sono.	*Let me see what time it is.*
Andiamoci!	*Let's go there.*

NUTS & BOLTS 1
THE PRESENT CONDITIONAL

The conditional mood expresses possible or hypothetical actions or states and translates into English as *would* + verb. Just like in English, there are two conditional tenses: present conditional and past conditional.

The present conditional is formed, just like the future tense, by dropping the final **-e** from the infinitive. Then the conditional endings **-ei, -esti, -ebbe, -emmo, -este, -ebbero** are added. As in the future, in verbs of the first conjugation, the **-a** of the infinitive ending changes to **-e**:

PARLARE	PRENDERE	DORMIRE	PULIRE
io parlerei	io prenderei	io dormirei	io pulirei
tu parleresti	tu prenderesti	tu dormiresti	tu puliresti
lui parlerebbe	lui prenderebbe	lui dormirebbe	lui pulirebbe
lei parlerebbe	lei prenderebbe	lei dormirebbe	lei pulirebbe
noi parleremmo	noi prenderemmo	noi dormiremmo	noi puliremmo
voi parlereste	voi prendereste	voi dormireste	voi pulireste
loro parlerebbero	loro prenderebbero	loro dormirebbero	loro pulirebbero

The present conditional is used to express actions that would occur in the present or in the future, if not for conditions or uncertainties that prevent them from occurring.

Prenderei un caffè, ma non ho tempo.
I would have a coffee, but I don't have time.
Usciremmo con voi, ma abbiamo già un altro impegno.
We would go out with you, but we already have a previous engagement.

Verbs with irregularities in the future (see Unit 6, Lesson 23) maintain the same irregularities in the conditional.

Andrei in vacanza, ma non ho abbastanza soldi.
I would go on vacation, but I don't have enough money.
Vorrei dormire, ma non ho tempo.
I would like to sleep, but I don't have time.

The present conditional can also be used to express polite requests and wishes. This is particularly true when using the conditional of **dovere, potere,** and **volere.**

Vorrei sapere se avete una camera disponibile.
I would like to know if you have a room available.
Potrei prenotare una stanza?
Could I reserve a room?

PRACTICE 1
Fill in the blanks with the present conditional of the verbs in parentheses.

1. Io _____ (uscire) volentieri con te, ma ho troppo lavoro.

2. Loro _____ (venire) a cena da noi, ma domani hanno già un impegno.

3. Noi _____ (comprare) quella macchina, ma non abbiamo abbastanza soldi.

4. Lui _____ (dovere) studiare, ma non ne ha voglia.

5. Voi lo _____ (invitare), ma lui non viene mai.

6. Tu mi _____ (potere) chiamare un po' più spesso!

SENTENCE GROUP 2

Ho appena saputo che ho bisogno di venire a Bologna.

I've just found out (that) I need to come to Bologna.

Vorrei sapere se avete una camera disponibile.

I would like to know if you have a room available.

Avrebbe dovuto chiamare prima.

You should have called sooner.

Ho una camera doppia, Le andrebbe bene?

I have a double room, would that be good for you?

La camera è al secondo piano.

The room is on the second floor.

Non avrei mai pensato di trovare una camera.

I would have never thought I would find a room.

A che ora pensa di arrivare?

At what time do you expect to arrive/get here?

Arriviamo domani mattina. Sarebbe un problema?

We arrive tomorrow morning. Will that be a problem?

NUTS & BOLTS 2
THE PAST CONDITIONAL

The past conditional is formed with the conditional of **essere** or **avere,** followed by the past participle. Just as is the case with the present perfect, past participles of **essere** verbs must agree with the subject.

PARLARE	ARRIVARE
io avrei parlato	io sarei arrivato/a
tu avresti parlato	ti saresti arrivato/a
lui avrebbe parlato	lui sarebbe arrivato
lei avrebbe parlato	lei sarebbe arrivata
noi avremmo parlato	noi saremmo arrivati/e
voi avreste parlato	voi sareste arrivati/e
loro avrebbero parlato	loro sarebbero arrivati/e

The past conditional in Italian is the same as the phrase *would have . . .* in English.

Ti avrei telefonato, ma non ho avuto tempo.
I would have called you, but I didn't have time.

In English, when expressing a future action from the point of view of the past, we use the present conditional; Italian uses the past conditional.

Ha detto che sarebbe arrivato presto.
He said he would arrive early.
Ha deciso che avrebbero mangiato fuori.
He decided they would eat out.

When using **dovere, potere,** and **volere** in the past conditional, they mean *should have, could have,* and *would have liked,* respectively. They are all followed by the main verb in the infinitive form, and the main verb determines which auxiliary to use.

Avrebbe dovuto chiamare prima.

You (fml.) should have called sooner.

Saremmo dovuti restare di più.

We should have stayed longer.

PRACTICE 2

Fill in the blank with the present or past conditional of the verb in parentheses as appropriate.

1. Io _____ (prendere) un aperitivo con te, ma ho fretta.

2. Noi _____ (venire) a casa tua, ma siamo tornati tardi.

3. Loro vi _____ (invitare), ma non vi hanno trovato.

4. Lui ti _____ (scrivere), ma non ha il tuo indirizzo.

5. Voi gli _____ (offrire) il lavoro, ma lui non è molto interessato.

6. Tu _____ (partire) con noi, ma dovevi finire quel lavoro.

Culture note

Bologna gave birth to many famous artists, most notably Guido Reni, the brothers Annibale, Lodovico, and Agostino Carracci, Giovanni Barbieri, known as il Guercino, and Giorgio Morandi.

ANSWERS

PRACTICE 1: 1. uscirei; 2. verrebbero; 3. compreremmo; 4. dovrebbe; 5. invitereste; 6. potresti.

PRACTICE 2: 1. prenderei; 2. saremmo venuti/e; 3. avrebbero invitato; 4. scriverebbe; 5. offrireste; 6. saresti partito/a.

CONVERSATION 1

Giorgio: Paola! Sei tu? Non posso crederci! Non ti vedo da una vita! Che cosa fai qui a Bologna?

Paola: Sono qui per un colloquio di lavoro! E tu?

Giorgio: Io abito qui da un anno. Non lo sapevi?

Paola: No, ho saputo che ti eri trasferito, ma non sapevo che abitavi a Bologna.

Giorgio: Dove vai per il colloquio?

Paola: Alla Pinacoteca. Cercano un esperto d'arte medievale e sono una delle finaliste.

Giorgio: Avresti il tempo di prendere un caffè con me? C'è un ottimo bar qui vicino.

Paola: Fammi vedere che ore sono, non vorrei arrivare in ritardo . . . no, mi dispiace, non ho tempo, il colloquio è fra tre quarti d'ora. Anzi, mi faresti un favore?

Giorgio: Certamente, se posso.

Paola: Sapresti dirmi come arrivare alla Pinacoteca da qui? È in via Belle Arti.

Giorgio: È molto facile: va' avanti cento metri fino a via Rizzoli. Volta a destra e davanti a te vedrai le due Torri. Quando arrivi sotto le due Torri, gira a sinistra e cammina lungo via Zamboni quasi fino in fondo, sulla sinistra troverai via Belle Arti. Da qui sono solo circa dieci minuti a piedi.

Paola: Beh, allora ho anche il tempo di bere un caffè in quel famoso bar. Andiamo!

Giorgio: Paola! Is that you? I can't believe it! I haven't seen you in ages! What are you doing here in Bologna?

Paola: I'm here for a job interview, and you?

Giorgio: I've lived here for a year. You didn't know?

Paola: No, I heard that you had moved, but I didn't know you lived in Bologna.

Giorgio:	Where do you have your interview?
Paola:	At the Pinacoteca. They're looking for an expert in Medieval art, and I'm one of the finalists.
Giorgio:	Would you have time to have coffee with me? There is a very good café nearby.
Paola:	Let me see what time it is, I wouldn't want to be late . . . no, I'm sorry, I don't have time, the interview is in forty-five minutes. Would you do me a favor, though?
Giorgio:	Certainly, if I can.
Paola:	Could you tell me how to get to the Pinacoteca from here? It's in via Belle Arti.
Giorgio:	It's very easy: go ahead for one hundred meters up to via Rizzoli. Turn right, and you'll see the two towers in front of you. When you get under the two Towers, turn left and walk along Zamboni Street almost until the end, and on your left you'll find via Belle Arti. It's about a ten-minute walk from here.
Paola:	Well, then I should have time for a coffee in that famous café. Let's go there.

NOTES

Riuscire a + infinitive is often used in Italian instead of **potere** to indicate *to be able to* or *to succeed in doing something*.

Da una vita idiomatically indicates *for a very long time (in ages)*.

Unlike other means of transportation that use the preposition **in**, **piedi** is used with the preposition **a**—**a piedi**—to indicate *on foot (walking)*.

NUTS & BOLTS 1
SUFFIXES

In Italian it is possible to slightly change the meaning of a word by adding a suffix to that word. These suffixes give emphasis to the size or quality of that word, or express the speaker's feeling concerning a person or object. As there are no specific rules governing these suffixes, it is advisable to learn to recognize the suffixes before using them. Please note that when adding a suffix most nouns maintain their gender, and that the final vowel is dropped before adding a suffix.

Three main categories of suffixes exist:

a) **-ino, -etto,** and **-ello** are called diminutives, indicating smallness or cuteness, or used to express the speaker's affection.

Tuo figlio è proprio un bravo bambino!
Your son is really a nice little boy!

b) **-one, -ona, -oni,** and **-one** *(f. pl.)* express largeness.

Suo marito è un omone.
Her husband is a big man.

c) **-accio, -astro,** and **-ucolo** express ugliness, roughness, or other negative qualities.

Non dire quelle parolacce!
Don't say such bad words.

PRACTICE 1
Change the underlined words into a word with a suffix.

1. Marco è un <u>ragazzo piccolo</u>.

2. Mirko è un <u>ragazzo cattivo</u>.

3. Loro hanno una bella <u>casa piccola</u>.

4. I bambini giocano con le <u>macchine piccole</u>.

5. Tu stai leggendo un <u>libro molto grosso</u>.

CONVERSATION 2

Receptionist:	Buongiorno, Hotel International, desidera?
Signora Bianchini:	Buon giorno, vorrei sapere se avete una camera disponibile per me e mio marito.
Receptionist:	Per quando?
Signora Bianchini:	Per due notti a partire da domani sera.
Receptionist:	Signora, controllo, ma siamo molto pieni. Avrebbe dovuto chiamare prima perché questa settimana c'è la fiera del mobile e Bologna è affollatissima.
Signora Bianchini:	Sì, lo so, ma purtroppo ho appena appreso di dover venire a Bologna.
Receptionist:	Signora, è la Sua giornata fortunata. Non ho una camera matrimoniale, ma ho una camera doppia, le andrebbe bene lo stesso?
Signora Bianchini:	Certamente, anzi, per noi va meglio.
Receptionist:	Signora, la camera è al secondo piano ed è un po' rumorosa, ma è spaziosa e ha l'aria condizionata.
Signora Bianchini:	Per me non è un problema. Abitiamo al terzo piano e anche il nostro appartamento è rumoroso. Non avrei mai pensato di trovare una stanza così in fretta all'ultimo minuto!
Receptionist:	Signora, Lei è molto accomodante. A che ora pensa di arrivare?
Signora Bianchini:	Arriviamo domani mattina. Per Lei sarebbe un problema?
Receptionist:	No signora, se la camera non è pronta può lasciare le valigie alla reception.
Signora Bianchini:	Grazie allora, a domani.

Receptionist:	*Good morning, Hotel International, how can I help you?*
Signora Bianchini:	*Good morning, I'd like to know if you have a room available for my husband and me.*

Receptionist:	For which date?
Signora Bianchini:	For two nights, starting tomorrow night.
Receptionist:	Madam, I will check, but we're very full. You should have called earlier because this is furniture-fair week, and Bologna is very crowded.
Signora Bianchini:	Yes, I know, but unfortunately I've just found out that I need to come to Bologna.
Receptionist:	Madam, you're lucky. I don't have a room with a queen-size bed, but I have one with two single beds; would that be okay by you?
Signora Bianchini:	Certainly, actually we'd prefer it.
Receptionist:	Madam, the room is on the second floor, and it's a bit noisy, but it's spacious and it has air conditioning.
Signora Bianchini:	It's fine by me. We live on the third floor and our apartment is also noisy. I would have never thought I would be able to find a room so quickly at last minute notice!
Receptionist:	Madam, you're very accommodating. At what time do you think you'll be checking in?
Signora Bianchini:	We arrive tomorrow morning. Would it be a problem?
Receptionist:	No Madam, if the room is not ready, you can leave your luggage with the reception.
Signora Bianchini:	Thank you, until tomorrow then.

NOTES

Two different words translate the English word *floor* in Italian: **piano** is the floor of a building with different floors, while **pavimento** is the floor inside a house or apartment, the surface on which we walk.

NUTS & BOLTS 2
ORDINAL NUMBERS

The ordinal numbers from first to tenth are as follows.

primo	*first*
secondo	*second*
terzo	*third*
quarto	*fourth*
quinto	*fifth*
sesto	*sixth*
settimo	*seventh*
ottavo	*eighth*
nono	*ninth*
decimo	*tenth*

Beginning with **undicesimo** *(eleventh)* ordinal numbers are formed by dropping the last vowel of the cardinal number, and by adding **-esimo.** If the cardinal number ends in **-tre,** then the final **-e** of the cardinal number is retained, as in **ventitreesimo.**

Remember that ordinal numbers are adjectives, and they must agree in gender and number with the noun they modify. Where English uses a superscript *-st, -nd, -rd,* or *-th* for ordinal numbers, Italian uses a degree symbol: **1°, 2°,** etc.

PRACTICE 2
Spell out the number given in parentheses.

1. Giulio è il suo (3°) figlio.

2. Loro festeggiano il loro (43°) anniversario di matrimonio.

3. Ieri sera abbiamo ascoltato la (9°) sinfonia di Beethoven.

4. Questo è il (18°) anno che lavoro in quest'ufficio.

5. Mia figlia fa la (5°) elementare.

Language link

For a very comprehensive and current site about Bologna, see **www.comune.bologna.It,** where you can find information about Bologna's history, main sights, culture, economics, cuisine, etc., and you will discover that Bologna is certainly well worth a visit!

ANSWERS
PRACTICE 1: 1. Marco è un ragazzino; **2.** Mirko è un ragazzaccio; **3.** Loro hanno una bella casetta; **4.** I bambini giocano con le macchinine; **5.** Tu stai leggendo un librone.

PRACTICE 2: 1. terzo; **2.** quarantatreesimo; **3.** nona; **4.** diciottesimo; **5.** quinta.

UNIT 8 ESSENTIALS

Abito qui da un anno.	*I've been living here for a year.*
Ho saputo che ti eri trasferito.	*I heard that you had moved.*
Avresti il tempo di prendere un caffè con me?	*Would you have time to have coffee with me?*
Non vorrei arrivare in ritardo.	*I wouldn't want to arrive late.*
Mi faresti un favore.	*Would you do me a favor?*
Sapresti dirmi come arrivare alla Pinacoteca?	*Could you tell me how to get to the Pinacoteca?*

Fammi vedere che ore sono.	*Let me see what time it is.*
Va' avanti cento metri.	*Go ahead for one hundred meters.*
Gira a sinistra e cammina lungo via Zamboni.	*Turn left and walk along Zamboni Street.*
Avrebbe dovuto chiamare prima.	*You should have called earlier/sooner.*
Non avrei mai pensato di trovare una camera così in fretta.	*I would never have thought I would find a room so quickly.*
La camera è al secondo piano.	*The room is on the second floor.*

UNIT 9
Talking about health

God forbid you might get sick while traveling in Italy! However, just in case you need to, we want to make sure you are going to be able to communicate with **un medico** *(a doctor)* or **un infermiere** *(a male nurse)* or **un'infermiera** *(a female nurse)* about what's troubling you. So you'll learn to name the different parts of the body, many of them irregular nouns, and how to describe **i sintomi,** your symptoms.

———————— Lesson 33 (Words) ————————

WORD LIST 1

ospedale	*hospital*
pronto soccorso	*emergency room*
testa	*head*
collo	*neck*
occhio	*eye*
naso	*nose*
bocca	*mouth*
schiena	*back*
stomaco	*stomach*
pancia	*belly*
intestino	*intestine*
gamba	*leg*
piede *(m.)*	*foot*
infarto	*heart attack*

NUTS & BOLTS 1
IRREGULAR PLURALS OF NOUNS

In Unit 2, you learned how to form the plural of nouns. There are, however, some nouns that have irregular plurals.

a. Nouns that end with an accent, such as **città, università, caffè,** etc. do not change in the plural: **una città → due città.**

b. Foreign words, which usually end in a consonant, such as **sport, film, week-end,** etc., do not change in the plural: **un film → due film.** Although the word **zoo** ends with a vowel, it is a foreign word, and its plural is **zoo.**

c. Words that are abbreviated, such as **cinematografo → cinema; fotografia → foto; motocicletta → moto; bicicletta → bici,** etc. do not change in the plural. Also, pay attention to the gender of these nouns, which is the gender of the original word: **il cinema → i cinema.**

d. A few words, particularly words indicating parts of the body, are masculine in the singular, but have an irregular feminine plural ending in -a:

SINGULAR	PLURAL	
il ciglio	le ciglia	*eyelash(es)*
il sopracciglio	le sopracciglia	*eyebrow(s)*
il braccio	le braccia	*arm(s)*
il ginocchio	le ginocchia	*knee(s)*
il dito	le dita	*finger(s)*
l'osso	le ossa	*bone(s)*

SINGULAR	PLURAL	
l'uovo	le uova	*egg(s)*
il lenzuolo	le lenzuola	*bed-sheet(s)/bed linen(s)*

L'orecchio *(ear)* has both a feminine and a masculine plural, respectively ending in **-e/-i: le orecchie/gli orecchi. La mano** *(hand)* is feminine but with an irregular ending in **-o**. The plural is also feminine, ending in **-i: la mano → le mani.**

PRACTICE 1
Provide the singular article for the following nouns, and then change both article and noun to the plural.

1. _____ braccio. _____

2. _____ foto. _____

3. _____ città. _____

4. _____ sport. _____

5. _____ zoo. _____

6. _____ mano. _____

7. _____ orecchio. _____

8. _____ lenzuolo. _____

WORD LIST 2
salute *(f.)*	*health*
febbre *(f.)*	*fever*
temperatura	*temperature*
pressione *(f.)*	*pressure*
sangue *(m.)*	*blood*
cuore *(m.)*	*heart*

polmone *(m.)*	*lung*
fegato	*liver*
rene *(m.)*	*kidney*
respirare	*to breath*
forma	*shape*
elettrocardiogramma *(m.)*	*electrocardiogram*
mancino	*left-handed*
atleta	*athlete*
sorprendere	*to surprise*

NUTS & BOLTS 2
IRREGULAR SINGULAR NOUNS WITH REGULAR PLURAL FORMS
In Italian there are nouns with an irregular singular form, but a regular plural form.

A few masculine nouns, usually derived from Greek, have an irregular singular ending in **-a**. Many of these nouns are cognates. The plural form ends regularly in **-i**. In addition to all those nouns ending in **-amma**, such as **programma** *(program)*, **telegramma** *(telegram)*, **elettrocardiogramma** *(electrocardiogram)*. Here are other common irregular nouns:

dramma	*drama*
aroma	*aroma*
diploma	*diploma*
panorama	*panorama*
poema	*poem*
problema	*problem*
clima	*climate*
pianeta	*planet*
sistema	*system*

Other irregular nouns include those nouns ending in **-ista** and **-iatra** (which usually indicate professions), and a few others such as **collega** *(colleague)* and **astronauta** *(astronaut)*, can be either masculine or feminine. The plural, however, ends regularly in **-i** in the masculine form, and in **-e** in the feminine form. Here are a few common nouns: **atleta** *(athlete)*, **giornalista** *(journalist)*, **pianista** *(pianist)*, **regista** *(movie director)*, **turista** *(tourist)*, **pediatra** *(pediatrician)*, **psichiatra** *(psychiatrist)*.

PRACTICE 2
Change the following sentences from the plural to the singular. Change everything possible.

1. I registi famosi hanno partecipato al Festival di Venezia.

2. Ci sono molti turisti a Roma.

3. Loro hanno molti problemi.

4. I programmi televisivi sono noiosi.

5. Sono due poemi epici famosi.

6. I giornalisti hanno scritto due articoli interessanti.

Culture note
Although named by Americans, the "Mediterranean diet" has been a staple in many southern European countries, such as Italy, Spain, and Greece. In the past 50 years or so, however, due to the increased wealth of the country, Italy's diet has become less healthy, and as a consequence there has been an increase in obesity and other diet related diseases. There has been an effort, both in Italy and the United States, to go back to a healthier way of eating in the hopes of reversing the current trend.

ANSWERS
PRACTICE 1: 1. il braccio, le braccia; **2.** la foto, le foto; **3.** la città, le città; **4.** lo sport, gli sport; **5.** lo zoo, gli zoo; **6.** la mano, le mani; **7.** l'orecchio, gli orecchi/le orecchie; **8.** il lenzuolo, le lenzuola.

PRACTICE 2: 1. Il regista famoso ha partecipato al Festival di Venezia; 2. C'è un turista a Roma; 3. Lui ha un problema; 4. Il programma televisivo è noioso; 5. È un poema epico famoso; 6. Il giornalista ha scritto un articolo interessante.

--------- Lesson 34 (Phrases) ---------

PHRASE LIST 1

sto bene	*I feel well*
mi sento bene	*I am well*
fa male	*it hurts*
ho un dolore a	*I have a pain in/my . . . hurts*
ho male a	*I have a pain in/my . . . hurts*
perdere tempo	*to waste time*
si telefona	*one calls*
si deve	*one must*
ogni volta	*every time*
nessuna idea	*no idea*
tanto vale	*(one) might as well*
sono preoccupato	*I'm worried*

NUTS & BOLTS 1

THE IMPERSONAL CONSTRUCTION

The impersonal construction (the equivalent to the English *one*, *they*, or *people* + verb) is formed in Italian with the impersonal pronoun **si** followed by the verb in the third person singular.

Quando si telefona a un medico si deve aspettare molto.

When one calls a doctor, one has to wait a long time.

Si legge che un dolore al braccio sinistro può essere un sintomo d'infarto.

One reads that a pain in the left arm can be a symptom of a heart attack.

If a plural noun follows the verb, then the verb is in the third person plural form.

In ospedale si mangia cibo molto leggero.
In the hospital one eats very light food.
In ospedale si curano molte malattie.
Hospitals (they) treat many diseases.

In compound tenses, the auxiliary in an impersonal construction is always **essere,** both with verbs that normally take **essere** as well as those that take **avere.**

Ieri si è mangiato molto.
Yesterday, people ate a lot.
Al Festival di Venezia si sono visti molti film interessanti.
People saw many interesting movies at the Venice Festival.

PRACTICE 1
Change the following sentences to the impersonal construction, following the example.

La gente mangia molta frutta in Italia → Si mangia molta frutta in Italia.

1. A Bologna la gente mangia tagliatelle e lasagne.

2. La gente aspetta molto tempo dal dottore.

3. La gente deve fare molto sport.

4. La gente spende molti soldi in vacanza.

5. La gente deve usare meno la macchina.

6. Ieri loro hanno letto molto.

7. L'anno scorso molta gente è andata in Grecia.

PHRASE LIST 2

ho esagerato	*I overreacted*
si legge che . . .	*one reads that . . .*
avere la febbre	*to have a fever*
misurare la pressione	*to check blood pressure*
faccio sport	*I practice sports, I play sports*
in ottima forma	*in great shape*
chi fa sport . . .	*those who play sports . . .*
con cui . . .	*with whom . . .*
è dovuto a . . .	*it's due to . . .*
visto che	*given that, since*

NUTS & BOLTS 2
RELATIVE PRONOUNS

A relative pronoun *(who, whom, whose, which, that)* connects a noun or a pronoun to a dependent clause. Although in English the relative pronoun is often omitted, in Italian it must always be expressed.

I medici che lavorano al pronto soccorso sono molto gentili.

Doctors who work at the emergency room are very kind.

In the sentence above, **che** connects the noun **i medici** to the sentence **lavorano al pronto soccorso.** The relative pronouns are **che** *(that, which, who, whom);* **cui** *(which, whom);* and **chi** *(he/she who, the one who, whoever).*

Che *(that, which, who, whom)* is invariable and is never used after a preposition.

Il medico che vedo normalmente è in vacanza.

The doctor (whom) I normally see is on vacation.

Gli esami che ha/hai fatto sono tutti normali.

The results of the tests you took are all normal./Your test results are all normal.

Cui *(which, whom)* is also invariable, and is always used after a preposition. **Cui** is also used in the expressions **la ragione/il motivo per cui** *(the reason why)*, and **il modo in cui** *(the way in which)*.

Sono uscito a cena con gli stessi amici con cui ho giocato a tennis.
I went out to dinner with my friends from the tennis game.
Mi piace il modo in cui quell'infermiera tratta i pazienti.
I like the way in which that nurse treats (her) patients.

Chi *(he/she who, the one who, whoever)* is invariable, is only used for people, and always takes a verb in the singular. **Chi** is often found in proverbs and popular sayings.

Chi fa sport alla Sua/tua età raramente ha un infarto.
People who play sports at your age rarely have heart attacks.
Chi rompe, paga.
You break it, you buy it. (lit., The one who breaks, pays.)

PRACTICE 2
Complete the following sentences with the appropriate relative pronoun.

1. Mi fa male il braccio _____ mi sono rotto l'anno scorso.

2. Il medico di _____ mi parli sempre non accetta nuovi pazienti.

3. _____ non ingrassa ha meno problemi di salute.

4. Ho telefonato al medico _____ ha lo studio vicino a casa tua.

5. Quel signore _____ abbiamo incontrato ieri è un infermiere.

6. Non capisco il motivo per _____ devo aspettare così a lungo.

7. Chi è quella signora con _____ parlavi?

Language link

In search of a healthy life style, Italians have embraced **i prodotti d'erboristeria** (*herbal products*). There are numerous stores in Italy where you can buy not only vitamins and supplements, but also dried herbs that can be mixed according to the individual needs. In the website below, if you click on **erbario** on the left, you can find a list of many different herbs, with a description of their properties and how to take them.

www.lerboristeria.com

ANSWERS

PRACTICE 1: 1. A Bologna si mangiano tagliatelle e lasagne; **2.** Si aspetta molto tempo dal dottore; **3.** Si deve fare molto sport; **4.** Si spendono molti soldi in vacanza; **5.** Si deve usare meno la macchina; **6.** Ieri si è letto molto; **7.** L'anno scorso si è andati in Grecia.

PRACTICE 2: 1. che; **2.** cui; **3.** chi; **4.** che; **5.** che; **6.** cui; **7.** cui.

───────────── Lesson 35 (Sentences) ─────────────

SENTENCE GROUP 1

Ho un problema.

I've a problem.

Non mi sento bene.

I don't feel good.

Che cosa ti fa male?

What hurts? Tell me about your ailment.

Muoviti lentamente!

Move slowly.

Il medico che vedo normalmente è in vacanza.

The doctor (whom) I normally see is on vacation.

Ogni volta che si telefona si deve aspettare.

Every time one calls, one has to wait.

Tanto vale andare all'ospedale.

One might as well go to the hospital.

Ho male al braccio sinistro.

My left arm hurts.

Non ne ho idea.

I have no idea (about it).

NUTS & BOLTS 1
ADVERBS

Adverbs modify verbs, adjectives, and other adverbs, and are invariable. Some common adverbs are **bene** *(well)*, **male** *(badly)*, **molto** *(very)*, **poco** *(little)*, **presto** *(early)*, **tardi** *(late)*, **spesso** *(often)*, **insieme** *(together)*, **così** *(so)*, and **volenticri** *(gladly)*.

Many adverbs are formed by adding the suffix **-mente** to the feminine singular form of an adjective.

lento ➔ lenta ➔ lentamente

veloce ➔ veloce ➔ velocemente

Muoviti lentamente!

Move slowly.

Chi fa sport raramente ha un infarto.

People who practice sports rarely have heart attacks.

If the adjective ends in **-le** or **-re**, the final **-e** is dropped before **-mente** is added.

normale ➔ normalmente

regolare ➔ regolarmente

Il medico che vedo normalmente è in vacanza.

My regular physician is on vacation. (lit., The doctor whom I normally see is on vacation.)

Faccio sport regolarmente.

I exercise regularly.

Some adjectives, such as **chiaro** *(clearly)*, **giusto** *(right)*, **forte** *(loudly)*, **piano** *(slowly, softly)*, **svelto** *(fast)*, **vicino** *(nearby)*, and **lontano** *(far)*, can also be used as adverbs.

Lui abita molto lontano.
He lives very far away.
Non camminare così svelto.
Don't walk so fast.

Adverbs usually follow the verb. In compound tenses, however, **ancora** *(still, yet)*, **già** *(already)*, **mai** *(never)*, **sempre** *(always)*, **più** *(any more)*, and **spesso** *(often)* are usually placed between the auxiliary and the past participle.

Ci siamo già conosciuti?
Have we already met?
Non sono mai stato in un ospedale.
I have never been in a hospital.

PRACTICE 1
Translate the following sentences.

1. She speaks very softly.

2. I play tennis regularly.

3. We run really fast.

4. They haven't seen that movie yet.

5. You play piano very well.

SENTENCE GROUP 2
Ci siamo già conosciuti?
Have we already met (each other)?

Mi fa male il braccio sinistro.

My left arm hurts.

Vediamo se ha/hai la febbre.

Let's see if you have a fever.

Le misuro la pressione.

I'll check your blood pressure.

Controlliamo il cuore e i polmoni.

Let's listen to your heart and lungs.

Lei mi sembra in ottima forma.

You appear to be in great shape.

Chi fa sport raramente ha un infarto.

People who practice sports rarely have heart attacks.

Sono uscito/a con gli amici con cui ho giocato.

I went out with my friends from the game.

Il mal di testa è probabilmente dovuto alla cena abbondante.

Your headache is probably due to the large dinner (you had).

NUTS & BOLTS 2
REFLEXIVE VERBS OF RECIPROCITY

You learned about reflexive verbs in Unit 6. The reflexive structure is used idiomatically also to express reciprocity *(one another, each other)*. In these cases the subject can only be plural. As with reflexive verbs, compound tenses are formed with **essere.** Some common verbs that express reciprocity are: **abbracciarsi** *(to hug)*, **aiutarsi** *(to help each other)*, **baciarsi** *(to kiss)*, **conoscersi** *(to know each other)*, **incontrarsi** *(to meet each other)*, **salutarsi** *(to greet each other)*, **telefonarsi** *(to call each other)*, **vedersi** *(to see each other)*.

Ci siamo già conosciuti?

Have we already met (each other)?

Loro si vedono oggi.

They see each other today.

PRACTICE 2
Change the following sentences into the past tense.

1. Ci vediamo spesso.

2. Non si baciano ancora.

3. Vi telefonate tutti i giorni.

4. Non si salutano mai.

5. Ci incontriamo regolarmente.

6. Vi aiutate sempre.

Language link

Italians have also embraced **la medicina omeopatica** *(homeo-pathic medicine)*. There are schools in Italy where medical doctors, pharmacists, or veterinarians can specialize in homeopathic medi-cine, and many people seek homeopathic treatment for their ail-ments. If you search **omeopatia** in **www.google.it,** you will get a sense of how popular this therapeutic method is in Italy.

ANSWERS
PRACTICE 1: 1. Lei parla molto piano; **2.** Gioco a tennis regolarmente; **3.** Corriamo molto forte (velocemente); **4.** Non hanno ancora visto quel film; **5.** Suoni/Suona il pianoforte molto bene.

PRACTICE 2: 1. Ci siamo visti/e spesso; **2.** Non si sono ancora baciati; **3.** Vi siete telefonati/e tutti i giorni; **4.** Non si sono mai salutati/e; **5.** Ci siamo incontrati/e regolarmente; **6.** Vi siete sempre aiutati/e.

———————— Lesson 36 (Conversations) ————————

CONVERSATION 1
Signor Pollini: **Luisa, ho un problema: non mi sento affatto bene; c'è qualcosa che non va e ho bisogno di vedere un medico.**

Signora Pollini: Cosa è successo, tu stai sempre bene, non hai mai niente. Che cosa ti senti? Che cosa ti fa male? Non ti agitare! Muoviti lentamente!

Signor Pollini: Ho mal di testa, mal di stomaco e ho anche un dolore in fondo alla schiena. Da chi posso andare?

Signora Pollini: Non lo so, il medico che vedo normalmente è in vacanza e non conosco il suo sostituto, ma possiamo telefonargli.

Signor Pollini: No, non voglio perdere tempo. Ogni volta che si telefona a un medico si deve aspettare un sacco di tempo. E poi visto che non lo conosco di persona, tanto vale andare all'ospedale.

Signora Pollini: Ma stai davvero così male?

Signor Pollini: Sì, ma soprattutto sono preoccupato. Ti devo confessare che mi fa anche male il braccio sinistro . . . magari sto avendo un infarto!

Signora Pollini: Sergio, hai trentasette anni! Sei un atleta, come puoi pensare a un infarto!

Signor Pollini: Se non è un infarto, allora che cos'è?

Signora Pollini: Non ne ho nessuna idea. Ma se ti tranquillizza, ti accompagno al pronto soccorso.

Signor Pollini: Luisa, I have a problem: I don't feel well at all; something is not right and I need to see a doctor.

Signora Pollini: What happened, you always feel well. There's never anything wrong with you. What do you feel? What hurts? Don't get nervous. Move slowly.

Signor Pollini: I have a headache, I have a stomachache, and I have a pain in my lower back. Who can I see?

Signora Pollini: I don't know; the doctor I normally see is on vacation, and I don't know his substitute, but we can call her.

Signor Pollini: No, I don't want to waste time. Every time you call a doctor, you have to wait for a long time. Then,

	since I don't know him personally, I might as well go to the hospital.
Signora Pollini:	*Are you really that sick?*
Signor Pollini:	*Yes, but above all I'm worried. I must confess that my left arm hurts as well . . . perhaps I'm having a heart attack!*
Signora Pollini:	*Sergio, you're thirty-seven! You're an athlete, how can you think you're having a heart attack!*
Signor Pollini:	*If it's not a heart attack, then what is it?*
Signora Pollini:	*I have no idea, but if it gives you peace of mind, I'll take you to the emergency room.*

NOTES

Both **fare male** and **avere male a/di** express that something hurts. **Fare male** works exactly like the verb **piacere: gli fa male lo stomaco;** but **ha male allo stomaco.** Note that Italian does not use the possessive adjective with parts of the body, but simply a definite article.

Fondo means bottom, and **in fondo a** is used to express at the bottom/end of something, such as **in fondo alla strada** *(at the end of the street),* **in fondo alla schiena** *(in the lower back),* **in fondo al bicchiere** *(at the bottom of the glass),* etc.

Tanto vale is an impersonal expression that can be translated into English as "subject + *might as well."* **Tanto vale andare in ospedale** *(one might as well go to the hospital).*

NUTS & BOLTS 1
INDEFINITE ADJECTIVES AND PRONOUNS
Indefinite adjectives and pronouns indicate an indeterminate quality or quantity, such as the English examples *some* or *any*. In Italian, some indefinites are used strictly as adjectives, some are used strictly as pronouns, and others can be used either as adjectives or pronouns.

The following indefinites can only be used as adjectives. They are invariable, and they can only modify singular nouns, although they can also express plural meaning.

ogni *(each, every)*
qualche *(some)*
qualsiasi/qualunque *(any, any kind of)*

Ogni volta che si telefona a un medico si deve aspettare.
Every time one calls a doctor one has to wait.
Ho invitato qualche amico a cena. Mi hanno detto che mangiano di tutto.
I invited some friends for dinner. They told me they eat anything.

The following indefinites can only be used as pronouns, and they are singular.

chiunque *(anyone)*
niente/nulla *(nothing)*
ognuno/ognuna *(everyone)*
qualcosa *(something, anything)*
qualcuno *(someone, anyone)*
uno/una *(one)*

Non hai mai niente.
You have never had any health problems.
C'è qualcosa che non va.
Something is not right.
Hai visto qualcuno che conosci a teatro ieri sera?
Did you see anyone you know at the theater, last night?

When an adjective follows **qualcosa** or **niente,** it is introduced by the preposition **di.** When a verb follows **qualcosa** or **niente** it is introduced by the preposition **da.**

C'è qualcosa di bello da fare questo weekend?
Is there anything interesting to do' this weekend?
Alla festa non c'era niente di buono da mangiare.
There was nothing good to eat at the party.

PRACTICE 1
Complete with either an indefinite adjective or pronoun.

1. In quel negozio non ho visto _____ che mi piaceva.

2. C'è _____ che parla inglese in quest'ospedale?

3. Gioco a tennis quasi _____ giorno.

4. _____ volta mangio dolci, ma di solito mangio frutta.

5. C'è _____ di interessante da fare stasera?

6. _____ sa cucinare in casa di Vittoria.

CONVERSATION 2

Medico: Buongiorno, ci siamo già conosciuti?

Signor Pollini: No, è la prima volta che vengo al pronto soccorso e forse non ce ne sarà bisogno, ma sono molto preoccupato . . . vede, mi fa male il braccio sinistro e si legge sempre che . . .

Medico: Prima di tutto vediamo se ha la febbre . . . no, ha trentesei e sette, la temperatura è normale. Adesso Le misuro la pressione . . . centoventi su setanta, è perfetta . . . Ascoltiamo il cuore e i polmoni . . . Respiri profondamente . . . tutto sembra normale . . . Guardi, Lei mi sembra in ottima forma, gli esami sono normali e mi sembra un tipo atletico . . .

Signor Pollini: Sì, faccio molto sport e gioco a tennis almeno due volte alla settimana.

Medico: Guardi, di solito chi fa sport alla sua età e non è in sovrappeso raramente ha un infarto,

	comunque Le faccio un elettrocardiogramma, così siamo sicuri . . . Anche l'elettrocardiogramma è normale. Mi dica, che cosa ha fatto ieri?
Signor Pollini:	Vediamo, ho lavorato, poi ho giocato per due ore a tennis e poi sono uscito a cena con gli stessi amici con cui ho giocato . . . beh, ora che ci penso celebravamo il compleanno di un amico e forse ho bevuto un po' troppo.
Medico:	E forse ha anche giocato a tennis un po' troppo entusiasticamente! Ho notato che Lei è mancino e dopo due ore di tennis non mi sorprende che abbia male al braccio e alla schiena. Il mal di stomaco e il mal di testa sono probabilmente dovuti alla cena abbondante. Visto che non Le ho trovato nessun problema grave, Le consiglio di andare a casa e di farsi una bella dormita!

Doctor:	*Good morning, have we met before?*
Signor Pollini:	*No, it's my first time at the emergency room, and perhaps I overreacted when I decided to come, but I'm very nervous . . . you see, my left arm hurts and one always reads that . . .*
Doctor:	*First of all, let's see if you've a fever . . . no, it's 36.7; your temperature is normal. Now I'm going to measure your blood pressure . . . 120 over 70; it's perfect . . . let's listen to your heart and lungs . . . take a deep breath . . . everything seems normal . . . Look, it seems to me that you are in excellent shape: all tests are normal, and you look athletic . . .*
Signor Pollini:	*Yes, I do a lot of sports and I play tennis at least twice a week.*
Doctor:	*Look, usually people of your age who exercise a lot and who are not overweight rarely have heart attacks; in any case we'll do an electrocardiogram, just to*

> *make sure . . . Even the electrocardiogram is normal.*
> *Tell me, what did you do yesterday?*

Signor Pollini: *Let's see; I worked, then I played tennis for two*
hours, and then I went out to dinner with my friends
from the tennis game . . . well, now that I think about
it we were celebrating a friend's birthday and perhaps
I drank a bit too much.

Doctor: *And perhaps you also played tennis a bit too*
enthusiastically. I noticed that you're left handed, and
after two hours of tennis I'm not surprised that your
left arm and your back hurt. Your stomachache and
headache are probably due to the big dinner. Since I
haven't found any serious problem, I'll advise you to
go home and take a nice long nap!

NOTES

Please note that **respiri, guardi, mi dica** are formal imperative that will be explained in the next unit.

È dovuto/a; sono dovuti/e a translate the English to *it's/they are due to*. **Il Suo mal di testa è dovuto alla cena abbondante.** *Your headache is due to the large dinner.*

Farsi una bella dormita *(to take a nice long nap)* and **farsi una bella mangiata** *(to have a nice big meal)* are idiomatic expressions using the past participle, **mangiato, dormito,** as feminine nouns.

NUTS & BOLTS 2
INDEFINITES USED AS EITHER ADJECTIVES OR PRONOUNS

The following indefinites, some of which you have already encountered, may be used as either adjectives or pronouns.

alcuni/e *(some, a few)*
certo/a/i/e *(certain, certain ones)*
ciascuno/a *(each, each one)*

molto/a/i/e *(much, many, a lot)*
nessuno/a *(no, none, no one)*
parecchio/a/i/e *(a lot, several)*
poco/a/chi/che *(little, few)*
quanto/a/i/e *(how much, how many)*
tanto/a/i/e *(so much, so many)*
troppo/a/i/e *(too much, too many)*

Non ho visto nessuno.
I didn't see anybody.
Non ho visto nessuna amica.
I didn't see any (of my female) friends.
Lui lavora tanto.
He works a lot.
Lui ha tanti libri.
He has many books.

PRACTICE 2
Replace the underlined expression with an indefinite pronoun.

1. <u>Alcune persone</u> vanno sempre al pronto soccorso.

2. In quell'ospedale <u>sono tutti gentili</u>.

3. <u>Molte persone</u> leggono poco.

4. Hanno mangiato <u>troppe cose</u> in quel ristorante.

5. <u>Nessuna persona</u> va mai in quel parco perché è pericoloso.

6. Marco non ha bevuto <u>nessuna cosa</u> perché non stava bene.

Long before herbs and homeopathic medicine became popular, Italians have always believed in the healing power of water. Most Italians go to the **Terme** (*spas*) every year to treat specific ailments, or simply to relax and detoxify. There are many **Terme** in Italy. If you are thinking about a very relaxing and beneficial vacation in an Italian spa, this is the site for you.

www.benessere.com/terme/italia

ANSWERS

PRACTICE 1: 1. niente/nulla; **2.** qualcuno; **3.** ogni; **4.** qualche; **5.** qualcosa; **6.** chiunque.

PRACTICE 2: 1. alcuni; **2.** ognuno; **3.** molti; **4.** troppo; **5.** nessuno; **6.** niente/nulla.

UNIT 9 ESSENTIALS

Ho un problema.	*I have a problem.*
Sei un atleta!	*You are an athlete!*
Ogni volta che si telefona si deve aspettare.	*Every time one calls, one must wait.*
Mi fa male la testa.	*My head hurts.*
Ho male alla testa.	*My head hurts.*
Ci siamo già conosciuti?	*Have we met before?*
Tanto vale andare all'ospedale.	*One might as well go to the hospital.*
Il medico che vedo normalmente è in vacanza.	*The doctor I normally see is on vacation./ My regular physician is on vacation.*
Chi fa sport raramente ha un infarto.	*People who play sports rarely have heart attacks.*
Sono uscito con gli amici con cui ho giocato.	*I went out with my friends from the game.*
Il mal di testa è probabilmente dovuto alla cena abbondante.	*Your headache is probably due to your large dinner.*

UNIT 10
Sports and hobbies

What's your outlook on life? Do you like to live in the country or in the city? Do you do any sports? Do you want to express your feelings and opinions? In this final unit you will learn a new mode, the subjunctive, which will allow you to speak about your feelings and ideas kindly and with more nuances.

―――――――― Lesson 37 (Words) ――――――――

WORD LIST 1

trasferirsi	*to transfer*
fine settimana	*weekend*
giardino	*garden*
orto	*vegetable garden*
cortile	*backyard, courtyard*
albero	*tree*
sapore	*taste*
sostanze chimiche	*chemicals, chemical substances*
follia	*folly*
amaramente	*bitterly*
pentirsi	*to repent; to regret*

NUTS & BOLTS 1
THE PRESENT SUBJUNCTIVE

While the indicative mood is used to express factual reality and certainty, the subjunctive mood (**il congiuntivo**) conveys uncertainty, possibility, and personal perspectives such as opinions and emotions. As we will see later in this unit, the subjunctive is primarily used in dependent clauses and is connected by **che** to an independent clause. We'll be learning the present and past tense of the subjunctive mood.

The **congiuntivo presente** is formed by adding the appropriate endings to the stem of the verb. Third conjugation verbs that insert -isc- (like **finire**) in the present indicative also insert it in the present subjunctive. Please note that the endings for the first, second, and third persons singular are identical and, therefore, the subject must be expressed if ambiguity arises. Also note that the **noi** form of the subjunctive, both of regular and irregular verbs, is identical to the **noi** indicative form.

PARLARE	RICEVERE	DORMIRE	FINIRE
(che) io parl-i	(che) io ricev-a	(che) io dorm-a	(che) io fin-isc-a
(che) tu parl-i	(che) tu ricev-a	(che) tu dorm-a	(che) tu fin-isc-a
(che) lui parl-i	(che) lui ricev-a	(che) lui dorm-a	(che) lui fin-isc-a
(che) lei parl-i	(che) lei ricev-a	(che) lei dorm-a	(che) lei fin-isc-a
(che) noi parl-iamo	(che) noi ricev-iamo	(che) noi dorm-iamo	(che) noi fin-iamo
(che) voi parl-iate	(che) voi ricev-iate	(che) voi dorm-iate	(che) voi fin-iate
(che) loro parl-ino	(che) loro ricev-ano	(che) loro dorm-ano	(che) loro fin-isc-ano

Note that verbs ending in **-care** or **-gare** add an **h** between the stem and the endings. Also note that verbs ending in **-iare** drop the **-i** of the stem before adding the subjunctive endings, unless the **-i** is stressed (like in **inviare**).

Voglio che i nostri bambini giochino insieme.
I want our children to play together.
Non voglio che lui paghi il conto.
I don't want him to pay the bill.
Penso che loro mangino troppo.
I think they eat too much.

Those irregular verbs that have an irregular present indicative also have an irregular present subjunctive. Here are the most common ones.

AVERE	abbia, abbiamo, abbiate, abbiano
ESSERE	sia, siamo, siate, siano
ANDARE	vada, andiamo, andiate, vadano
BERE	beva, beviamo, beviate, bevano
DARE	dia, diamo, diate, diano
DIRE	dica, diciamo, diciate, dicano
DOVERE	debba, dobbiamo, dobbiate, debbano
FARE	faccia, facciamo, facciate, facciano
PIACERE	piaccia, piacciamo, piacciate, piacciano
POTERE	possa, possiamo, possiate, possano
SAPERE	sappia, sappiamo, sappiate, sappiano
STARE	stia, stiamo, stiate, stiano
USCIRE	esca, usciamo, usciate, escano
VENIRE	venga, veniamo, veniate, vengano
VOLERE	voglia, vogliamo, vogliate, vogliano

PRACTICE 1

Complete the following sentences with the present subjunctive of the verb in parentheses.

1. È importante che voi _____ (volere) imparare una lingua straniera.

2. Voglio che lui _____ (scrivere) una lettera a suo nonno.

3. Pensiamo che loro _____ (arrivare) domani sera.

4. Non credo che tu _____ (dire) la verità.

5. Loro desiderano che io li _____ (andare) a trovare presto.

6. Tu pensi che noi non _____ (sapere) niente.

7. Dubito che lei _____ (venire) al cinema con noi.

8. Sono felice che voi _____ (laurearsi) fra un mese.

WORD LIST 2

traslocare	to move
quartiere	neighborhood
maschio	male
femmina	female
palestra	gym(nasium), health club
calcio	soccer
pallacanestro	basketball
palla a volo	volleyball
nuotare	to swim
correre	to run

NUTS & BOLTS 2
THE PAST SUBJUNCTIVE

The **congiuntivo passato** *(past subjunctive)* is the equivalent of the **passato prossimo**. It is formed with the present subjunctive of **avere** and **essere** followed by the past participle of the verb. It is used to express past actions when the verb of the main clause is in the present, the future, or the imperative.

PARLARE	ANDARE
(che) io abbia parlato	(che) io sia andato/a
(che) tu abbia parlato	(che) tu sia andato/a
(che) lui abbia parlato	(che) lui sia andato
(che) lei abbia parlato	(che) lei sia andata
(che) noi abbiamo parlato	(che) noi siamo andati/e
(che) voi abbiate parlato	(che) voi siate andati/e
(che) loro abbiano parlato	(che) loro siano andati/e

Penso che loro abbiano traslocato un mese fa.
I think they moved (out) a month ago.
Ci dispiace che lui non sia uscito con noi ieri sera.
We are sorry he didn't go out with us last night.

PRACTICE 2
Complete the following sentences with the past subjunctive of the verb in parentheses.

1. Sono contenta che loro _____ (andare) in vacanza.
2. Penso che lei _____ (arrivare) ieri sera.

3. È importante che tu _____ (studiare) per l'esame.

4. Mi dispiace che voi _____ (perdere) il lavoro.

5. Spero che lui _____ (comprare) un dolce.

Language link

Do you want to learn more about Italian art, cinema, music, and culture in general? Here's a great site, available in both Italian and English; for English, just click on the word "English" on the top left of the page.

www.italica.rai.it

ANSWERS

PRACTICE 1: 1. vogliate; **2.** scriva; **3.** arrivino; **4.** dica; **5.** vada; **6.** sappiamo; **7.** venga; **8.** vi laureiate.

PRACTICE 2: 1. siano andati/e; **2.** sia arrivata; **3.** abbia studiato; **4.** abbiate perso; **5.** abbia comprato.

—————— Lesson 38 (Phrases) ——————

PHRASE LIST 1

decidere di . . .	to decide to . . .
cercare di . . .	to try to . . .
cominciare a . . .	to begin to . . .
convincere a . . .	to convince to . . .
trasferirsi in campagna	to move to the country
ne ha affittata una	he rented one
fare giardinaggio	to do gardening
a casa sua	to/at his/her house
si pentirà amaramente	he will bitterly regret it
prima che trovi	before he finds
è una follia	it's a folly, it's crazy

NUTS & BOLTS 1
Verbs that require the subjunctive

As mentioned before, the subjunctive is primarily used in dependent clauses and is connected by **che** to an independent clause.
The choice of the indicative or subjunctive mood in a dependent
clause is determined by the verb or the expression used in the independent clause. The following verbs require the subjunctive in
a dependent clause:

a) verbs that express emotions, such as **avere paura** *(to be afraid),*
essere felice/contento *(to be happy),* **sperare** *(to hope);*

b) verbs that express opinion, such as **credere** *(to believe),* **pensare**
(to think);

c) verbs that express doubt or uncertainty, such as **dubitare** *(to doubt);*

d) verbs that express wish or command, such as **ordinare** *(to
order),* **comandare** *(to command),* **proibire** *(to prohibit),* **permettere**
(to allow), **lasciare** *(to let),* **volere** *(to want),* **desiderare** *(to desire).*

Sono felice che lui non abbia traslocato.
I'm happy he didn't move (out).
Penso che gli piaccia la campagna.
I think he likes the country.
Dubito che lei voglia uscire con noi.
I doubt that she would (want to) go out with us.
Voglio che tu lo convinca a rimanere in città.
I want you to convince him to stay in the city.

By contrast, assertions expressing certainty, such as **sono sicuro
che** *(I'm sure/certain that),* **so che** *(I know that),* **è ovvio che** *(it is obvious that),* **è vero che** *(it's true that),* etc., do not require the subjunctive.

Sono sicuro/a che lei vuole uscire con noi.
I'm certain that she wants to go out with us.
È vero che gli piace la campagna.
It is true that he likes the country.

PRACTICE 1
Complete the following sentences with either the present indicative or subjunctive of the verb in parentheses.

1. So che loro _____ (partire) stasera.

2. Penso che tu _____ (essere) molto stanco.

3. Dubito che lui _____ (arrivare) in orario.

4. Siamo sicuri che voi _____ (avere) molti amici.

5. Siamo felici che lei non _____ (trasferirsi).

6. Vogliono che io _____ (coltivare) un orto

PHRASE LIST 2

finire di . . .	*to finish . . .*
mi dica	*tell me*
guardi	*look*
mi scusi	*excuse me*
ce ne sono tre	*there are three of them*
della stessa età	*of the same age*
fare footing	*to jog*
saltare la corda	*to jump rope*
fare ginnastica aerobica	*to do aerobics*
mi sembra eccezionale	*it sounds great, it looks great*

NUTS & BOLTS 2
IMPERSONAL EXPRESSIONS WITH THE SUBJUNCTIVE
Impersonal expressions implying doubt, necessity, desire, or emotion, also require the subjunctive: **è importante che** *(it is im-*

portant that), è **necessario che** *(it is necessary that)*, è **possibile che** *(it is possible that)*, è **probabile che** *(it is likely that)*, è **meglio che** *(it is better that)*, è **strano che** *(it is strange that)*, etc.

È **importante che i bambini facciano ginnastica.**
It is important that children exercise.
È **meglio che lui ci pensi bene prima di trasferirsi.**
He'd better think long and hard before moving.
È **strano che voi preferiate la campagna alla città.**
How odd that you'd prefer the country to the city.

The subjunctive is also used after the following conjunctions: **affinché** *(in order that, so that)*, **a meno che . . . non** *(unless)*, **benché** *(although)*, **a condizione che/a patto che/purché** *(provided that)*, **prima che** *(before)*, and **senza che** *(without)*.

Dobbiamo parlargli prima che lui trovi una casa.
We must talk to him before he finds a house.
Benché lui ami la città, preferisce vivere in campagna.
Although he loves the city, he prefers to live in the country.
Andrò a casa sua a meno che lei non mi telefoni.
I'll go to her house unless she calls me.

PRACTICE 2
Translate the following sentences into Italian.

1. I am sure she is leaving tomorrow.

2. We think she is leaving today.

3. It's interesting that he likes to live in the country.

4. Do you think the children want to play together?

5. I must call her before she goes out.

6. Although sometimes he feels lonely **(solo),** he likes the country.

ANSWERS

PRACTICE 1: 1. partono; **2.** sia; **3.** arrivi; **4.** avete; **5.** si trasferisca; **6.** coltivi.

PRACTICE 2: 1. Sono sicuro/a che lei parte domani; **2.** Noi pensiamo che lei parta oggi; **3.** È interessante che gli piaccia vivere in campagna; **4.** Pensi che i bambini vogliano giocare insieme? **5.** Devo chiamarla prima che lei esca; **6.** Benché a volte si senta solo, gli piace la campagna.

—————— Lesson 39 (Sentences) ——————

SENTENCE GROUP 1

Ha deciso di trasferirsi in campagna.

He decided to move to the country.

Vuole comprare una casa.

He wants to buy a house.

Penso che gli piaccia abitare in città.

I think he likes living in the city.

Credo che il suo interesse per la natura sia cominciato così.

I believe this is how his interest in nature got started.

Credo che faccia molto giardinaggio.

I believe he does a lot of gardening.

Ha cominciato a coltivare un po' di verdura.

He began growing some vegetables.

Crede che la verdura sia piena di sostanze chimiche.

He believes vegetables are steeped in chemicals.

Sono sicuro/a che si pentirà amaramente.

I'm sure he will bitterly regret it.

Dobbiamo parlargli prima che lui trovi una casa.

We must talk to him before he finds a house.

Voglio che tu lo convinca a rimanere in città.

I want you to convince him to stay in the city.

NUTS & BOLTS 1
INFINITIVE CONSTRUCTIONS

Please note that the subjunctive is used when the subject of the independent clause is different from the subject in the dependent clause. When the subject is the same in both clauses, Italian uses an infinitive construction. Consider the examples below.

Vuole comprare una casa.

He/she wants to buy a house.

Voglio che tu lo convinca a rimanere in città.

I want you to convince him to stay in the city.

Spero di divertirmi al parco giochi.

I hope I'll have fun at the playground.

Spero che i bambini si divertano al parco giochi.

I hope the children will have fun at the playground.

Dubito di arrivare per cena.

I doubt I will get there by dinner.

Dubito che lui arrivi per cena.

I doubt he will get there by dinner.

Ti telefono prima di uscire di casa.

I'll call you before I leave the house.

Ti telefono prima che tu esca di casa.

I'll call you before you leave the house.

È importante imparare le lingue straniere.

It's important to learn foreign languages.

È importante che loro imparino le lingue straniere.

It's important that they learn foreign languages.

PRACTICE 1

Translate the following sentences into Italian.

1. He wants to go to the mountains this summer.

2. They want me to go with them to the country.

3. I hope you'll come to my party.

4. We hope to buy a new house.

5. They are happy that you're graduating.

6. We are happy we are eating in a restaurant tonight.

SENTENCE GROUP 2

Abbiamo appena finito di traslocare.

We've just finished moving (out).

Ci abbiamo messo una settimana.

It took us a week.

Credo che abbia i prezzi più bassi.

I think (lit., I believe) it/he/she has the lowest prices.

Ci vogliono solo pochi minuti a piedi.

It is only a few minutes' walk.

È necessario che i bambini facciano sport tutti i giorni.

It's necessary that children exercise daily.

Li voglio iscrivere in questa palestra.

I want to enroll them at this gym.

Voglio che i Suoi bambini conoscano i miei.

I want your (fml.) children to meet mine.

Li vuole mandare a casa mia domani?

Do you want to send them to my house tomorrow?

Sono felici di avere nuovi amici.

They are happy to have new friends.

NUTS & BOLTS 2
EXPRESSING TO TAKE TIME

To take (time) is rendered in Italian by two different expressions: **volerci** and **metterci**. **Volerci** is always used impersonally.

Ci vogliono solo pochi minuti a piedi.

It's only a few minutes' walk.

Ci vuole molto tempo per traslocare.

It takes a long time to move.

In the compound tenses, **volerci** is conjugated with **essere**.

C'è voluto un mese per finire questo lavoro.

It took a month to finish this job.

Metterci, however, is always used with a personal subject.

(Noi) ci abbiamo messo una settimana.

It took us a week.

(Io) ci metto poco tempo a fare la spesa.

It takes me little time to shop.

In compound tenses, **metterci** is conjugated with **avere**.

Ci hanno messo tre ore ad arrivare.

It took them three hours to arrive (to get there/here).

PRACTICE 2

Complete the following sentences with the correct form of either **metterci** or **volerci**.

1. Ieri siamo andati a Roma e _____ due ore.

2. Quanto tempo _____ per cucinare un arrosto?

3. _____ cinque ore per finire la maratona la settimana scorsa.

4. Io non _____ molto a pulire la casa.

5. Loro _____ sempre poco tempo a preparare un programma.

Language link

Are you an opera enthusiast, and are planning to see an opera during your stay in Italy? Here are the sites for the most important opera theaters or events in Italy:

Arena di Verona: **www.arena.it**

Teatro alla Scala di Milano: **www.teatroallascala.org**

Puccini Opera Festival: **www.puccinifestival.it**

Rossini Opera Festival in Pesaro: **www.rossinioperafestival.it**

And if your hobby is opera singing, on this website you can find teachers, schools, or just online Italian pronunciation exercises using opera arias: **www.cantarelopera.com**.

ANSWERS

PRACTICE 1: 1. Vuole andare in montagna quest'estate;
2. Vogliono che io vada con loro in campagna; **3.** Spero che tu venga alla mia festa; **4.** Speriamo di comprare una casa nuova; **5.** Sono felici che ti laurei; **6.** Siamo felici di mangiare in un ristorante stasera.

PRACTICE 2: 1. ci abbiamo messo; **2.** ci vuole; **3.** ci sono volute; **4.** ci metto; **5.** ci mettono.

CONVERSATION 1

Michele: Hai saputo che Vittorio ha deciso di trasferirsi in campagna?

Enza: Si, vuole comprare una casa, ma non penso che l'abbia ancora trovata. Però ne ha affittata una per l'estate.

Michele: Non capisco questa decisione, non gli piace abitare in città?

Enza: Penso che gli piaccia, qui ci sono tutte le cose cha ama fare. Gli piace andare al cinema e a teatro, gli piacciono i musei e gli piace molto uscire con gli amici, mangiare al ristorante e andare in discoteca. Però l'anno scorso ha incontrato un vecchio amico che l'ha invitato a casa sua in campagna e credo che da lì sia nato questo nuovo interesse per la natura. Sai, ormai passa quasi tutti i fine settimana in campagna.

Michele: Ma che cosa fa in campagna tutto quel tempo?

Enza: Credo che faccia molto giardinaggio. Ha piantato fiori attorno a tutta la casa e ha cominciato anche a coltivare un po' di verdura in un orto. Sostiene che la verdura che si compra nei negozi sia insipida e che sia piena di sostanze chimiche nocive per la salute. So che vuole anche piantare dei peschi e degli albicocchi, ma penso che aspetterà di aver la sua propria casa.

Michele: Senti, a me pare una follia. Sono sicuro che dopo un anno di vita di campagna si pentirà amaramente. Dobbiamo parlargli prima che trovi una casa. Voglio che tu lo convinca a rimanere in città. Lo sai, se si trasferisce non lo vedremo più e allora con chi giocheremo a poker il giovedì sera?

Michele: Did you hear that Vittorio decided to move to the country?

Enza: Yes, he wants to buy a house, but I don't think he has found one yet. Though he rented one for the summer.

Michele: I don't understand his decision. Doesn't he like living in the city?

Enza: I think he does, all the things he loves to do are here. He likes to go to the movies and to the theater, he likes museums, and he really likes to go out with friends, eat in restaurants, and dance in clubs. But last year he met an old friend who invited him to his house in the country, and I believe that's when his new interest in nature started. You know, he now spends almost all (of his) weekends in the country.

Michele: But what does he do in the country all that time?

Enza: I believe he does a lot of gardening. He planted flowers all around the house and he also began planting some vegetables in an orchard. He believes that the vegetables you buy in the stores are flavorless, and that they are full of chemicals that are harmful to the health. I know he also wants to plant peach and apricot trees, but I think he'll wait until he has his own house.

Michele: Listen, it's crazy. I'm sure that after a year of life in the country he'll bitterly regret it. We must talk to him before he finds a house. I want you to convince him to stay in the city. You know, if he moves we're not going to see him any more, and who will we play poker with on Thursday nights?

NOTES

The verb **giocare** *(to play)* always takes the preposition **a** before the name of the game. **Giocare a carte** *(to play cards)*, **giocare a tennis** *(to play tennis)*, etc. The verb **suonare** translates as *to play* *music/an instrument:* **Mario suona il pianoforte** *(Mario plays the piano).*

NUTS & BOLTS 1
VERBS FOLLOWED BY VERBS IN THE INFINITIVE

As you might have already noticed, when a verb governs another verb, this second verb is always in the infinitive form in Italian.

Voglio giocare a carte.
I want to play cards.
Preferisco vivere in città.
I prefer living in the city.
Devo traslocare.
I must move (out).

Often, however, between the first and the second verb there is a preposition, usually **a** or **di.**

A few common verbs that require the preposition **a** before an infinitive are: **aiutare** *(to help),* **andare** *(to go),* **cominciare** *(to begin),* **continuare** *(to continue),* **imparare** *(to learn),* **insegnare** *(to teach),* **riuscire** *(to succeed).*

Io vado a ballare in discoteca.
I'm going dancing.
Vittorio ha cominciato a coltivare verdura.
Vittorio has started growing vegetables.
Loro mi aiutano a piantare fiori.
They help me planting flowers.

Among those verbs that require the preposition **di** before an infinitive are: **cercare** *(to try),* **decidere** *(to decide),* **dimenticare** *(to forget),* **finire** *(to finish),* **promettere** *(to promise),* **ricordare** *(to remember),* **smettere** *(to quit, to stop),* **sperare** *(to hope).*

PRACTICE 1
Complete the following sentences with **a, di,** or leave an empty space, appropriately.

1. Desidero _____ comprare una casa al mare.

2. Speriamo _____ andarlo a trovare in campagna.

3. Cominciano _____ lavorare alle 9 e finiscono _____ lavorare alle 6.

4. Loro mi insegnano _____ giocare a golf.

5. Lui ha deciso _____ andare in vacanza in Italia.

6. Imparate _____ parlare l'italiano.

CONVERSATION 2

Signora Fucini: Buongiorno, mi chiamo Laura Fucini. Finalmente io e mio marito abbiamo appena finito di traslocare nell'appartamento di fronte al Suo. Ci abbiamo messo un'intera settimana!

Signor Dondi: Ah, piacere signora, sono Giovanni Dondi. Benvenuti nel nostro palazzo.

Signora Fucini: Grazie mille. Mi dica, visto che questo è un nuovo quartiere per noi, saprebbe indicarmi un buon negozio di alimentari?

Signor Dondi: Guardi, ce ne sono tre, tutti molto buoni. Io credo però che Pollini abbia i prezzi più bassi e la frutta e la verdura più fresche. È qui vicino, in via Arno, ci vogliono solo pochi minuti a piedi.

Signora Fucini: Mi scusi se Le faccio un'altra domanda. Lei ha bambini?

Signor Dondi: Sì, ne ho due, un maschio e una femmina di sei e nove anni.

Signora Fucini: Davvero? Anch'io ne ho due della stessa età. I suoi dove vanno a giocare di solito?

Signor Dondi: C'è un parco giochi qui vicino e quando posso li porto lì. Visto che è necessario per i bambini fare moto tutti i giorni, li ho iscritti a una palestra dove il pomeriggio si tengono classi per i bambini.

Signora Fucini: Guardi, anch'io ritengo sia molto importante che i bambini facciano ginnastica. Quali altre attività sono offerte in questa palestra?

Signor Dondi: Possono giocare a calcio, a pallacanestro o a pallavolo. Hanno anche una piscina e due pomeriggi alla settimana possono anche nuotare. E poi corrono, saltano la corda e fanno anche ginnastica aerobica. C'è un' ampia varietà di scelta.

Signora Fucini: Mi sembra eccezionale, anch'io li voglio iscrivere a questa palestra. Voglio anche che i nostri bambini si conoscano, che abbiano la possibilità di diventare amici e di giocare insieme. Li vuole mandare a casa mia domani pomeriggio?

Signor Dondi: Certamente, saranno molto contenti di avere nuovi amici nel palazzo!

Signora Fucini: Good morning Sir, my name is Laura Fucini. My husband and I have finally just finished moving into the apartment across from yours. It took us a whole week!

Signor Dondi: Ah, nice to meet you, Madam, I'm Giovanni Dondi, welcome to our building.

Signora Fucini: Thank you so much. As we are new to the neighborhood, could you please tell us where we can find a good grocery store?

Signor Dondi: Look, there are three very good ones in the area. But I think Pollini has the lowest prices and the freshest fruit and vegetables. It's nearby, in Arno Street, it's only a few minutes' walk from here.

Signora Fucini:	Excuse me if I ask yet another question. Do you have any children?
Signor Dondi:	Yes, I have two of them, a boy and a girl; they're six and nine.
Signora Fucini:	Really? I have two of the same age. Where do they usually play?
Signor Dondi:	There's a playground nearby, and when I can I take them there. But since it's necessary that children move every day, I enrolled them in a gym where they have classes for children in the afternoon.
Signora Fucini:	Look, I also believe that it's important that children exercise. What other activities are available at this gym?
Signor Dondi:	They can play soccer, basketball, and volleyball. They also have a swimming pool and they swim two afternoons a week. And then they run, jump rope, and they also do aerobic exercise. There's a wide variety of choices.
Signora Fucini:	It seems great; I want to enroll them at this gym as well. I also want your children to meet mine, so they can become friends and play together. Do you want to send them to my house tomorrow afternoon?
Signor Dondi:	Sure, they'll be very happy to have new friends in the building!

NOTES

Two verbs indicate *to move* in Italian, **traslocare** and **trasferirsi.** They are sometimes interchangeable, however **traslocare,** and also **fare il trasloco,** indicate the actual moving of furniture, whereas **trasferirsi** has a more generic meaning.

NUTS & BOLTS 2
THE FORMAL IMPERATIVE

In Unit 8 we studied the informal forms of command. The forms of the formal imperative are the same as the **Lei** form of the present subjunctive. Thus, verbs that have irregular forms in the subjunctive will also have irregular forms of the formal imperative.

PARLARE	SCRIVERE	SENTIRE	FINIRE
Parli!	Scriva!	Senta!	Finisca!

Guardi, ci sono tre negozi.
Actually, there are three stores.
Signora, scriva il Suo nome per favore.
Madam, please sign your name.

The negative formal imperative is formed by placing **non** in front of the imperative.

Per favore, non fumi in quest'ufficio.
Please, don't smoke in this office.

Direct and indirect object pronouns, as well as reflexive pronouns, always precede the formal imperative.

Mi scusi, posso farLe una domanda?
Excuse me, may I ask you a question?
Mi dica, ha bambini?
Tell me, do you have children?

PRACTICE 2
Change the following informal sentence into formal ones.

1. Dimmi quando arrivi domani.

2. Non parlare così velocemente.

3. Ascolta, devo dirti una cosa importante.

4. Parlami del film che hai visto ieri.

5. Non vestirti in modo sportivo: sarà una festa elegante.

6. Fammi un favore!

Language link

If instead you are interested in pop music, the site of the **Festival-bar** is probably for you. Here you will find biographical information on the most popular Italian and international pop singers, videos, concerts dates, and so on.

it.festivalbar.music.yahoo.net

ANSWERS

PRACTICE 1: 1. -; 2. di; 3. a, di; 4. a; 5. di; 6. a.

PRACTICE 2: 1. Mi dica quando arriva domani; 2. Non parli così velocemente; 3. Ascolti, devo dirLe una cosa importante; 4. Mi parli del film che ha visto ieri; 5. Non si vesta in modo sportivo: sarà una festa elegante; 6. Mi faccia un favore!

UNIT 10 ESSENTIALS

Non penso che lui abbia ancora trovato una casa.	*I don't think he has found a house yet.*
Credo che lui faccia molto giardinaggio.	*I believe he does a lot of gardening.*
Voglio che tu lo convinca a rimanere in città.	*I want you to convince him to stay in the city.*
Li voglio iscrivere a questa palestra.	*I want to enroll them at this gym.*
È importante che i bambini facciano ginnastica.	*It's important that children exercise.*
Credo che il suo interesse per la natura sia cominciato così.	*I believe that's how his interest in nature began (got started).*
Sono sicuro/a che si pentirà amaramente.	*I'm sure he will bitterly regret it.*
Ha cominciato a coltivare verdura.	*He has started growing vegetables.*
Ha deciso di trasferirsi in campagna.	*He decided to move to the country.*

Ci vogliono solo pochi minuti a piedi.	*It is only a few minutes' walk.*
Ci abbiamo messo una settimana.	*It took us a week.*
Mi dica, signora/signore.	*Tell me, Madam/Sir.*

Vendesi in provincia di Verona villetta su tre livelli: taverna e bagno al sottopiano; ampio salone, camera da pranzo, cucina abitabile e servizio al piano terra; 4 camere da letto, due con balcone e doppi servizi al primo piano. Mq. 310. Ampio giardino e garage con due posti macchina. 890.000€.

VOCABULARY

sottopiano	*basement*
piano terra	*first floor*
primo piano	*second floor*
cucina abitabile	*eat-in kitchen*
servizio	*bathroom*
doppi servizi	*two bathrooms*

Please answer the following questions.

1. What is this?
2. Does the ad speak of a house, an apartment, or an office building?
3. How large is the living space?
4. How many cars does the garage hold?

ANSWERS

1. A real estate ad.
2. A house.
3. 310 square meters.
4. Two.

For sale in the province of Verona a three-story house: finished basement with one bathroom; large living room, dining room, eat-in kitchen and bathroom on the first floor; 4 bedrooms, two with balcony, and two bathrooms on the second floor. 310 square meters. Large garden with a 2-car garage. €890,000.

───────── ITALIAN IN ACTION 2 ─────────

Spaghetti alla carbonara
Tempo necessario: circa 40 minuti
Ingredienti per quattro persone:
400 g. di spaghetti
100 g. di pancetta affumicata, tagliata in piccoli pezzi
1 piccola cipolla affettata sottile
30 g. di burro
3/4 bicchiere di vino bianco secco
50 g. di parmigiano grattugiato
Un uovo intero + tre tuorli
Olio extra vergine d'oliva, sale, pepe

Far bollire circa 5 litri d'acqua salata in una pentola e cucinare la pasta. Nel frattempo, far rosolare la cipolla nel burro e un po' di olio finché diventa trasparente. Aggiungere la pancetta e far rosolare per qualche minuto. Aggiungere il vino bianco, farlo assorbire. In una terrina grande sbattere le uova e aggiungere pepe a piacere. Quando gli spaghetti sono cotti, scolarli, versarli nella terrina con le uova e mescolare bene e velocemente. Versare la pancetta con il grasso di cottura molto caldo, mescolare e aggiungere il parmigiano alla fine. Servire subito.

VOCABULARY

pancetta affumicata	*smoked bacon*
cipolla	*onion*
tuorlo	*yolk*
bollire	*to boil*
rosolare	*sauté*
aggiungere	*to add*

| mescolare | to mix |
| sbattere | to beat |

Please answer the following questions.

1. How many eggs do you need?
2. What do you add the wine to?
3. Do you cook the eggs?
4. After cooking this dish, when do you serve it?

ANSWERS

1. One whole egg and three yolks.
2. You add the wine to the sautéed onions and bacon.
3. No, the hot pasta slightly cooks the eggs.
4. Right away.

Spaghetti alla carbonara
Preparation time: around 40 minutes
Ingredients for 4 people:
400 grams spaghetti
100 grams smoked bacon, diced
1 small onion, sliced thin
30 grams butter
3/4 cup dry white wine
50 grams grated Parmesan cheese
one egg + three yolks
extra virgin olive oil, salt, pepper

Boil 5 quarts of salted water in a pot and cook the pasta. In the mean-time, sauté the onion until translucent. Add the bacon and sauté for a few minutes. Add the white wine and let it evaporate. In a large bowl beat the eggs and add pepper to taste. When the spaghetti is cooked, drain it, pour it in the bowl over the eggs, and mix well and quickly. Pour the bacon with its reduced hot juices, mix, and add the Parmesan cheese last. Serve promptly.

-------------------- ITALIAN IN ACTION 3 --------------------

DATI ANAGRAFICI

Luisa Rosselli
Residenza: Milano, via Cavour, 2, Tel. 06/654321–0437/1234456
Luogo e data di nascita: Vicenza, 6 gennaio 1982
Stato civile: Nubile
Cittadinanza: Italiana

FORMAZIONE SCOLASTICA
- **Scuole Superiori: Maturità classica presso l'Istituto Galvani di Milano, 2001. Votazione 58/60.**
- **Laurea in Economia e Commercio presso l'Università Bocconi, 2005. Votazione 110/110 e lode. Titolo tesi: "La Cina e la Comunità Europea".**

ESPERIENZE PROFESSIONALI
- **Stage presso la Chase Bank di New York, durata 6 mesi (2006).**

CAPACITÀ GENERALI
Lingue conosciute:
- **Inglese: ottimo livello, parlato e scritto**
- **Francese: buon livello, parlato e scritto**
Competenze informatiche: Office 2000
Hobbies: vela, lettura, cinema, chitarra

CONDIZIONE ATTUALE
Stage presso l'UniCredit a Milano fino al 31/10/07.

DISPONIBILITÀ
Dal 1° novembre 2007. Disponibile a lavorare e viaggiare anche all'estero.

VOCABULARY

nubile	*single (woman)*
celibe	*single (man)*
maturità	*high school degree*
laurea	*university degree, equivalent to an MA*
stage	*internship*
informatica	*computer science*
vela	*sailing*
disponibilità	*availability*

Please answer the following questions.

1. Where does Luisa Rosselli live?

2. Is she married?

3. Is she working now?

4. Which foreign languages does she speak?

ANSWERS

1. She lives in Milan.

2. No, she's single.

3. She is doing an internship at UniCredit.

4. She speaks English and French.

PERSONAL INFORMATION
Luisa Rosselli
Residence: Milano, via Cavour, 2, Tel. 06/654321–0437/1234456
Place and Date of Birth: Vicenza, January 6, 1982
Marital Status: Single
Citizenship: Italian

EDUCATION
• *High School: Diploma in Classical Studies from Liceo Classico Galvani in Milan, 2001. Grade: 58/60.*

• MA in Economics and Business from Bocconi University, 2005. Grade 110/110 cum laude. Thesis title: "China and the European Community."

PROFESSIONAL EXPERIENCE
• Internship at Chase Bank in New York, 6 months (2006).

GENERAL SKILLS
Foreign Languages:
• English: Excellent, spoken and written
• French: Good, spoken and written
Computer skills: Office 2000
Hobbies: Sailing, reading, cinema, and guitar

CURRENT STATUS
Internship at UniCredit in Milan until 10/31/07

AVAILABILITY
From November 1, 2007. Available to work and travel abroad

Alcuni ricervatori norvegesi hanno pubblicato un articolo sulla rivista *Science* del 22 giugno, in cui si afferma che i figli primogeniti tendono ad avere un quoziente intellettivo più alto dei loro fratelli minori. Questa indagine ha infatti mostrato che fra i fratelli presi in esame, la media del quoziente intellettivo dei primogeniti era 103,2, mentre quella dei secondo e terzogeniti era rispettivamante 102,9 e 100.

Quest'indagine ha inoltre mostrato che nei casi in cui il figlio primogenito fosse morto da piccolo, il quoziente intellettivo del secondogenito raggiungeva la stessa media di quello dei primogeniti.

Secondo gli autori di questa indagine, dunque, quello che conta non è l'ordine di nascita in sé, ma il fatto di essere cresciuti come primogeniti. La differenza nel quoziente intellettivo quindi sembra non essere genetica, ma piuttosto determinata da fattori sociali.

VOCABULARY

ricercatore	*researcher, scientist*
primogenito	*first-born*
secondogenito	*second-born*
tendere	*to have a tendency*
maggiore	*older (sibling)*
minore	*younger (sibling)*
indagine	*study, research*
crescere	*to grow, to raise*

Please answer the following questions.

1. What is this article about?

2. Where are the scientists from?

3. What seems to be the most important factor determining IQ difference among siblings?

4. Do the scientists believe that the IQ difference in siblings is genetically determined?

ANSWERS

1. The difference in IQ among siblings.

2. Norway.

3. Having being raised as first-born.

4. No, their study points to social, rather than genetic factors.

Norwegian scientists have published an article in the June 22 issue of the journal Science, *where they claim that first-born children have a higher IQ than their younger siblings. This study has in fact shown that among the children in the study, the average of the first-born IQ was 103.2, while the average for second and third-born children was 102.9 and 100, respectively.*

This study has also shown that when a first-born child died young, the second-born IQ would reach the same average as that of first-born children.

According to the authors of the study, then, what counts is not the order of birth per se, but rather the fact of having been raised as a first-born. Thus, the difference in IQ does not seem to be genetic, but rather determined by social factors.

SUPPLEMENTAL VOCABULARY

1. FAMILY AND RELATIONSHIPS

mother	la madre
father	il padre
son	il figlio
daughter	la figlia
sister	la sorella
baby	il bambino
brother	il fratello
husband	il marito
wife	la moglie
aunt	la zia
uncle	lo zio
grandmother	la nonna
grandfather	il nonno
cousin (male)	il cugino
cousin (female)	la cugina
mother-in-law	la suocera
father-in-law	il suocero
stepmother	la moglie di mio padre
stepfather	il marito di mia madre
stepson	il figlio di mia moglie (di mio marito)
stepdaughter	la figlia di mia moglie (di mio marito)
boyfriend	il mio ragazzo
girlfriend	la mia ragazza
fiancé(e)	il fidanzato, la fidanzata
friend	l'amico/l'amica (amici/amiche)
relative	il/la parente
to love	amare
to know (a person)	conoscere
to meet (a person)	conoscere *(for the first time)*, incontrare *(casually)*, vedere

to marry (someone)	sposarsi (con qualcuno)
to divorce (someone)	divorziarsi (da qualcuno)
to get a divorce	divorziarsi
to inherit	ereditare

2. PEOPLE

person	la persona
man	l'uomo
woman	la donna
adult	l'adulto
child	il bambino *(from 0 to 10 years old)*
boy	il ragazzino *(from 11 to 13)* il ragazzo *(from 14 to 35)*
girl	la bambina *(from 0 to 10 years old)* la ragazzina *(from 11 to 13)* la ragazza *(from 14 to 35)*
teenager	l'adolescente, il teenager
tall/short	alto/basso
old/young	vecchio/giovane
fat/thin	grasso/magro
friendly/unfriendly	simpatico/antipatico
happy/sad	felice/triste
beautiful/ugly	bello/brutto
sick/healthy	malato/sano
strong/weak	forte/debole
famous	famoso
intelligent	intelligente
talented	con talento, in gamba *(coll.)*

3. AT HOME

house	la casa
apartment	l'appartamento, l'alloggio
room	la camera, la stanza

living room	**il soggiorno**
dining room	**la sala da pranzo**
kitchen	**la cucina**
bedroom	**la camera da letto, la stanza da letto**
bathroom	**il bagno**
hall	**l'ingresso**
closet	**l'armadio**
window	**la finestra**
door	**la porta**
table	**il tavolo**
chair	**la sedia**
sofa	**il sofà**
couch	**il divano**
curtain	**la tenda**
carpet	**il tappeto** *(rug),* **la moquette** *(wall-to-wall carpet)*
television	**la televisione**
CD player	**il lettore di CD (ci-di)**
lamp	**la lampada**
DVD player	**il lettore di DVD (di-vu-di)**
sound system	**lo stereo**
painting/picture	**il quadro**
shelf	**lo scaffale**
stairs	**la scala (le scale)**
ceiling	**il soffitto**
wall	**il muro, la parete**
floor	**il pavimento**
big/small	**grande/piccolo**
new/old	**nuovo/vecchio**
wood	**il legno**
wooden	**di legno**
plastic	**la plastica**
made from plastic	**di plastica**

4. IN THE KITCHEN

refrigerator	il frigorifero (il frigo)
(kitchen) sink	il lavandino
counter	il piano
stove	la cucina elettrica, la cucina a gas
oven	il forno
microwave	il forno a microonde
cupboard	la credenza
drawer	il cassetto
plate	il piatto
cup	la tazza
bowl	la scodella *(small, for one person)* la ciotola, la terrina
glass	il bicchiere
spoon	il cucchiaio
knife	il coltello
can	la lattina
box	la scatola
bottle	la bottiglia
carton	la scatola di cartone
coffee maker	la caffettiera *(stovetop)*, la macchina del caffè *(espresso machine)*
tea kettle	il bollitore
blender	il frullatore
iron	il ferro da stiro
ironing board	l'asse da stiro
broom	la scopa
dishwasher	la lavapiatti, la lavastoviglie
washing machine	la lavatrice, la lavabiancheria
dryer	l'essiccatrice
to cook	cucinare
to do the dishes	lavare i piatti

to do the laundry	**fare la lavanderia, fare il bucato**
dishwashing detergent	**il detersivo per i piatti**
laundy detergent	**il detersivo per il bucato**
bleach	**la candeggina**
clean/dirty	**pulito/sporco**

5. IN THE BATHROOM

toilet	**il water**
sink (wash basin)	**il lavandino, il lavabo**
bath tub	**la vasca (da bagno)**
shower	**la doccia**
mirror	**lo specchio**
medicine cabinet	**l'armadietto**
towel	**l'asciugamano**
toilet paper	**la carta igienica**
shampoo	**lo shampoo**
soap	**la saponetta**
bath gel	**il bagnoschiuma**
shower gel	**il docciaschiuma**
shaving cream	**la crema da barba**
razor	**il rasoio**
to wash oneself	**lavarsi**
to take a shower	**farsi la doccia**
to take a bath	**farsi il bagno**
to shave	**farsi la barba, radersi**
cologne	**l'acqua colonia**
perfume	**il profumo**
deodorant	**il deodorante**
bandage	**la benda, il cerotto**
powder	**il borotalco**

6. IN THE OFFICE

office	**l'ufficio**
desk	**la scrivania**

computer	il computer
telephone	il telefono
cell phone	il cellulare, il telefonino
fax machine	il fax
shelf	lo scaffale
bookshelf	lo scaffale dei libri
file cabinet	lo schedario
file	la cartella
boss	il capo
colleague	il/la collega
employee	l'impiegato
staff	lo staff
company	la compagnia
business	il business
factory	la fabbrica
meeting room	la sala delle riunioni
meeting	la riunione
appointment	l'appuntamento
salary	il salario, lo stipendio
job	il lavoro
busy	occupato, impegnato
to work	lavorare
to earn	guadagnare

7. AT SCHOOL

school	la scuola
university	l'università
classroom	la classe
course	il corso
teacher	l'insegnante, il maestro/la maestra *(nursery school and elementary school)*
professor	il professore/la professoressa *(from junior high to university)*
student	lo studente/la studentessa

subject	la materia
notebook	il quaderno
textbook	il libro di testo
math	la matematica
history	la storia
chemistry	la chimica
biology	la biologia
literature	la letteratura
language	la lingua
art	l'arte *(f.)*
music	la musica
gym	la palestra
recess	la vacanza
exam	l'esame *(m.)*
test	il test
grade	il voto
report card	la scheda
diploma	il diploma
degree	la laurea
difficult/easy	difficile/facile
to study	studiare
to learn	imparare
to pass	passare (l'esame), essere promosso
to fail	essere bocciato

8. NATURE

tree	l'albero
flower	il fiore
forest	la foresta
mountain	la montagna
field	il campo
river	il fiume

lake	il lago
ocean	l'oceano
sea	il mare
beach	la spiaggia
desert	il deserto
rock	la roccia
sand	la sabbia
sky	il cielo
sun	il sole
moon	la luna
star	la stella
water	l'acqua
land	la terra
plant	la pianta
hill	la collina
pond	lo stagno

9. WEATHER

It's raining.	Piove.
It's snowing.	Nevica.
It's hailing.	Grandina.
It's windy.	C'è vento. Tira vento.
It's hot.	Fa caldo.
It's cold.	Fa freddo.
It's sunny.	C'è il sole.
It's cloudy.	È nuvolóso.
It's beautiful.	Fa bello.
It's stormy.	C'è un temporale.
It's foggy.	C'è nebbia.
storm	il temporale
wind	il vento
sun	il sole

thunder	il tuono
lightning	il lampo
hurricane	l'uragano
temperature	la temperatura
degree	il grado
rain	la pioggia
snow	la neve
cloud	la nuvola
fog	la nebbia
smog	lo smog
umbrella	l'ombrello

10. AROUND TOWN

town	la cittadina *(town)*, il paese *(small town)*
city	la città
village	il paese *(village)*, il paesino *(small village)*
car	la macchina
bus	l'autobus *(m.)*
train	il treno
taxi	il taxi
subway/metro	il metro *(Milan)*, la metro *(Rome)*
traffic	il traffico
building	l'edificio, il palazzo *(old building)*
apartment building	il condominio, la palazzina/ il palazzo *(4–5 story old building)*
library	la biblioteca
restaurant	il ristorante
store	il negozio
street	la strada
park	il parco
train station	la stazione ferroviaria

airport	l'aeroporto
airplane	l'aereo
intersection	l'incrocio
lamp post	il lampione
street light	il semaforo
bank	la banca
church	la chiesa
temple	il tempio
synagogue	la sinagoga
mosque	la moschea
sidewalk	il marciapiede
bakery	la pasticceria
butcher shop	la macelleria
café	il bar
coffee shop	il caffè
drugstore/pharmacy	la farmacia
supermarket	il supermercato
market	il mercato
shoe store	il negozio di scarpe
clothing store	il negozio di abbigliamento
electronics store	il negozio di elettronica
bookstore	la libreria
department store	il grande magazzino
shopping mall	il centro acquisti, il centro commerciale
mayor	il sindaco
city hall/municipal building	il municipio, il comune
to buy	comprare
to go shopping	fare le spese
near/far	vicino/lontano
urban	urbano
suburban	periferico
rural	rurale

11. OCCUPATIONS

policeman/policewoman	**il poliziotto/la donna poliziotto**
lawyer	**l'avvocato**
doctor	**il dottore/la dottoressa, il medico**
engineer	**l'ingegnere**
businessman/woman	**l'uomo d'affari/la donna d'affari**
salesman/woman	**il commesso/la commessa**
teacher	**l'insegnante**
professor	**il professore/la professoressa**
banker	**il banchiere/la banchiera**
architect	**l'architetto**
veterinarian	**il veterinario/la veterinaria**
dentist	**il/la dentista**
stay-at-home dad/mom	**il casalingo/la casalinga**
carpenter	**il falegname**
construction worker	**il muratore/la muratrice**
taxi driver	**il/la tassista**
artist	**l'artista**
writer	**il scrittore/la scrittrice**
plumber	**l'idraulico/l'idraulica**
electrician	**l'elettricista**
journalist	**il/la giornalista**
actor/actress	**l'attore/l'attrice**
musician	**il/la musicista**
farmer	**il contadino/la contadina**
secretary	**il segretario/la segretaria**
assistant	**l'assistente**
unemployed	**il disoccupato/la disoccupata**
retired	**il pensionato/la pensionata**
full-time	**a pieno tempo**
part-time	**part time**
steady job	**lavoro fisso**

12. COMPUTERS AND THE INTERNET

computer	il computer
keyboard	la tastiera
monitor/screen	il monitor, lo schermo
printer	la stampante
mouse	il mouse
mouse pad	il mousepad
modem	il modem
memory	la memoria
CD-ROM	il CD rom
CD ROM drive	l'unitta CD
file	il file, il documento
document	il documento
cable (DSL)	il cavo ASDL
internet	internet
website	il sito web
webpage	la web page, la pagina web
e-mail	l'email (f.), la posta elettronica
chatroom	la chatroom
blog	il blog
instant message	il messaggio instantanio
attachment	l'allegato
to send an e-mail	mandare un'email, mandare una mail
to send a file	inviare un file, inviare un documento
to forward	inoltrare
to reply	rispondere
to delete	cancellare, eliminare
to save a document	salvare un documento
to open a file	aprire un file, aprire un documento
to close a file	chiudere un file, chiudere un documento

to attach a file	allegare un file, allegare un documento

13. SPORTS AND RECREATION

soccer	il calcio
basketball	la pallacanestro
baseball	il baseball
American football	il futbol americano
ice hockey	l'hockey sulle ghiaccio
tennis	il tennis
swimming	il nuoto
biking	il ciclismo
game	la partita
team	la squadra
stadium	lo stadio
coach	l'allenatore/l'allenatrice
player	il giocatore/la giocatrice
champion	il campione/la campionessa
ball	la palla/il pallone
(to go) hiking	camminare in montagna
(to go) camping	andare in campeggio
to play (a sport)	praticare uno sport
to play (a game)	giocare
to win	vincere
to lose	perdere
to draw/tie	pareggiare
cards	(giocare a) carte
pool/billiards	(giocare a) biliardo

14. ENTERTAINMENT

movie/film	il film
to go to the movies	andare al cinema
to see a movie	vedere un film

theater	il teatro, la salle cinematografia (movie theater)
cinema	il cinema
to see a play	vedere uno spettacolo
opera	l'opera
concert	il concerto
club	il club
restaurant	il ristorante
circus	il circo
ticket	il biglietto
museum	il museo
gallery	la galleria
painting	il quadro
sculpture	la scultura
television program	la trasmissione televisiva
to watch television	guardare la tivù (la televisione)
comedy	la commedia
documentary	il documentario
drama	il dramma
book	il libro
magazine	la rivista
to read a book	leggere un libro
to read a magazine	leggere una rivista
to listen to music	ascoltare la musica
song	la canzone
band	il gruppo musicale
the news	le notizie, il telegiornale/il TG (ti-gi) (on TV), il giornale radio (on the radio)
tto flip channels	cambiare canale
to have fun	divertirsi
to be bored	annoiarsi

funny	**divertente**
interesting	**interessante**
exciting	**stimolante**
scary	**pauroso/a**
party	**la festa**
to go to a party	**andare a una festa**
to have a party	**dare una festa**
to dance	**ballare**

15. FOOD

dinner	**la cena**
lunch	**il pranzo**
breakfast	**la colazione**
meat	**la carne**
chicken	**il pollo**
beef	**il manzo**
veal	**il vitello**
pork	**il maiale**
fish	**il pesce**
shrimp	**il gambero**
lobster	**l'aragosta**
bread	**il pane**
egg	**l'uovo *(m.)*, le uova *(f.)***
cheese	**il formaggio**
rice	**il riso**
vegetable	**la verdura**
lettuce	**la lattuga**
tomato	**il pomodoro**
zucchini	**lo zucchino, la zucchina**
eggplant	**la melanzana**
carrot	**la carota**
cucumber	**il cetriolo**

pepper	il peperone
fruit	la frutta
apple	la mela
orange	l'arancia
banana	la banana
pear	la pera
peach	la pesca
apricot	l'albicocca
grapes	l'uva
drink	la bevanda
water	l'acqua
milk	il latte
juice	il succo
coffee	il caffè
tea	il tè
wine	il vino
beer	la birra
soft drink/soda	la bibita
salt	il sale
pepper	il pepe
sugar	lo zucchero
honey	il miele
hot/cold	caldo/freddo
sweet/sour	dolce/aspero

16. CLOTHING

shirt	la camicia
pants	i pantaloni
jeans	i blue jeans
T-shirt	la maglietta
shoe(s)	le scarpe
sock(s)	le calze

belt	la cintura
sneaker/tennis shoe	le scarpe da ginnastica, le scarpe da tennis, gli sneaker
dress	il vestito
skirt	la gonna
blouse	la camicetta
suit	l'abito da uomo *(men)*, il tailleur/il tailleur pantalone *(women)*
hat	il cappello
glove(s)	i guanti
scarf	il foulard *(if square)*, la sciarpa *(if long)*
jacket	la giacca
coat	il cappotto *(if to the knees or longer)*, la giacca/il giaccone *(if shorter)*
earrings	gli orecchini
bracelet	il braccialetto
necklace	la collana
eyeglasses	gli occhiali
sunglasses	gli occhiali da sole
watch	l'orologio
ring	l'anello
underpants	le mutande, gli slip *(for men)*, le mutandine *(for women)*
boxers	i boxer
undershirt	la canottiera
bra	il reggiseno
bathing trunks	il pantaloncihi da bagno
bathing suit	il costume da bagno
bikini	il bikini
pajamas	il pigiama
cotton	(di) il cotone
leather	(di) la pelle
silk	(di) la seta

wool	(di) la lana
size	la misura *(shirts)*, la taglia *(dresses, pants)*, il numero *(shoes)*
to wear	portare, indossare

17. THE HUMAN BODY

head	la testa
face	la faccia
forehead	la fronte
eye	l'occhio
eyebrow(s)	il sopracciglio *(m.)*, le sopracciglia *(f.)*
eyelash(es)	il ciglio *(m.)*, le ciglia *(f.)*
ear(s)	l'orecchio *(m.)*, le orecchie *(f.)*
nose	il naso
mouth	la bocca
tooth	il dente
tongue	la lingua
cheek(s)	la guancia *(m.)*, le guance *(f.)*
chin	il mento
hair	i capelli
neck	il collo
chest	il petto
breast	il seno
shoulders	le spalle
arm(s)	il braccio *(m.)*, le braccia *(f.)*
elbow	il gomito
wrist	il polso
hand(s)	la mano *(m.)*, le mani *(f.)*
waist	la vita
hips	i fianchi

stomach/abdomen	lo stomaco *(above the waist)*, la pancia *(below the waist)*, il ventre *(below the waist)*
behind	il sedere
leg	la gamba
knee(s)	il ginocchio *(m.)*, le ginocchia *(f.)*
ankle	la caviglia
foot	il piede
finger(s)	il dito *(m.)*, le dita *(f.)*
toe	l'alluce *(m.)*
thumb	il pollice
skin	la pelle
blood	il sangue
brain	il cervello
heart	il cuore
lungs	i polmoni
bone(s)	l'osso *(m.)*, le ossa *(f.)*
muscle	il muscolo
tendon	il tendine

18. TRAVEL AND TOURISM

tourist	il/la turista
hotel	l'albergo, l'hotel *(m.)*
youth hostel	l'ostello
reception desk	la reception, l'accettazione
to check in	registrarsi (all'hotel)
to check out	pagare il conto (dell'hotel)
reservation	la prenotazione
passport	il passaporto
tour bus	il pullman
guided tour	il viaggio organizzato
camera (digital)	la macchina fotografica (digitale)
information center	il centro informazioni

map	la piantina, la cartina, la mappa
brochure	l'opuscolo
monument	il monumento
to go sightseeing	visitare
to take a picture	fare una fotografia (delle fotografie)
Can you take our picture?	Può farci una foto(grafia)?

Internet Resources

The following is a list of Italian language websites and other informational websites that students of Italian may find interesting and useful.

www.livinglanguage.com	The Living Language site offers online courses, descriptions of supplemental learning material, resources for teachers and librarians, and much more.
www.italiantourism.com	Italian Government Tourist Board
www.corriere.it	Italian newspaper from Milan
www.rai.it	Italian television and radio
it.yahoo.com	The Italian version of Yahoo!
www.google.it	Italian Google
www.allaboutitaly.com	Events, food, sport
www.initaly.com	Events, accommodations, and general information
www.discoveritalia.com	Information on all of Italy
www.museionline.com	The museums of Italy
www.romaturismo.com	Rome
www.firenze.net	Florence
www.turismovenezia.it	Venice
www.touristbureau.com/indexIta.asp	Amalfi Coast
www.bestofsicily.com	Sicily

Summary of Italian Grammar

1. ALPHABET

LETTER	NAME	LETTER	NAME	LETTER	NAME
a	*a*	h	*acca*	q	*qu*
b	*bi*	i	*i*	r	*erre*
c	*ci*	l	*elle*	s	*esse*
d	*di*	m	*emme*	t	*ti*
e	*e*	n	*enne*	u	*u*
f	*effe*	o	*o*	v	*vu/vi*
g	*gi*	p	*pi*	z	*zeta*

2. PRONUNCIATION
SIMPLE VOWELS

a	as in *ah* or *father*
e	as in *day, ace*
i	as in *machine, police*
o	as in *no, note*
u	as in *rule*

Vowel combinations

ai	*ai* in *aisle*
au	*ou* in *out*
ei	*ay-ee*
eu	*ay-oo*
ia	*ya* in *yard*
ie	*ye* in *yes*
io	*yo* in *yoke*
iu	*you*
oi	*oy* in *boy*
ua	*wah*
ue	*way*
ui	*oo-ee*
uo	*oo-oh*

Consonants

Most Italian consonants are the same as those in English. The differences are discussed below.

The consonant **h** is never pronounced.

Italian has a series of double consonants: **ll, mm, nn, rr,** and **ss.**
Notice the difference between the following:

caro *(dear)*	**carro** *(truck)*
casa *(house)*	**cassa** *(crate, cash register)*
pala *(shovel)*	**palla** *(ball)*

The doubled consonants are pronounced with more force and are held longer than the simple consonants.

SPECIAL ITALIAN LETTER COMBINATIONS AND SOUNDS

1. **ci, ce** is pronounced like the English **ch** in **chair**:

cacciatorc	*hunter*

2. **ch** before **e** and **i** is pronounced like the English **k** in **key**:

chitarra	*guitar*

3. **gi, ge** is pronounced like **j** in jail:

generoso	*generous*

4. **gh** before **e** and **i** is pronounced like the English **g** in **gate**:

ghirlanda	*wreath*

5. **gli** is pronounced similar to **lli** as in **million**:

figlio	*son*
paglia	*straw*

6. **gn** is always pronounced as one letter, similar to the English **ni** in **onion** or **ny** in **canyon**:

segno	*sign*
Spagna	*Spain*

7. **sc** before **e** and **i** is pronounced like the English **sh** in **shoe**:

scendere	*(to) descend/(to) get off/down*
sciroppo	*syrup*

8. **sc** before **a, o,** and **u** is pronounced like the English **sk** in **sky**:

scuola	*school*
scarpa	*shoe*

9. **z** is pronounced similar to **ds** at the end of English **rods**:
zoccolo clog

10. **zz** is pronounced similar to **ts** at the end of **lots**:
tazza cup

3. STRESS
1. Words of two syllables are generally stressed on the first syllable, unless the other one bears an accent mark:

tazza	cup	città	city
penna	pen	virtù	virtue
meta	goal	metà	half

2. Words of more than two syllables are generally stressed either on the syllable before the last, or on the syllable before that:

ancora	more	ancora	anchor
dolore	grief	amore	love
scatola	box	automobile	car

4. THE DEFINITE ARTICLE

	MASCULINE	FEMININE
SINGULAR	il, l', and lo	la and l'
PLURAL	i and gli	le

L' is used before masculine or feminine nouns beginning with a vowel:

l'arrivo *(m.)* the arrival
l'uscita *(f.)* the exit

Lo is used before masculine nouns beginning with an **s** plus consonant or with a **z**:

lo studente	*the student*
lo zoccolo	*the clog*

Gli is used before plural nouns beginning with an **s** plus consonant, a **z** or a vowel:

gli studenti	*the students*
gli zoccoli	*the clogs*
gli arrivi	*the arrivals*

There are many instances (such as expressing general truth) in which Italian uses a definite article where no article is used in English:

Il tempo è denaro.	*Time is money.*
La vita è piena di guai.	*Life is full of troubles.*
I lupi sono feroci.	*Wolves are ferocious.*
I cani sono fedeli.	*Dogs are faithful.*
L'oro è un metallo prezioso.	*Gold is a precious metal.*
Il ferro è duro.	*Iron is hard.*
Gli affari sono affari.	*Business is business.*
La necessità non conosce legge.	*Necessity knows no law.*

Remember that in Italian the definite article is also used in front of a possessive adjective or pronoun:

Il mio libro è nero, il tuo rosso.	*My book is black, yours is red.*

But with nouns indicating a family member in the singular, no article is used in front of the possessive adjective:

mio padre	*my father*
tuo fratello	*your brother*
nostro zio	*our uncle*

When **loro** (their, your) is used or when the kinship term is followed by an adjective, the definite article precedes the possessive:

la loro mamma	*their mother*
il mio padre generoso	*my generous father*

In expressions like the following, Italian uses the definite article:

Tre volte la settimana	*Three times a week.*
Due euro al kilo.	*Two euros per kilo.*

The definite article is used when talking about parts of the human body:

Ha il naso lungo.	*He/she has a long nose.*

The definite article is always used with expressions of time:

Sono le due.	*It is two o'clock.*

And with some geographical expressions:

L'Europa è un continente.	*Europe is a continent.*
La Toscana è bella.	*Tuscany is beautiful.*

5. THE INDEFINITE ARTICLE

	MASCULINE	FEMININE
SINGULAR	**un, uno**	**una, un'**

un uomo	*a man*
una donna	*a woman*

Uno is used before words beginning with an **s** plus another consonant and with **z**:

uno sciopero	*a strike*
uno zoccolo	*a clog*

Un' is used before feminine nouns beginning with a vowel:

un'aranciata	*an orange soda (orangeade)*

Italian uses no indefinite article in cases like the following ones:

Io sono maestro.	*I am a teacher.*
Che donna!	*What a woman!*
mezzo chilo	*half a kilo*
cento uomini	*a hundred men*

6. MASCULINE AND FEMININE

Nouns referring to males are masculine; nouns referring to females are feminine:

MASCULINE		FEMININE	
il padre	*the father*	la madre	*the mother*
il figlio	*the son*	la figlia	*the daughter*
l'uomo	*the man*	la donna	*the woman*
il toro	*the bull*	la vacca	*the cow*
il gatto	*the tomcat*	la gatta	*the female cat*

But all nouns in Italian, including those that do not refer to animate beings, have gender. A noun is either masculine or feminine depending on its ending.

MASCULINE NOUNS

1. Nouns ending in **-o** are usually masculine:

il corpo	*the body*
il cielo	*the sky*
il denaro	*the money*

2. The names of the months and the names of the days (except Sunday) are masculine:

il gennaio scorso	*last January*
il lunedì	*on Mondays*

3. The names of lakes and some names of mountains are masculine:

il Garda	*Lake Garda*
gli Appennini	*the Apennines*

FEMININE NOUNS
Nouns ending in **-a** are usually feminine:

la testa	*the head*
la città	*the city*
la macchina	*the car*

NOUNS ENDING IN -E
Nouns ending in **-e** in the singular may be either masculine or feminine:

la madre	*the mother*
il padre	*the father*
la legge *(f.)*	*the law*
il piede *(m.)*	*the foot*

NOUNS WITH MASCULINE OR FEMININE FORMS
1. Some masculine nouns ending in **-a, -e, -o**, mostly professions, form their feminine in **-essa**:

il poeta	*the poet*	**la poetessa**	*the poetess*
il professore	*the (male) professor*	**la professoressa**	*the (female) professor*

2. Masculine nouns ending in **-tore** form their feminine in **-trice**:

l'attore	*the actor*	**l'attrice**	*the actress*

7. PLURALS OF NOUNS

1. Nouns ending in **-o**, mostly masculine, form their plural in **-i**:

il bambino	*the child*	i bambini	*the children*

Some exceptions:

A few nouns ending in **-o** are feminine:

la mano	*the hand*	le mani	*the hands*
la radio	*the radio*	le radio	*the radios*
la dinamo	*the dynamo*	le dinamo	*the dynamos*

Some masculine nouns ending in **-o** have two plurals, with different meanings for each:

il braccio	*the arm*
i bracci	*the arms (of a stream)*
le braccia	*the arms (of the body)*

2. Nouns ending in **-a**, usually feminine, form their plural in **-e**:

la rosa	*the rose*	le rose	*the roses*

Masculine nouns ending in **-a** form their plural in **-i**:

il poeta	*the poet*	i poeti	*the poets*

3. Nouns ending in **-e**, which can be masculine or feminine, form their plural in **-i**:

il nipote	*the nephew or grandson/ grandchild*	i nipoti	*the nephews or grandsons/ grandchildren*
la nipote	*the niece or granddaughter*	le nipoti	*the nieces or granddaughters*

SPECIAL CASES

1. Nouns ending in **-ca** or **-ga** insert **h** in the plural in order to keep the "**k**" and "**g**" sound in the plural:

la barca	*the boat*	le barche	*the boats*
il monarca	*the monarch*	i monarchi	*the monarchs*

Exceptions:

un belga	*a Belgian*	**i belgi**	*the Belgians*
un amico	*a friend*	**gli amici**	*the friends*

2. Nouns ending in **-cia** or **-gia** (with unaccented **i**) form their plural in **-ce** or **-ge** if the **c** or **g** is double or is preceded by another consonant:

la spiaggia	*the seashore*	**le spiagge**	*the seashores*
la guancia	*the cheek*	**le guance**	*the cheeks*

Nouns ending in **-cia** or **-gia** form their plural in **-cie** or **-gie** if **c** or **g** is preceded by a vowel or if the **i** is accented:

la bugia	*the lie*	**le bugie**	*the lies*

3. Nouns ending in **-io** (without an accent on the **i**) have a single **i** in the plural:

il figlio	*the son*	**i figli**	*the sons*

If the **i** is accented, the plural has **ii**:

lo zio	*the uncle*	**gli zii**	*the uncles*

4. Nouns ending in **-co** or **-go** form their plural in **-chi** or **-ghi** if the accent falls on the syllable before the last:

il fico	*the fig*	**i fichi**	*the figs*

Exception:

l'amico	*the friend*	**gli amici**	*the friends*

If the accent falls on the third-to-last syllable, the plural is in **-ci** or **-gi**:

il medico	*the doctor*	**i medici**	*the doctors*

5. Nouns in the singular with the accent on the last vowel do not change in the plural:

la città	*the city*	**le città**	*the cities*

There is no special plural form for:

1. Nouns with a written accent on the last vowel:

la città	*the city*
le città	*the cities*
il caffè	*the coffee*
i caffè	*the coffees*

2. Nouns ending in **i** in the singular, and almost all the nouns in **ie**:

il brindisi	*the toast*
i brindisi	*the toasts*
la crisi	*the crisis*
le crisi	*the crises*
la superficie	*the surface*
le superficie	*the surfaces*

3. Nouns ending in a consonant:

il bar	*the bar*
i bar	*the bars*
il computer	*the computer*
i computer	*the computers*

8. THE PARTITIVE

The partitive (i.e., words expressing a partial quantity of an item that cannot be counted) can be expressed in Italian in several ways:

a. With the preposition **di** + a form of the definite article **il, lo, la, l', i, le, gli**:

Io mangio del pane.	*I eat some (of the) bread.*
Io mangio della carne.	*I eat some meat.*
Io prendo dell'acqua.	*I take some water.*
Io prendo dello zucchero.	*I take some sugar.*
Io leggo dei libri.	*I read some books.*

| Io scrivo degli esercizi. | *I write some exercises.* |
| Io compro delle sedie. | *I buy some chairs.* |

b. By using **qualche** (only with singular nouns):

| Io scrivo qualche lettera. | *I write a few (some) letters.* |
| Io leggo qualche giornale. | *I read a few (some) newspapers.* |

c. By using **alcuni, alcune** (only in the plural):

| Io ho alcuni amici. | *I have a few (some) friends.* |
| Io scrivo alcune poesie. | *I write a few (some) poems.* |

d. By using **un po' di**:

| Io prendo un po' di zucchero. | *I'll take some sugar.* |

SPECIAL USES OF THE PARTITIVE

Some expressions with the partitive:

ancora del	*(some) more*
(dello, della, dell', dei, etc.)	
un po' più di	*a little more*
Voglio ancora del pane.	*I want more bread.*
Prendo un po' più di carne.	*I take a little more meat.*
non . . . di più	*no more (quantity)*
Volete di più? No, non ne vogliamo più.	*Do you want more? No, we don't want any more.*

Note that **più** can also be used to express time:

| non . . . più | *no longer (time)* |
| Lei non canta più. | *She doesn't sing any longer.* |

9. ADJECTIVES

The endings used with adjectives are similar to those used with nouns (see 6 above).

1. Most singular adjectives end in **-o** for the masculine and **-a** for the feminine:

| un caro amico *(m.)* | *a dear friend* |
| una cara amica *(f.)* | *a dear friend* |

2. Most plural adjectives end in **-i** for the masculine and **-e** for the feminine:

| cari amici *(m.)* | *dear friends* |
| care amiche *(f.)* | *dear friends* |

3. Some singular adjectives end in **-e** in the masculine and in the feminine:

| un uomo gentile | *a kind man* |
| una donna gentile | *a kind woman* |

In the plural these same adjectives end in **i** in both the masculine and the feminine:

| uomini gentili | *kind men* |
| donne gentili | *kind women* |

10. POSITION OF THE ADJECTIVE

In general, adjectives follow the noun. Some common exceptions are: **buono** (*good*), **cattivo** (*bad*), **nuovo** (*new*), **bello** (*beautiful*), and **brutto** (*ugly*).

la musica italiana	*Italian music*
il libro nero	*the black book*
una brutta giornata	*an awful day*
un nuovo libro	*a new book*

Possessive adjectives, demonstrative adjectives, numerals, and indefinite adjectives generally precede the noun:

il mio amico	*my friend*
questo libro	*this book*
due penne	*two pens*
alcuni signori	*a few (some) men*

11. COMPARISON

Different forms of comparison are formed in the following way:

Equality	(così) . . . come	as . . . as
Equality	tanto . . . quanto	as much/as many . . . as
Superiority	più . . . di or che	more . . . than
Inferiority	meno . . . di or che	less/fewer . . . than

Il mio appartamento è grande come il tuo. *My apartment is as large as yours.*

Luigi legge tanto quanto Paola. *Luigi reads as much as Paola.*

After **più** and **meno**, either **di** or **che** can be used, but if the comparison is between two adjectives, or if there is a preposition, only **che** can be used:

Franco è più studioso di Carlo. *Frank is more studious than Charles.*

Franco è meno alto di Luca. *Carlo is less tall than Luca.*

Giacomo è più studioso che intelligente. *James is more studious than intelligent.*

Ci sono meno bambini in campagna che in città. *There are fewer children in the country than in the city.*

If the second term of the comparison is expressed by a clause, **di quello che** must be used.

Studia più di quello che (tu) pensi. *He studies more than you think.*

If the second term of the comparison is expressed by a pronoun, the object form of the pronoun is used:

Lui è più alto di me. *He is taller than I (am).*

Io sono meno ricco di te. *I am less rich than you (are).*

Lei è coraggiosa come lui. *She is as brave as he (is).*

12. RELATIVE SUPERLATIVE

The relative superlative (expressed in English using *the most/the least/the . . . -est of/in*) is formed by placing the appropriate definite article before **più** or **meno** followed by the adjective. *Of/in* is translated with **di**, whether by itself or combined with the definite article:

Quest'uomo è il più ricco del mondo.	*This man is the richest in the world.*
Lei è la più famosa delle sorelle.	*She is the most famous among her sisters.*
Marco è il meno timido di tutti.	*Marco is the least shy of all.*

If a clause follows the superlative, the verb is often in the subjunctive form:

È il quadro più bello che io abbia mai visto.	*It's the most beautiful painting I have ever seen.*

With the superlative of adverbs, the definite article is often omitted, unless **possibile** is added to the adverb:

Parla più chiaramente di tutti.	*She is the clearest speaker of (them) all.*
Parliamo il più chiaramente possibile.	*We're speaking as clearly as possible.*

13. ABSOLUTE SUPERLATIVE

1. The absolute superlative is formed by dropping the last vowel of the adjective and adding **-issimo, -issima, -issimi, -issime**:

L'esercizio è facilissimo.	*The exercise is very easy.*

2. By putting the words **molto, troppo,** or **assai** in front of the adjectives:

La poesia è molto bella.	*The poem is very beautiful.*

3. By using a second adjective of almost the same meaning, or by repeating the adjective:

La casa è piena zeppa di amici. *The house is full of (loaded with) friends.*

La macchina è nuova nuova. *The car is brand new.*

4. By using **stra-, arci-, sopra-, super-, extra-**:

Il signore è straricco. *The gentleman is loaded with money.*

Il signore è arciricco.

Questa seta è sopraffina. *This silk is extra fine.*

14. IRREGULAR COMPARATIVES AND SUPERLATIVES

Some adjectives and adverbs have irregular comparatives and superlatives in addition to their regular forms.

ADJECTIVE	COMPARATIVE	SUPERLATIVE
good: **buono(a)**	*better:* **più buono(a)** **migliore**	*the best:* **il più buono** **buonissimo(a)** **ottimo(a)** **il/la migliore**
bad: **cattivo(a)**	*worse:* **peggiore** **più cattivo(a)** **peggio di**	*the worst:* **il/la peggiore** **il/la più cattivo(a)** **pessimo(a)** **cattivissimo(a)**
big/great: **grande**	*bigger/greater:* **maggiore** **più grande**	*the biggest/greatest:* **il/la maggiore** **grandissimo(a)** **il/la più grande** **massimo(a)**
small/little: **piccolo(a)**	*smaller/lesser:* **minore** **più piccolo(a)**	*the smallest/least:* **il/la minore** **il/la più piccolo(a)** **piccolissimo(a)** **minimo(a)**

ADVERB	COMPARATIVE	SUPERLATIVE
well: **bene**	*better:* **meglio (il migliore)**	*the best:* **il meglio**
badly: **male**	*worse:* **peggio (il peggiore)**	*the worst:* **il peggio**

15. DIMINUTIVES AND AUGMENTATIVES

1. The endings **-ino, -ina, -ello, -ella, -etto, -etta, -uccio, -uccia** imply smallness:

gattino	*kitten (kitty cat)*
casetta	*pretty little house*

2. The endings **-one, -ona, -otta** imply largeness or hyperbole:

donnona	*big woman*
stupidone	*big fool*

3. The endings **-uccia, -uccio** indicate endearment:

tesoruccio	*little treasure*
boccuccia	*sweet little mouth*

4. The endings **-accio, -accia, -astro, -astra, -azzo, -azza** indicate depreciation:

parolaccia	*curse word*
cagnaccio	*ugly/bad dog*

16. DAYS OF THE WEEK

The days of the week (except Sunday) are masculine, and are not capitalized unless they begin a sentence. The article is only used when referring to a repeated, habitual event, as in "on Sundays" "on Mondays," etc.

lunedì	*Monday*
martedì	*Tuesday*
mercoledì	*Wednesday*
giovedì	*Thursday*
venerdì	*Friday*
sabato	*Saturday*
domenica *(f.)*	*Sunday*

Vengo lunedì. — *I'm coming on Monday.*

Gli andranno a fare visita domenica. — *They're going to pay them a visit on Sunday.*

La vedo sabato. — *I'll see her on Saturday.*

La domenica vado in chiesa. — *On Sundays I go to church.*

Vado a scuola il venerdì. — *I go to school on Fridays.*

Note: The word *on* is not translated before the days of the week or a date.

il 15 febbraio — *on February 15*

17. MONTHS OF THE YEAR

The names of the months are masculine and are not capitalized unless they begin a sentence. They are usually used without the definite article:

gennaio	*January*
febbraio	*February*
marzo	*March*
aprile	*April*
maggio	*May*
giugno	*June*
luglio	*July*

agosto	August
settembre	September
ottobre	October
novembre	November
dicembre	December

18. THE SEASONS

l'inverno *(m.)*	*winter*
la primavera	*spring*
l'estate *(f.)*	*summer*
l'autunno *(m.)*	*fall*

The names of the seasons are usually not capitalized. They are preceded by the definite article, but after **di** the article may or may not be used:

L'inverno è una brutta stagione.	*Winter is an ugly season.*
Fa freddo d'inverno.	*It's cold in (the) winter.*
Io lavoro durante i mesi estivi (or, dell'estate).	*I work during summer months (or, during the summer).*

19. NUMBERS

The plural of **mille** *(thousand)* is **mila**: **duemila**, *two thousand;* **seimila**, *six thousand.*

After **milione** the preposition **di** is used:

un milione di soldati	*one million soldiers*
tre milioni di dollari	*three million dollars*

In writing a date, give the day first and then the month:

il 5 (cinque) agosto	*August 5th*
il 10 (dieci) novembre	*November 10th*

The ordinal numeral is used only for the first of the month:

il primo novembre	*November 1st*
il tre agosto	*August 3rd*

20. DEMONSTRATIVES

questo, -a, -i, -e	*this, these*
quello, -a, -i, -e	*that, those*

The pronoun *this* is **questo**:

Questo è l'uomo che cerchiamo.	*This is the man we are looking for.*

Besides the forms of **quello** already given, there are also the forms **quel, quei, quegli.** Here is how they are used:

1. If the article **il** is used before the noun, use **quel**:

il libro	*the book*
quel libro	*that book*

2. If the article **l'** is used before the noun, then use **quell'**:

l'orologio	*the watch*
quell'orologio	*that watch*

3. If **i** is used before the noun, use **quei**:

i maestri	*the teachers*
quei maestri	*those teachers*

4. If **gli** is used before the noun, use **quegli**:

gli studenti	*the students*
quegli studenti	*those students*

Note that the same rules apply to **bel, bell', bei, begli,** from **bello, -a, -i, -e** (*beautiful*).

21. POSSESSIVE ADJECTIVES

MASCULINE SINGULAR	FEMININE SINGULAR	MASCULINE PLURAL	FEMININE PLURAL
mio	mia	miei *(irregular)*	mie
tuo	tua	tuoi *(irregular)*	tue
suo	sua	suoi *(irregular)*	sue
nostro	nostra	nostri	nostre
vostro	vostra	vostri	vostre
loro	loro	loro	loro

Always use the article in front of a possessive adjective:

il mio denaro   *my money*
la tua sedia   *your chair*
la vostra borsa   *your pocketbook*

Except for members of the family in the singular:

mia madre   *my mother*

The possessive adjective agrees with the thing possessed and not with the possessor:

la sua casa   *(his, her) house*

Suo may mean *his* or *her*, or, with the polite form, *your*. If confusion should arise because of the use of **suo, di lui, di lei,** etc., can be used for disambiguation.

22. INDEFINITE ADJECTIVES

1. *Some*—**qualche** (used only in **sing.**) **alcuni** (used only in *pl.*)

qualche lettera	*some letters*
alcuni dollari	*some dollars*

2. *Any*—**qualunque, qualsiasi** (has no *pl.*)

qualunque mese	*any month*
qualsiasi ragazzo	*any boy*

3. *Each, every*—**ogni** (has no *pl.*), **ciascun, ciascuno, ciascuna** (no *pl.*)

Ogni ragazzo parla.	*Every boy talks.*
Ogni ragazza parla.	*Every girl talks.*
Diciamo una parola a ciascun signore.	*Let's say a word to each of the gentlemen.*
Raccontate tutto a ciascuna signora.	*Tell everything to each of the/every lady.*

4. *Other, more*—**altro (l'altro), altra, altri, altre**

Mandiamo gli altri libri?	*Do we send the other books?*
Vuole altro denaro?	*Do you want more money?*

5. *No, no one, none of*—**nessuno, nessun, nessuna**

Nessuno zio ha scritto.	*None of the uncles wrote.*
Nessun soldato ha paura.	*No soldier is afraid.*
Nessuna sedia è buona.	*None of the (these/those) chairs is good.*

23. INDEFINITE PRONOUNS

1. *Some*—**alcuni, alcuni . . . altri**

alcuni dei suoi discorsi	*some of his speeches*
Di questi libri, alcuni sono buoni, altri pessimi.	*Of these books, some are good, some bad.*

2. *Someone, somebody*—**qualcuno**

Qualcuno è venuto.	*Somebody came.*

3. *Anybody, anyone*—**chiunque**

Chiunque dice così.	*Anybody says (would say) so.*

4. *Each one, each person*—**ognuno**; *everybody, everyone*—**tutti** (only *pl.*); *each, each one*—**ciascuno**; *everything*—**tutto**

Tutti corrono.	*Everybody runs. (All run.)*
Ho dato un biscotto ciascuno.	*I gave each a cookie.*

5. *The other, the others, else* (in interrogative or negative sentences), *anything else* (in interrogative or negative sentences)—**l'altro, l'altra, gli altri, le altre, altro**; *another one*—**un altro**

Lui dice una cosa ma l'altro non è d'accordo.	*He says one thing, but the other one does not agree.*
Volete altro?	*Do you want something else?*
Non vogliamo altro.	*We do not want anything else.*

6. *Nothing*—**niente, nulla**; *nobody, no one*—**nessuno** (no *m.*, no *pl.*)

Niente (nulla) lo consola.	*Nothing comforts him.*
Nessuno conosce questa regola.	*Nobody knows this rule.*

24. INTERROGATIVE PRONOUNS AND ADJECTIVES

1. The interrogative pronoun **chi** refers to persons, and corresponds to *who, whom,* or *which:*

Chi vi scrive?	*Who writes to you?*
Chi vediamo?	*Whom do we see?*
Chi di noi ha parlato?	*Which one of us has talked?*

2. **Che, cosa,** or **che cosa** translates as *what:*

Che facciamo?	*What are we going to do?*
Che cosa leggete?	*What are you reading?*
Cosa studi?	*What do you study (in college)?*

3. The two interrogative adjectives **quale** and **che** mean *which, what:*

Quale dei due giornali compra Lei?	*Which of the two newspapers do you buy?*
Che colore desiderate?	*What color would you like?*

25. RELATIVE PRONOUNS

chi	*who*
che	*who, whom, that, which*
cui	*(used with prepositions)*
a cui	*to whom*
di cui	*of whom, of which*
in cui	*in which*

Chi studia impara.	*He who studies, learns.*
l'uomo che ho visto	*the man (whom) I saw*
la donna di cui parlo	*the woman (of whom) I speak of*
la ragazza a cui parlo	*the girl (to whom) I'm speaking to*

1. **che**: For masculine, feminine, singular, plural; for persons, animals, things. Do not use this pronoun if there is a preposition.

2. **cui**: Masculine, feminine, singular, plural; for persons, animals, things; substitutes **che** when there is a preposition.

3. **il quale, la quale, i quali, le quali**: For persons, animals, things, with the same English meanings as **che**; can be used with or without prepositions. When used with prepositions, the contracted forms are used, e.g., **alla quale, dei quali**, etc.

26. PERSONAL PRONOUNS

Pronouns have different forms depending on whether they are:

1. The subject of a verb

2. The direct object of a verb

3. The indirect object of a verb

4. Used after a preposition

5. Used with reflexive verbs

a. The subject pronouns are:

SINGULAR	
io	*I*
tu	*you* (infml.)
lui	*he*
lei	*she*
Lei	*you* (fml.)
esso	*it* (m.)
essa	*it* (f.)

PLURAL	
noi	*we*
voi	*you*
loro	*they*
Loro	*you* (fml. pl.)

Subject pronouns are optional in Italian as the verb ending indicates who is speaking or being spoken about.

b. The direct object pronouns are:

mi	*me*
ti	*you* (infml.)
lo	*him, it*
la	*her, it, you* (fml.)
ci	*us*
vi	*you*
li	*them, you*
le	*them, you* (fml.)

| Ci vede. | *He sees us.* |
| Lo scrive. | *He writes it.* |

c. The indirect object pronouns are:

mi	*to me*
ti	*to you* (infml.)
gli	*to him*
le	*to her*
Le	*to you* (fml.)
ci	*to us*
vi	*to you*
gli/Loro	*to them, to you* (fml.)

Lui mi scrive una lettera.	*He writes me a letter.*
Io ti regalo una bambola.	*I give you a doll (as a present).*
Noi gli parliamo.	*We speak to them.*

d. The pronouns used after a preposition are:

me	*me*
te	*you* (infml.)
lui	*him*
lei	*her, you* (fml.)
noi	*us*
voi	*you*
loro	*them, you* (fml.)

| Io verrò con te. | *I will come with you.* |
| Lui parla sempre di lei. | *He always speaks about her.* |

e. The reflexive pronouns are:

mi	*myself*
ti	*yourself* (infml.)
si	*himself, herself, itself, yourself* (fml.)
ci	*ourselves*
vi	*yourselves*
si	*themselves, yourselves* (fml.)

Io mi lavo.	*I wash myself.*
Noi ci alziamo alle nove.	*We get up at nine.*
Loro si alzano.	*They get up.*

27. POSITION OF PRONOUNS

1. Pronouns are written as separate words, before the verb, except with the imperative, infinitive, and gerund, where they follow the verbal form and are written as one word with it:

Ditelo.	*Say it.*
Fatemi un favore.	*Do me a favor.*
per scriverle una lettera	*to write her a letter*
dopo avermi chiamato	*after having called me*
facendolo	*doing it*
chiamandolo	*calling him*

2. In the imperative, when the formal form is used, the pronouns are never attached to the verb:

Mi faccia un favore *(fml.).*	*Do me a favor (please).*

3. Some verbs of one syllable in the imperative double the initial consonant of the pronoun:

Dimmi una cosa.	*Tell me one thing.*
Facci una cortesia.	*Do us a favor.*

4. In the compound infinitive the pronoun is attached to the auxiliary:

Credo di averti dato tutto. *I think I gave you everything.*

The simple infinitive drops the final **e** before the pronoun:

per leggere un articolo *to read an article*
per leggerti un articolo *to read you an article*

5. When two object pronouns are used with the same verb, the indirect object pronoun precedes the direct object pronoun:

Te lo voglio dire. *I want to tell you about it.*

Observe the following changes in the pronouns that occur in this case:

The **i** in **mi, ti, ci, vi, si** changes to **e** before **lo, la, le, li, ne**, while **gli** takes an additional **e** and is written as one word with the following pronoun. **Le** also becomes **glie** before **lo, la, li, le, ne**:

Ce lo dà. *He gives it to us.*

Glielo mando a casa. *I send it to his (her, your) home.*

Glielo dicono. *They tell him about it (to her, to you, to them).*

28. NE

1. Used as a pronoun meaning *of him, of her, of them, of it*:

Parla del mio amico? *Are you talking of my friend?*

Sì, ne parlo. *Yes, I am talking of him.*

Parliamo di questa cosa? *Are we talking of this thing?*

Sì, ne parliamo. *Yes, we are talking of it.*

2. Used as a partitive meaning *some* or *any*:

Mangia del pesce la signorina? *Does the young lady like to eat any fish?*

Sì, ne gradisce (un po'). *Yes, she does. (lit., Yes, she does some of it.)*

29. SI

1. Si can be used as a reflexive pronoun:

Lui si lava.	*He washes himself.*
Loro si lavano.	*They wash themselves.*

2. Si is used as an impersonal pronoun:

Non sempre si riflette su quel che si dice.	*One doesn't always ponder over what one says.*
Qui si mangia bene.	*One eats well here.*

3. Si is sometimes used to translate the English passive:

Come si manda questa lettera?	*How is this letter supposed to be mailed?*

30. ADVERBS

1. Many adverbs end in -**mente**:

caramente	*dearly*
dolcemente	*sweetly*

These adverbs are easily formed; take the feminine singular form of the adjective and add -**mente**. For instance, *dear* is **caro, cara, cari, care**; the feminine singular form is **cara,** and so the adverb is **caramente.** *Sweet* is **dolce, dolci** (there is no difference between the masculine and feminine); the feminine singular is **dolce,** and so the adverb is **dolcemente.**

2. Adjectives ending in -**le** or -**re** drop the final **e** before -**mente** if the **l** or **r** is preceded by a vowel; thus the adverb corresponding to **facile** is **facilmente** (*easily*). The adverbs corresponding to **buono** (*good*) and **cattivo** (*bad*) are **bene** and **male.**

3. Adverbs may have a comparative and superlative form: **Caramente, più caramente, molto caramente,** or **carissimamente.**

Observe these irregular comparative and superlative forms of adverbs:

meglio	*better*
peggio	*worse*
maggiormente	*more greatly*
massimamente	*very greatly*
minimamente	*in the least, minimally*
ottimamente	*very well, with excellence*
pessimamente	*very bad*

31. PREPOSITIONS

1. The most common prepositions in Italian are:

di	*of*
a	*at, to*
da	*from*
in	*in*
con	*with*
su	*above*
per	*through, by means of, on*
tra, fra	*between, among*

2. When used before a definite article, these prepositions are often contracted. Here are the most common of these combinations:

	DI	A	SU	CON
IL	del	al	sul	col
LO	dello	allo	sullo	–
LA	della	alla	sulla	–
L'	dell'	all'	sull'	–
I	dei	ai	sui	coi
GLI	degli	agli	sugli	–
LE	delle	alle	sulle	–

Io ho del denaro.	*I have some money.*
il cavallo dello zio	*our uncle's horse*
Io regalo un dollaro al ragazzo.	*I give a dollar to the boy.*
Il professore risponde agli studenti.	*The professor answers the students.*

32. NEGATION

1. **Non** (*not*) comes before the verb:

Io non vedo.	*I don't see.*
Lui non parla.	*He doesn't speak.*

2. *Nothing, never, no one*:

Non vedo nulla.	*I see nothing.*
Non vado mai.	*I never go.*
Non viene nessuno.	*No one comes.*

Note that **non** can be combined with negative pronouns in the same sentence.

If the negative pronoun begins the sentence, **non** is not used.

Nessuno viene.	No one comes.

33. QUESTION WORDS

Interrogative pronouns and adjectives were introduced above. Here are more interrogative adverbs and adjectives.

Perché?	*Why?*
Come?	*How?*
Quando?	*When?*
Dove?	*Where?*
Quanto/quanta?	*How much?*
Quanti/quante?	*How many?*

Perché non entriamo.	*Why don't we go in?*
Come stai?	*How are you?*
Quando vieni?	*When are you coming?*
Dove vai?	*Where are you going?*

| Quanto caffè compri? | *How much coffee are you buying?* |
| Quanti dollari hai? | *How many dollars do you have?* |

34. THE TENSES OF VERBS

Italian verbs are divided into three classes (conjugations) according to their infinitives:

Class I (-are): **parlare, amare**
Class II (-ere): **scrivere, temere**
Class III (-ire): **partire, sentire**

1. The present:

To form the **present** tense, take off the infinitive ending **(-are, -ere, -ire)** and add the following present tense endings:

CLASS I	CLASS II	CLASS III
-o	-o	-o
-i	-i	-i
-a	-e	-e
-iamo	-iamo	-iamo
-ate	-ete	-ite
-ano	-ono	-ono

The present tense can be translated in several ways:

| Io parlo italiano. | *I speak Italian./I am speaking Italian./I do speak Italian.* |

2. The imperfect:

To form the **imperfect** tense, take off the infinitive ending **(-are, -ere, -ire)** and add the following imperfect tense endings:

I	II	III
-avo	-evo	-ivo
-avi	-evi	-ivi
-ava	-eva	-iva
-avamo	-evamo	-ivamo
-avate	-evate	-ivate
-avano	-evano	-ivano

The imperfect is used:

a. To indicate continued or customary action in the past:

Quando ero a Roma andavo sempre a visitare i musei.	*When I was in Rome, I would always visit museums.*
Lo incontravo ogni giorno.	*I used to meet him every day./ I would meet him every day.*

b. To indicate what was happening when something else happened:

Lui scriveva quando lei è entrata.	*He was writing when she entered (the room).*

3. The future:

The **future** of regular verbs is formed by adding to the infinitive (after the final **e** is dropped) the endings -**ò**, -**ai**, -**à**, -**emo**, -**ete**, -**anno**. For the class I verbs, the **a** of the infinitive changes to **e**.

The future generally expresses actions that will take place in the future:

Lo comprerò.	*I'll buy it.*
Andrò domani.	*I'll go tomorrow.*

Sometimes it expresses probability or conjecture:

Che ora sarà?	*What time can it be? What time do you think it is?*
Sarà l'una.	*It must be one o'clock.*
Starà mangiando ora.	*He's probably eating (right) now.*

4. Passato remoto (preterit):

This tense indicates an action that happened in a period of time completely finished now. Although there are some regions in Italy where the **passato remoto** is used in conversation, it is chiefly a literary tense, and the **passato prossimo** is used in conversation instead.

Romolo fondò Roma.	*Romulus founded Rome.*
Dante nacque nel 1265.	*Dante was born in 1265.*
Garibaldi combattè per l'unità d'Italia.	*Garibaldi fought for the unification of Italy.*

5. Passato prossimo (present perfect):

The **passato prossimo** is formed by adding the past participle to the present indicative of **avere** or **essere**. It is used to indicate a past action and corresponds to the English preterit or present perfect:

Io ho finito il mio lavoro.	*I finished my work.*
	(I have finished my work.)
L'hai visto?	*Have you seen him?*
Sono arrivati.	*They arrived.*

6. Past perfect:

The **past perfect** or **pluperfect** tense is formed by adding the past participle to the imperfect of **avere** or **essere**.

Lui l'aveva fatto.	*He had done it.*

7. Trapassato remoto (preterit perfect):

The **trapassato remoto** (preterit perfect) is formed by adding the past participle to the **passato remoto** (preterit) of **avere** or **essere**.

It is a rare, literary tense used to indicate an event that had happened just before another event:

Quando uscì ebbe finito.   *When he went out, he had finished.*

8. Future perfect:
The **future perfect** tense is a literary tense formed by adding the past participle to the future of **avere** or **essere**.

Lui avrà finito presto.   *He will soon have finished.*

The future perfect can also be used to indicate probability:

Lui sarà stato ammalato.   *He might have been sick.*

Saranno già partiti.   *They probably/might have left already.*

35. THE PAST PARTICIPLE

1. The past participle, the form used to form compound tenses, ends in:

Class I: **-ato (-ata, -ati, -ate)**   **parl-ato** *(spoken)*
Class II: **-uto (-uta, -uti, -ute)**   **bev-uto** *(drunk)*
Class III: **-ito (-ita, -iti, -ite)**   **part-ito** *(left)*

2. The past participle used with **essere** agrees with the subject of the verb in number and gender:

Marco è andato.   *Marco (has) left.*

Le bambine sono andate.   *The girls (have) left.*

All reflexive verbs also conjugate with **essere**.

Mi sono divertito/a.   *I enjoyed myself/I had fun. (m./f.)*

3. The past participle used with **avere** changes its form only when it follows a direct object pronoun with which it must agree.

Ho comprato i CD.   *I bought the CDs.*

Li ho comprati.   *I bought them.*

Ho visto Anna.   *I saw Anna.*

L'ho vista.   *I saw her.*

36. USE OF THE AUXILIARIES

The most common intransitive verbs that are conjugated with the verb **essere** in the compound tenses are the following:

andare, arrivare, scendere, entrare, salire, morire, nascere, partire, restare, ritornare, uscire, cadere, venire.

Io sono venuto(-a).	*I have come.*
Lui è arrivato.	*He has arrived.*
Noi siamo partiti(-e).	*We have left.*

Reflexive verbs form their compound tenses with **essere**. The past participle agrees with the subject.

La signorina si è rotta il braccio.	*The young lady broke her arm.*

The past tenses of passive constructions are formed with **essere**:

Il ragazzo è amato.	*The boy is loved.*
La ragazza è stata amata.	*The girl has been loved.*
I ragazzi furono amati.	*The boys were loved.*
Le ragazze saranno amate.	*The girls will be loved.*

Sometimes the verb **venire** is used instead of **essere** in a passive construction:

La poesia è letta dal maestro.	*The poem is read by the teacher.*
La poesia viene letta dal maestro.	*The poem is read by the teacher.*

37. THE PRESENT PROGRESSIVE

Io fumo means *I smoke* or *I am smoking,* but there is also a special way of translating *I am smoking*–**Io sto fumando.** In other words, Italian uses the verb **stare** with the present gerund of the main verb to emphasize that an action is in progress:

Noi stiamo leggendo.	*We are reading.*
Lui stava scrivendo.	*He was writing.*

This form is generally used only in the simple tenses.

38. THE SUBJUNCTIVE
FORMATION OF THE SUBJUNCTIVE
1. The present tense

a. Class I: Drop the **-are** from the infinitive and add **-i, -i, -i, -iamo, -iate, -ino.**

Penso che lui parli troppo.	*I think (that) he speaks too much.*

b. Class II and III: Drop the **-ere** and **-ire** and add **-a, -a, -a, -iamo, -iate, -iano.**

Sebbene Lei scriva in fretta non fa errori.	*Although you write fast, you make no mistakes.*

2. The imperfect tense

a. Class I: Drop the **-are** and add **-assi, -assi, -asse, -assimo, -aste, -asscro.**

Credevo che il ragazzo lavorasse molto.	*I thought (that) the boy was working hard.*

b. Class II: Drop the **-ere** and add **-essi, -essi, -esse, -essimo, -este, -essero.**

Prima che la signorina scrivesse la lettera il padre la chiamò.	*Before the girl wrote the letter, her father called her.*

c. Class III: Drop the **-ire** and add **-issi, -issi, -isse, -issimo, -iste, -issero.**

Ero del parere che il mio amico si sentisse male.	*I was under the impression that my friend did not feel well.*

3. The compound tenses (perfect and past perfect)
These are formed with the present and imperfect of the subjunctive of **avere** (*to have*) and **essere** (*to be*) and the past participle.

Credo che gli studenti abbiano finito la lezione.	*I think (that) the students have finished their lesson.*

Era possibile che i mei amici fossero già arrivati in città.	*It was possible that my friends had already arrived in town.*

USES OF THE SUBJUNCTIVE

The subjunctive mood expresses doubt, uncertainty, hope, fear, desire, supposition, possibility, probability, or granting. It is mostly found in clauses dependent upon another verb.

The subjunctive is used in dependent clauses in the following ways:

a. After verbs expressing hope, wish, desire, command, doubt:

Voglio che tu ci vada.	*I want you to go there.*

b. After verbs expressing an opinion (**penso, credo**):

Penso che sia vero.	*I think it is true.*

c. After expressions made with a form of **essere** and an adjective or an adverb (**è necessario, è facile, è possibile**), or some impersonal expressions like **bisogna, importa**, etc.:

È necessario che io parta subito.	*It is necessary that I leave immediately.*
È impossibile che noi veniamo questa sera.	*It is impossible for us to come over, this evening.*

d. After some conjunctions—**sebbene, quantunque, per quanto, benché, affinché, prima che** (subjunctive to express a possibility; indicative to express a fact):

Sebbene non sia guarito, devo uscire.	*Although I am not well yet, I must go out.*
Benché io te l'abbia già detto, ricordati di andare alla posta.	*Although I told you already, remember to go to the Post Office.*

39. THE CONDITIONAL
The conditional is formed:

1. In the present tense:

a. First and Second Conjugations: by dropping the **are**, or **ere** and adding **-erei, -ereste, -erebbe, -eremmo, -ereste, -erebbero.**

La signora parlerebbe molto, se potesse. *The lady would say a lot if she could.*

b. Third Conjugation: by dropping the **-ire** and adding **-irei, -iresti, -irebbe, -iremmo, -ireste, -irebbero.**

Il signore si sentirebbe bene se prendesse le pillole. *The gentleman would feel well if he took his pills.*

2. In the past tense:
By using the present conditional of *to have* or *to be* and the past participle.

Mio cugino non avrebbe investito il suo denaro in questo, se l'avesse saputo prima. *My cousin would not have invested his money in this, had he known about it sooner.*

40. "IF" CLAUSES
An "if" clause can express:

1. REALITY. In this case, the indicative present and future is used:

Se studio, imparo. *If I study, I learn.*

Se oggi pioverà, non uscirò. *If it rains today, I won't go out.*

2. POSSIBILITY. The imperfect subjunctive and the conditional present are used to express possibility in the present:

Se studiassi, imparerei. *If I studied, I would learn.*

Se tu leggessi, impareresti. *If you read, you would learn.*

(The idea is that it is possible that you may read and so you may learn.)

The past perfect subjunctive and the past conditional are used to express a possibility in the past:

Se tu avessi letto, avresti imparato.   *If you had read, you would have learned. (The idea is that you might have read and so might have learned.)*

3. IMPOSSIBILITY or COUNTERFACTUALITY. Use the same construction as in number 2; the only difference is that we know that the condition cannot be fulfilled.

Se avessi studiato, avrei imparato.   *If I had studied, I would have learned. (But it's a fact that I did not study, and so I did not learn.)*

Se l'uomo vivesse mille anni, imparerebbe molte cose.   *If man lived a thousand years, he would learn many things. (But it's a fact that people don't live a thousand years, and so don't learn many things.)*

41. THE IMPERATIVE

The forms of the imperative are normally taken from the present indicative:

leggi   *read (infml.)*
leggiamo   *let's read*
leggete   *read (pl.)*

For the First Conjugation, however, note:

canta   *sing*

The formal forms of the imperative are taken from the present subjunctive:

canti   *sing*
cantino   *sing (pl.)*
legga   *read*
leggano   *read (pl.)*

VERB CHARTS

COMPLETE CONJUGATION OF SAMPLE VERBS

Here are complete conjugations of sample verbs from each class.

Class I, -are verbs

amare (to love, to like)

	INFINITIVE	PARTICIPLE	GERUND
PRESENT	amare	amante	amando
PERFECT	avere amato	amato	avendo amato

	PRESENT	IMPERFECT	FUTURE	PRESENT PERFECT	PRETERIT	PAST PERFECT	PRETERIT PERFECT	FUTURE PERFECT
io	amo	amavo	amerò	ho amato	amai	avevo amato	ebbi amato	avrò amato
tu	ami	amavi	amerai	hai amato	amasti	avevi amato	avesti amato	avrai amato
lui/lei/Lei	ama	amava	amerà	ha amato	amò	aveva amato	ebbe amato	avrà amato
noi	amiamo	amavamo	ameremo	abbiamo amato	amammo	avevamo amato	avemmo amato	avremo amato
voi	amate	amavate	amerete	avete amato	amaste	avevate amato	aveste amato	avrete amato
loro	amano	amavano	ameranno	hanno amato	amarono	avevano amato	ebbero amato	avranno amato

	PRESENT SUBJUNCTIVE	IMPERFECT SUBJUNCTIVE	PERFECT SUBJUNCTIVE	PAST PERFECT SUBJUNCTIVE	PRESENT CONDITIONAL	PERFECT CONDITIONAL
io	ami	amassi	abbia amato	avessi amato	amerei	avrei amato
tu	ami	amassi	abbia amato	avessi amato	ameresti	avresti amato
lui/lei/Lei	ami	amasse	abbia amato	avesse amato	amerebbe	avrebbe amato
noi	amiamo	amassimo	abbiamo amato	avessimo amato	ameremmo	avremmo amato
voi	amiate	amaste	abbiate amato	aveste amato	amereste	avreste amato
loro	amino	amassero	abbiano amato	avessero amato	amerebbero	avrebbero amato

IMPERATIVE: ama (tu); ami (Lei); amiamo (noi); amate (voi); amino (Loro)

Class II, -ere verbs

amare (to love, to like)	INFINITIVE	PARTICIPLE	GERUND
PRESENT	temere	temente	temendo
PERFECT	avere temuto	temuto	avendo temuto

	PRESENT	IMPERFECT	FUTURE	PRESENT PERFECT	PRETERIT	PAST PERFECT	PRETERIT PERFECT	FUTURE PERFECT
io	temo	temevo	temerò	ho temuto	temei	avevo temuto	ebbi temuto	avrò temuto
tu	temi	temevi	temerai	hai temuto	temesti	avevi temuto	avesti temuto	avrai temuto
lui/lei/Lei	teme	temeva	temerà	ha temuto	temè (or -ette)	aveva temuto	ebbe temuto	avrà temuto
noi	temiamo	temevamo	temeremo	abbiamo temuto	tememmo	avevamo temuto	avemmo temuto	avremo temuto
voi	temete	temevate	temerete	avete temuto	temeste	avevate temuto	aveste temuto	avrete temuto
loro	temono	temevano	temeranno	hanno temuto	temerono (or -ettero)	avevano temuto	ebbero temuto	avranno temuto

	PRESENT SUBJUNCTIVE	IMPERFECT SUBJUNCTIVE	PERFECT SUBJUNCTIVE	PAST PERFECT SUBJUNCTIVE	PRESENT CONDITIONAL	PERFECT CONDITIONAL
io	tema	temessi	abbia temuto	avessi temuto	temerei	avrei temuto
tu	tema	temessi	abbia temuto	avessi temuto	temeresti	avresti temuto
lui/lei/Lei	tema	temesse	abbia temuto	avesse temuto	temerebbe	avrebbe temuto
noi	temiamo	temessimo	abbiamo temuto	avessimo temuto	temeremmo	avremmo temuto
voi	temiate	temeste	abbiate temuto	aveste temuto	temereste	avreste temuto
loro	temano	temessero	abbiano temuto	avessero temuto	temerebbero	avrebbero temuto

IMPERATIVE: temi (tu); tema (Lei); temiamo (noi); temete (voi); temano (Loro)

Class III, -ire verbs

	INFINITIVE	PARTICIPLE	GERUND.
sentire *(to bear)*	sentire	sentente	sentendo
PRESENT			
PERFECT	avere sentito	sentito	avendo sentito

	PRESENT	IMPERFECT	FUTURE	PRESENT PERFECT	PRETERIT	PAST PERFECT	PRETERIT PERFECT	FUTURE PERFECT
io	sento	sentivo	sentirò	ho sentito	sentii	avevo sentito	ebbi sentito	avrò sentito
tu	senti	sentivi	sentirai	hai sentito	sentisti	avevi sentito	avesti sentito	avrai sentito
lui/lei/Lei	sente	sentiva	sentirà	ha sentito	sentì	aveva sentito	ebbe sentito	avrà sentito
noi	sentiamo	sentivamo	sentiremo	abbiamo sentito	sentimmo	avevamo sentito	avemmo sentito	avremo sentito
voi	sentite	sentivate	sentirete	avete sentito	sentiste	avevate sentito	aveste sentito	avrete sentito
loro	sentono	sentivano	sentiranno	hanno sentito	sentirono	avevano sentito	ebbero sentito	avranno sentito

	PRESENT SUBJUNCTIVE	IMPERFECT SUBJUNCTIVE	PERFECT SUBJUNCTIVE.	PAST PERFECT SUBJUNCTIVE	PRESENT CONDITIONAL	PERFECT CONDITIONAL
io	senta	sentissi	abbia sentito	avessi sentito	sentirei	avrei sentito
tu	senta	sentissi	abbia sentito	avessi sentito	sentiresti	avresti sentito
lui/lei/Lei	senta	sentisse	abbia sentito	avesse sentito	sentirebbe	avrebbe sentito
noi	sentiamo	sentissimo	abbiamo sentito	avessimo sentito	sentiremmo	avremmo sentito
voi	sentiate	sentiste	abbiate sentito	aveste sentito	sentireste	avreste sentito
loro	sentano	sentissero	abbiano sentito	avessero sentito	sentirebbero	avrebbero sentito

IMPERATIVE: senti (tu); senta (Lei); sentiamo (noi); sentite (voi); sentano (Loro)

TO BE AND TO HAVE

Essere and avere, to be and to have, are very irregular. Here are their complete conjugations.

essere (to be)

	INFINITIVE	PARTICIPLE	GERUND
PRESENT	essere	sentente	sentendo
PERFECT	essere stato/a/i/e	stato/a/i/e	essendo stato/a/i/e

	PRESENT	IMPERFECT	FUTURE	PRESENT PERFECT	PRETERIT	PAST PERFECT	PRETERIT PERFECT	FUTURE PERFECT
io	sono	ero	sarò	sono stato/a	fui	ero stato/a	fui stato/a	sarò stato/a
tu	sei	eri	sarai	sei stato/a	fosti	eri stato/a	fosti stato/a	sarai stato/a
lui/lei/Lei	è	era	sarà	è stato	fu	era stato/a	fu stato/a	sarà stato
noi	siamo	eravamo	saremo	siamo stati/e	fummo	eravamo stati/e	fummo stati/e	saremo stati/e
voi	siete	eravate	sarete	siete stati/e	foste	eravate stati/e	foste stati/e	sarete stati/e
loro	sono	erano	saranno	sono stati/e	furono	erano stati/e	furono stati/e	saranno stati/e

	PRESENT SUBJUNCTIVE	IMPERFECT SUBJUNCTIVE	PERFECT SUBJUNCTIVE	PAST PERFECT SUBJUNCTIVE	PRESENT CONDITIONAL	PERFECT CONDITIONAL
io	sia	fossi	stato/a	fossi stato/a	sarei	sarei stato/a
tu	sia	fossi	stato/a	fossi stato/a	saresti	saresti stato/a
lui/lei/Lei	sia	fosse	sia stato	fosse stato/a	sarebbe	sarebbe stato/a
noi	siamo	fossimo	siamo stati/e	fossimo stati/e	saremmo	saremmo stati/e
voi	siete	foste	siate stati/e	foste stati/e	sareste	sareste stati/e
loro	siano	fossero	siano stati/e	fossero stati/e	sarebbero	sarebbero stati/e

IMPERATIVE: sii (tu); sia (Lei); siamo (noi); siate (voi); siano (Loro)

Avere (to have)

	INFINITIVE	PARTICIPLE	GERUND
PRESENT	avere	sentente	sentendo
PERFECT	avere avuto	avente	avendo avuto

	PRESENT	IMPERFECT	FUTURE	PRESENT PERFECT	PRETERIT	PAST PERFECT	PRETERIT PERFECT	FUTURE PERFECT
io	ho	avevo	avrò	ho avuto	ebbi	avevo avuto	ebbi avuto	avrò avuto
tu	hai	avevi	avrai	hai avuto	avesti	avevi avuto	avesti avuto	avrai avuto
lui/lei/Lei	ha	aveva	avrà	ha avuto	ebbe	aveva avuto	ebbe avuto	avrà avuto
noi	abbiamo	avevamo	avremo	abbiamo avuto	avemmo	avevamo avuto	avemmo avuto	avremo avuto
voi	avete	avevate	avrete	avete avuto	aveste	avevate avuto	aveste avuto	avrete avuto
loro	hanno	avevano	avranno	hanno avuto	ebbero	avevano avuto	ebbero avuto	avranno avuto

	PRESENT SUBJUNCTIVE	IMPERFECT SUBJUNCTIVE	PERFECT SUBJUNCTIVE	PAST PERFECT SUBJUNCTIVE	PRESENT CONDITIONAL	PERFECT CONDITIONAL
io	abbia	avessi	abbia avuto	avessi avuto	avrei	avrei avuto
tu	abbia	avessi	abbia avuto	avessi avuto	avresti	avresti avuto
lui/lei/Lei	abbia	avesse	abbia avuto	avesse avuto	avrebbe	avrebbe avuto
noi	abbiamo	avessimo	abbiamo avuto	avessimo avuto	avremmo	avremmo avuto
voi	abbiate	aveste	abbiate avuto	aveste avuto	avreste	avreste avuto
loro	abbiano	avessero	abbiano avuto	avessero avuto	avrebbero	avrebbero avuto

IMPERATIVE: abbi (tu); abbia (Lei); abbiamo (noi); abbiate (voi); abbiano (Loro)

SOME IRREGULAR VERBS

Only irregular tenses are indicated here. Other tenses follow the regular pattern of the conjugation as shown above.

Andare *(to go)*

Indicative present	**vado, vai, va, andiamo, andate, vanno**
Future	**andrò, andrai, andrà, andremo, andrete, andranno**
Subjunctive present	**vada, vada, vada, andiamo, andiate, vadano**
Imperative	**va', vada, andiamo, andate, vadano**
Present conditional	**andrei, andresti, andrebbe, andremmo, andreste, andrebbero**
Past participle	**andato**

Bere *(to drink)*

Indicative present	**bevo, bevi, beve, beviamo, bevete, bevono**
Imperfect	**bevevo, bevevi, etc.**
Preterit	**bevvi, bevesti, bevve, bevemmo, beveste, bevvero**
Future	**berrò, berrai, berrà, berremo, berrete, berranno**
Subjunctive imperfect	**bevessi, bevessi, bevesse, bevessimo, beveste, bevessero**
Conditional present	**berrei, berresti, berrebbe, berremmo, berreste, berrebbero**
Past participle	**bevuto**

Cadere *(to fall)*

Future	cadrò, cadrai, cadrà, cadremo, cadrete, cadranno
Preterit	caddi, cadesti, cadde, cademmo, cadeste, caddero
Conditional present	cadrei, cadresti, cadrebbe, cadremmo, cadreste, cadrebbero
Past participle	caduto

Chiedere *(to ask)*

Preterit	chiesi, chiedesti, chiese, chiedemmo, chiedeste, chiesero
Past participle	chiesto

Chiudere *(to shut)*

Preterit	chiusi, chiudesti, chiuse, chiudemmo, chiudeste, chiusero
Past participle	chiuso

Conoscere *(to know)*

Preterit	conobbi, conoscesti, conobbe, conoscemmo, conosceste, conobbero
Past participle	conosciuto

Cuocere *(to cook)*

Indicative present	cuocio, cuoci, cuoce, cociamo, cocete, cuociono
Preterit	cossi, cocesti, cosse, cocemmo, coceste, cossero
Subjunctive present	cuocia or cuoca, cuocia/cuoca, cuocia/cuoca, c(u)ociamo, c(u)ociate, cuociano
Imperative	cuoci, cuoc(i)a, c(u)ociamo, c(u)ociete, cuoc(i)ano
Past participle	cotto

Dare *(to give)*

Indicative present	do, dai, dà, diamo, date, danno
Preterit	diedi or detti, desti, diede or dette, demmo, deste, dettero or diedero
Subjunctive present	dia, dia, dia, diamo, diate, diano
Subjunctive imperfect	dessi, dessi, desse, dessimo, deste, dessero
Imperative	da', dia, diamo, date, diano
Past participle	dato

Dire *(to say)*

Indicative present	dico, dici, dice, diciamo, dite, dicono
Imperfect	dicevo, dicevi, diceva, dicevamo, dicevate, dicevano
Preterit	dissi, dicesti, disse, dicemmo, diceste, dissero

Subjunctive present	dica, dica, dica, diciamo, diciate, dicano
Subjunctive imperfect	dicessi, dicessi, dicesse, dicessimo, diceste, dicessero
Imperative	di', dica, diciamo, dite, dicano
Past participle	detto

Dovere *(to owe, to be obliged, to have to)*

Indicative present	devo or debbo, devi, deve, dobbiamo, dovete, devono or debbono
Future	dovrò, dovrai, dovrà, dovremo, dovrete, dovranno
Subjunctive present	deva or debba, deva or debba, deva or debba, dobbiamo, dobbiate, devano or debbano
Conditional present	dovrei, dovresti, dovrebbe, dovremmo, dovreste, dovrebbero
Past participle	dovuto

Fare *(to do)*

Indicative present	faccio, fai, fa, facciamo, fate, fanno
Imperfect	facevo, facevi, faceva, facevamo, facevate, facevano
Preterit	feci, facesti, fece, facemmo, faceste, fecero
Subjunctive present	faccia, faccia, faccia, facciamo, facciate, facciano
Subjunctive imperfect	facessi, facessi, facesse, facessimo, faceste, facessero

Imperative present	fa', faccia, facciamo, fate, facciano
Past participle	fatto

Leggere *(to read)*

Preterit	lessi, leggesti, lesse, leggemmo, leggeste, lessero
Past participle	letto

Mettere *(to put)*

Preterit	misi, mettesti, mise, mettemmo, metteste, misero
Past participle	messo

Morire *(to die)*

Indicative present	muoio, muori, muore, moriamo, morite, muoiono
Future	morirò or morrò, mor(i)rai, mor(i)rà, mor(i)remo, mor(i)rete, mor(i)ranno
Subjunctive present	muoia, muoia, muoia, moriamo, moriate, muoiano
Conditional present	morirei or morrei, mor(i)resti, mor(i)rebbe, mor(i)remmo, mor(i)reste, mor(i)rebbero
Past participle	morto

Nascere *(to be born)*

Preterit	nacqui, nascesti, nacque, nascemmo, nasceste, nacquero
Past participle	nato

Piacere *(to please, to like)*

Indicative present	piaccio, piaci, piace, piacciamo, piacete, piacciono
Preterit	piacqui, piacesti, piacque, piacemmo, piaceste, piacquero
Subjunctive present	piaccia, piaccia, piaccia, piac(c)iamo, piac(c)iate, piacessero
Past participle	piaciuto

Piovere *(to rain)*

Preterit	piovve, piovvero
Past participle	piovuto

Potere *(to be able, can)*

Indicative present	posso, puoi, può, possiamo, potete, possono
Future	potrò, potrai, potrà, potremo, potrete, potranno
Subjunctive present	possa, possa, possa, possiamo, possiate, possano

Conditional present	**potrei, potresti, potrebbe, potremmo, potreste, potrebbero**
Past participle	**potuto**

Ridere *(to laugh)*

Preterit	**risi, ridesti, rise, ridemmo, rideste, risero**
Past participle	**riso**

Rimanere *(to stay)*

Indicative present	**rimango, rimani, rimane, rimaniamo, rimanete, rimangono**
Preterit	**rimasi, rimanesti, rimase, rimanemmo, rimaneste, rimasero**
Future	**rimarrò, rimarrai, rimarrà, rimarremo, rimarrete, rimarranno**
Subjunctive present	**rimanga, rimanga, rimanga, rimaniamo, rimaniate, rimangano**
Conditional present	**rimarrei, rimarresti, rimarrebbe, rimarremmo, rimarreste, rimarrebbero**
Past participle	**rimasto**

Rispondere *(to answer)*

Preterit	risposi, rispondesti, rispose, rispondemmo, rispondeste, risposero
Past participle	risposto

Salire *(to go up, to climb)*

Indicative present	salgo, sali, sale, saliamo, salite, salgono
Subjunctive present	salga, salga, salga, saliamo, saliate, salgano
Imperative	sali, salga, saliamo, salite, salgano
Past participle	salito

Sapere *(to know)*

Indicative present	so, sai, sa, sappiamo, sapete, sanno
Future	saprò, saprai, saprà, sapremo, saprete, sapranno
Preterit	seppi, sapesti, seppe, sapemmo, sapeste, seppero
Subjunctive present	sappia, sappia, sappia, sappiamo, sappiate, sappiano
Imperative	sappi, sappia, sappiamo, sappiate, sappiano
Conditional present	saprei, sapresti, saprebbe, sapremmo, sapreste, saprebbero
Past participle	saputo

Scegliere *(to choose, select)*

Indicative present	scelgo, scegli, sceglie, scegliamo, scegliete, scelgono
Preterit	scelsi, scegliesti, scelse, scegliemmo, sceglieste, scelsero
Subjunctive present	scelga, scelga, scelga, scegliamo, scegliate, scelgano
Imperative	scegli, scelga, scegliamo, scegliete, scelgano
Past participle	scelto

Scendere *(to go down, descend)*

Preterit	scesi, scendeste, scese, scendemmo, scendeste, scesero
Past participle	sceso

Scrivere *(to write)*

Preterit	scrissi, scrivesti, scrisse, scrivemmo, scriveste, scrissero
Past participle	scritto

Sedere *(to sit)*

Indicative present	siedo, siedi, siede, sediamo, sedete, siedono
Subjunctive present	sieda, sieda, sieda, sediamo, sediate, siedano
Imperative	siedi, sieda, sediamo, sedete, siedano
Past participle	seduto

Stare *(to stay; to remain)*

Indicative present	sto, stai, sta, stiamo, state, stanno
Preterit	stetti, stesti, stette, stemmo, steste, stettero
Future	starò, starai, starà, staremo, starete, staranno
Subjunctive present	stia, stia, stia, stiamo, stiate, stiano
Subjunctive imperative	stessi, stessi, stesse, stessimo, steste, stessero
Imperative	sta', stia, stiamo, stiate, stiano
Conditional present	starei, staresti, starebbe, staremmo, stareste, starebbero
Past participle	stato

Uscire *(to go out)*

Indicative present	esco, esci, esce, usciamo, uscite, escono
Subjunctive present	esca, esca, esca, usciamo, usciate, escano
Imperative	esci, esca, usciamo, uscite, escano
Past participle	uscito

Vedere *(to see)*

Indicative present	vedo, vedi, vede, vediamo, vedete, vedono
Preterit	vidi, vedesti, vide, vedemmo, vedeste, videro
Future	vedrò, vedrai, vedrà, vedremo, vedrete, vedranno
Past participle	visto or veduto

Venire *(to come)*

Indicative present	vengo, vieni, viene, veniamo, venite, vengono
Preterit	venni, venisti, venne, venimmo, veniste, vennero
Future	verrò, verrai, verrà, verremo, verrete, verranno
Subjunctive present	venga, venga, venga, veniamo, veniate, vengano
Imperative	vieni, venga, veniamo, venite, vengano
Conditional present	verrei, verresti, verrebbe, verremmo, verreste, verrebbero
Present participle	veniente
Past participle	venuto

Vivere *(to live)*

Preterit	vissi, vivesti, visse, vivemmo, viveste, vissero
Future	vivrò, vivrai, vivrà, vivremo, vivrete, vivranno
Conditional present	vivrei, vivresti, vivrebbe, vivremmo, vivreste, vivrebbero
Past participle	vissuto

Volere *(to want)*

Indicative present	**voglio, vuoi, vuole, vogliamo, volete, vogliono**
Preterit	**volli, volesti, volle, volemmo, voleste, vollero**
Future	**vorrò, vorrai, vorrà, vorremo, vorrete, vorranno**
Subjunctive present	**voglia, voglia, voglia, vogliamo, vogliate, vogliano**
Conditional present	**vorrei, vorresti, vorrebbe, vorremmo, vorreste, vorrebbero**
Past participle	**voluto**